Dakota Pheasant

...and Iowa Too!

Ed McGaa, J.D. with Dr. Joel Tate

Editors: Pamela Cosgrove, Denise Dodson,
Diane Elliott and Pam Hanway

Cover illustrated by Marie Buchfink

Four Directions Publishing, Rapid City, South Dakota

Four Directions Publishing

Dakota Pheasants...and Iowa Too! © 2008 by Ed McGaa J.D.

All Rights Reserved. No part of this book may be used or repro-
duced in any manner whatsoever, without permission, except in
the case of quotations embodied in articles, books and reviews.

For information, address:
1117 Silver Street
Rapid City, SD 57701
www.edmcgaa.com

Cover illustrated by Marie Buchfink

ISBN: 978-1-57579-383-2

Printed in the United States of America

PINE HILL PRESS
4000 West 57th Street
Sioux Falls, SD 57106

Table of Contents

Preface

Foreword

Introduction

South Dakota Hunting Business Directory

Notes

Appendixes

Special Appreciation

To nephew David Ressl, for all his computer help and his DVD of my "Chief Crazy Horse" book.

To John, Mark and Kyle McGaa – My three hunting sons. To their friends who went on many Pheasant hunts including Prairie Dog forays into the Badlands and Sioux Reservations. To all Rattlesnake Eaters from those hunts.

To daughters, Julie, Mary Pat, Kibbe, Karen and Paula, my right hand girl.

To brother-in-law Mark Heiter, Sister LaVerne and their dog, my youthful, devoted companion, wonderful, unforgettable Cedric, Emery, South Dakota.

To a good Dad, Jim Gehrke and son, Chris and Kyle's pal, Rolf Ulvin.

To Todd Gifford who expanded my hunting after he came of age.

To Gary Black of Black's Pheasant Farms. Wirehair, Wolfman and Al, German Shorthair. To Momma and Poppa Black.

To Dr. Joel Tate for good hunting and his CRP research and publication.

To Dennis Armstrong, my Tucson Buddy.

To all my hunting buddies out of Emery, South Dakota: Dennis Burckhardt. (Big Bird), the Hunt Organizer and Hunting Birds Garage owner and his Brother Lennie and son Dr. Darrell, two of the best shots I've seen in the field along with Jim Kressman…and of course their great Labs. To Turtle and the two Detterman sons, Steve and Kevin. To Bob Detterman for the many acres of his land and corn we have hunted upon. The Kayser brothers, Kenny and David who started me out at Emery, and Nick Ernester and Poobly's Husband–Kenny Gemar. To Big Bird's girlfriend, Bonnie Harvey for a lot of cooking.

To my Iowa Buddies from Eagle Grove, Iowa. John Jacobson, the Hunt Organizer and Tim Reams, better known as 'Rooster' and his 'Rooster's Gathering Den'–his comfortable 'after hunting hours' shop and cleaning station: also two good shooters. To Steve Nelson, Tommy Merrick, Danny Elkin, another great shooter and his two fabulous Boykin Spaniels.

To all the good dogs we have hunted over with special recognition to John Jacobson's Weimaraner/Black Lab, Angus, The Legend.

To Rex II, Rex III and Rex IV (Puppy), Golden Retrievers.

To Don and Mary Smith for Pheasant Nirvana, Emery, South Dakota.

To neighbor, Helen Neitzel, for her babysitting, dog-sitting and generous sharing of her lake frontage land for the dog.

To the resorts, farmers and ranchers who are keeping this great sport alive and ongoing.

To the United States Marine Corps for giving me great adventure starting from a boot camp P.F.C. stripe to that big Phantom F-4 to fly.

Preface

I was inspired to write this book when I realized the way pheasant hunting has recently evolved. Four subjects alone have altered upland game hunting to a high degree:

1. Land availability (or rather un-availability).
2. Resort hunting.
3. More efficient firearms.
4. More efficient ammunition. ('Three-and-a-half inchers,' steel shot and higher velocity shells).

Regarding firearms for example, faster firing semi-automatic shotguns that are so reliable you can fire them in freezing rain without worry of jamming. Couple such new reliability with high velocity shells, and you are making your shooting more effective and reaching out with longer distance shots. I also must add, with a huge smile, the increased numbers in pheasant populations that abound in the Dakotas...and Iowa too. Historically, both of our Dakota states have had larger bird populations in comparison to others. Lately – due to habitat programs with state, local and private involvement – the pheasant population increase has drawn out-of-state hunters by the thousands. The privately owned resorts must also be commended for a goodly portion of the increase in both hunters and birds due to the assimilation of the released birds with the wild ones. 'Come out and find out' is my challenge to hunters across America. How this unique series of events occurred will receive careful coverage within these pages.

In my research, I browsed through several related writings, read several of the better ones, and then reflected upon what I consider some neglected areas. One book (a darn good book), Chris Dorsey's *Pheasant Days*, I found as interesting reading. It lists three states in its 'Table of Contents' regarding, what I assumed, were the states with the highest populations of pheasants. The states were listed as:

- Montana
- Kansas
- Iowa
- The North

In the 'North' portion of the chapter titled; *Pheasant Hunting Across America*, he centers on Wisconsin.[1] I was surprised, perturbed, and eventually downright disappointed that the author dared to leave out the Dakotas entirely. I believe right then and there the earliest seeds of this book were cast.

Dorsey did make up for this projection, however, when regarding dogs, he stated; "Not to be outdone, the Golden Retriever is also a fine bird retriever and fetcher. I've hunted with two – one a Kansas whizbang named Mysti and the other a veteran Montana hunter that were as effective a pair of pheasant dogs as I've ever run across."[2]

I do not intend to get involved in any 'Which is the better dog?' or 'Which is the best breed for upland birds?' arguments, as we all seem to have our favorites. But then again, I was a bit perturbed when I found in another pheasant book, that Golden Retrievers – these wonderful companions which I have enjoyed decades of rewarding hunting with – were listed quite briefly, in and among the 'Other Breeds,' category.

Another breed, which was the particular author's favorite, I personally consider a bit small for bucking through heavy brush, broom and leg-holding, leg-tiring, waist high canary grass; and those other two 'leg grabbers' I term as 'Vietnam style cattails' and the toughest of all: 'Iowa snakeweed.' And when it comes to running down a lightly-wounded, speeding cock, they don't have much of a chance. Worse yet, I have observed that particular breed as one you cannot count on for retrieving. Even the author admitted that 'some' of that particular breed does not retrieve. A ring neck dog that does not retrieve? What about those birds that hit the ground, get up and keep on running? It is often what I call a 'way-out' as well – a term given to far too many inexperienced, uncontrollable dogs that flush birds out of gun range. I should call the breed by name and quit trying to be so polite. From what I have seen of it, this breed is often a 'way, way out,' and I have often wondered, "How in the world does it get any birds for you?" Yet, their owners seem to be loyal and quite content with them. The Golden on the other hand – when properly trained – possesses an inherent, close-hunting characteristic. It is a free country, but I must admit I was a bit disappointed when that author placed that breed far above my Golden Retrievers.

I have to hunt with one of those 'way-outs' at an annual gathering. When we start a hunting drive in a new field, I check to see where the way-out dog is at; then I go to the opposite end of the line. The dog must love me however, because within a couple hundred yards or so into the drive, every year, there is old 'Wanderer' right over in front of me, getting up birds just a bit out of range. Once, we had to go through a rugged slough on a big drive and the birds were holding tight back in the thick of it. Who shows up just before we were able get in position for a big flock to erupt – yup! 'Wanderer,' and the birds exploded, just out of range of course.

Many critics will point to the Golden's coat as being unsuitable to the rigors of pheasant hunting. "Their coats attract burs and they have no strong advantage over labs." One author, Steve Grooms, *Modern Pheasant Hunting*, issued that statement about Goldens.[3] There exists a simple invention called a hair-clipper.

You simply plug it into an electrical outlet and 'Presto,' your dog soon resembles a burr resistant Yellow Lab. "Goldens have suffered from breeding problems based on good looks instead of performance" is another common criticism. [4] Again, I counter that you simply avoid that 'show dog' line completely (and also save yourself a bundle of money) and pick out your Golden puppy from a hunting line instead. Seed #2 for this book was planted once I read these types of criticisms, which I regard as omissions of the true characteristics of an excellent breed, a reliable breed that will hunt for you all day long and not play itself out by being a bit on the 'zippy' side. Goldens, like Labs, have the size to bust through heavy brush and that blood hound nose to stay with birds in thick cattail cover that will stop smaller breeds.

The serious and effective hunter that comes to the South Dakota Opener will usually trailer two to four Labradors. He will have a goodly parcel of land he has hunting rights leased for years and usually will have the latest shock collars, that are quite effective. One well trained Lab or a pair will work the morning hunt and the other Labs will work the afternoon hunt. I have been privileged to hunt along side of some very effective 'vacuum cleaners' to observe them work their magic and have to give credit where credit is due. Labs, are by far the most popular breed visible on Opening Day.

More important than what other authors write, compare or criticize, are two other highly rewarding subjects I felt needed more emphasis in pheasant hunting books. The positive reward of taking a boy hunting will have its own chapter, and prior to that inclusion, will be the influence of some truly remarkable dogs, not all Goldens or Labs that I have been so privileged to know. I also included a sobering, real life story that was a result of a father neglecting a son's appeal to take him hunting.

We pheasant hunters all owe a debt to a man named Judge Owen Denny for our great Autumn past time. He was our country's emissary to China back in the latter 1800s. If the good judge had not the foresight to bring eight pheasants to our land from Shanghai, China back in 1882, you would not be reading this book; and most likely, would never have had the exciting adrenalin rushes that wily 'Wigmunke Zintkala' provides for us. In Sioux, Wigmunke Zintkala' (pronounced, Wig-muunk-kee Zinnt-kaah lah) means Rainbow Winged. Indeed, he is a beautiful creature of many colors and provides endless thrills for us as we seek to find and flush him from cornfields, bean fields, wheat fields, sloughs, shelter belts, and just plain cover – the weedier and thicker the better, according to his preference.

Those first 'Chinese *Ringnecks' brought to America by Judge Owen perished. Undaunted, he brought over sixty more on his second attempt. The majority of these Chinese birds managed to survive on his homestead in the Willamette Valley of Oregon. It did not take long for these birds to adapt to America. This might lead us to believe that our entire pheasant stock is from these first immigrants. Such is not the case however; the birds we shoot at now are a mix of many strains brought over later, from Europe and even Arabia.

* Both spellings; ring neck and ringneck will be used since various authors employ one or the other.

Within a decade, the less than one hundred birds initiated into our continent multiplied enough to allow a seventy-five day hunting season. Another fifteen years after that first season, they were spread out to four out of five states in America. Where there was ample grain raised, they thrived, exploding in population. However, they did not do well in the southern states, where quail were considered the King of upland birds.

My sister and I did our part to help out the Pheasant population. We ordered 200 baby chicks from McFarland Pheasants in Wisconsin. We raised those birds all summer long despite a Rapid City ordinance that declared raising of chickens and related such fowl to be banned from city limits. Well, everyone in the political circle of the city knew what we were doing and just looked the other way despite the fact that my sister had fenced off her lawn and nothing but young growing pheasants were running around on it. Yes, at times, a small town has common sense exceptions to the rule.

Midway through our attempt at raising them we went off to a big pheasant grower's conference in Minneapolis. I'm an enrolled member of the Oglala tribe, in those days the tribe would match your landholdings (and then some) in the form of a lease. This meant that for every acre you owned, the tribe would let you have at least an equal amount of tribal land for lease. We wound up with well over 10,000 acres under our control for cattle raising (Our reservation is 100 miles by 100 miles so we do have plenty of land). This amount really impressed the conference people, as we had to put down how many acres we were raising our pheasants on. When they found out how much land my sister had they thought we were big time operators. Little did they know that we had ordered only 200 baby chicks. When it got to the percentage surviving into adulthood, we calculated that we were in the upper 90 percent range. My sister put medicine in the chicks' water two times a day, and even wiped their butts twice a day with Kleenex – she always was a stickler for hygiene. Those pheasant high-monkey-monks at the conference thought we were doing a fantastic job with those figures and treated us pretty well. In the end, when the pheasants grew enough into maturity to be released, we turned them loose, but all we wound up doing was feeding the coyotes. The reservation is simply not grain land. Within two years none of our pheasants survived in the Badlands of South Dakota, but at least we tried.

The hunting writers of decades past have rushed to proclaim the quail and the grouse as the Upland Kings and threw snobbish phrases at our heavier and trickier ringneck. That is until the resurgence of the wild turkey that had been reduced considerably by early hunters and such curtailment of these 'vacuum cleaners' allowed the quail back then to hold their own. The South is fairly scarce now with these exciting little creatures that can give you as much of an adrenaline rush as the mighty pheasant when they leap skyward, all darting together except magically parting as you pull the trigger. A quail burst covey is just as exciting as the rooster, in my experience, and we used to find them quite abundant in Southern Iowa down by the Missouri border until the turkeys moved in. Takes quite few of those cute little things to feed hungry hunters, however, whereas many a rooster will come in at three pounds and some a bit more. A four pounder is generally into his third year and that is about as long as a pheasant will live. I have heard of a few five-pounders and possibly an aged cock can make it to four years. A retired game warden told me five.

I have wondered if the Turkey poses a serious threat to upland hunting, first to the quail and now to our pheasants. The Southern Iowa story possibly could have some merit. Northern Iowa has few turkeys and plenty of pheasants, at least at the time of this writing. Iowa Turkey adherents tell me a different story and blame the quail disappearance and pheasants too on the lack of habitat and 'differing farming procedures.' Odd, however: Northern Iowa farming isn't much different. In South Dakota, the turkeys are starting to move into pheasant country from where they belong; in the Black Hills. I was shocked this past season to come across a flock of wild turkeys deep into eastern Dakota where wild Turkeys have never roamed. That gnawing question keeps coming up when I look at what has happened to once pheasant and quail abundant Southern Iowa where Tom and Lucy Turkey have moved in with all their relatives in tow. Not only have the quail vanished but the pheasants have too. Some folks downplay Planetary Heating and even Over Population as serious planetary catastrophe. Others send out scientific data that the planet is cooling instead of warming. I hate to be one of those portraying 'the sky is falling' but something that could be a possible serious threat, and especially when obvious detrimental change is happening right before us, such threat, from a common sense stand point at least, bears watching. DNR (Department of Natural Resources) is the counterpart in most states and the present head of the South Dakota Game, Fish & Parks Department was a former honcho from Iowa who probably will not share my worry. I am comforted by the fact that if our Game, Fish & Parks bureaucrats do not get alarmed, I am sure that the resort folks will eventually exert their influence if the Southern Iowa pheasant affliction moves up to the Dakotas. Free enterprise has its merits.

Too many hunting writers will give you the impression that they never miss a shot, that their super-dog finds every bird, and nary a wounded bird is left behind. If any misses do occur…it will always be his partner, but never the author. Hmmmm…. when that kind of propaganda is delivered on paper, this old Dakotan suspects strongly that he just might be getting exposed to some sure fire, ego soaked …'Hollywood writing.' Check out the hunting books and see for yourself. Hence another reason for this book; someone has to include some comments contrary to what I term, 'Hollywood' or 'Soap Opera' writing. Life may be inexorable but it certainly isn't like the movies!

'Wily' the pheasant is adept at ruining your day, if you let him. He will be right there in front of you on a 'sure point' by your dog and then slip out slowly and just flat disappear. You will moan and groan at times and embarrass yourself before your hunting buddies or your kids, if you think you are going to impress them with your 'dead eye' shooting. Wily will cackle defiantly, and in a split second explode into the sun, while you send a barrage of ammunition after him, unscathed. You will bemoan for days, maybe even years afterwards, wishing you had never occasioned that easy miss and worse yet – while your hunting companions all looked on. Woe to the braggart who declares 'I never miss,' when it comes to Upland Bird shooting.

This is a book based on quite a few decades of wonderful experiences, but many a bird will be missed and many will go down and not be found. Am I the bearer of that much bad luck? An unskilled hack with the reflexes of a three-toed sloth perhaps? Maybe I should tell a few lies and write a 'John Wayne' style hunting book: A 'Never Miss' and 'Always Found' pheasant book! Lots of folks accustomed to movies, soap operas and happy endings would appreciate that. When I read through those types of hunting books I can almost believe they are totally true. It is human nature to wish for episodes of exaggerated, perfect-life to be true – is it not? In comparison, I must be one helluva poor shot with a dog that does not have a nose (and my friends' dogs as well) despite the many birds we seem to harvest each season. Movies employ exceptional exaggeration and outright lies. It has become a trademark custom. I will leave it up to the reader. What kind of 'luck' do you have? Maybe if we have had similar experiences, then you will also be dubbing that ringneck 'Wily.'

I have hunted Iowa and Dakota Territory for quite some time, and no other states can boast the hunting land availability that South and North Dakota provides along with Northern Iowa and their deep drainage ditch bird havens. I base that declaration on the numbers of out-state hunters who practically flood our state (South Dakota) come fall every year. Our bird population does a great job of pleasing most all of those anxious hunters. Neither state yet suffers humanity's over population, human expansion which is steadily creeping across America (the entire planet as well). The CRP (Conservation Reserve Program) has also done wonders for the pheasant population within our borders. Dakota farm and ranch land is not being 'ploughed right up to the centerline' of the highway or gravel road as I figuratively observe in so many other states.

In the Dakotas, wide expanses of fertile, bird-producing roadside ditches are in abundance, along with excellent cover left to stand for healthy habitat. Public wildlife areas also abound. Barring a horrible winter, the Dakotas continue to provide excellent hunting and outdraw any other state come opening season. The 'proof is in the pudding' to put it bluntly, and I simply re-issue the challenge to come out and see for yourself come opening day. I have a few other petty grievances from other writings, but one will have to turn the pages to find those. Lastly, I do not intend this work to be a pheasant 'how to' book. It still remains an individual's sport, full of personal choices; for myself, one which completes the end of a rewarding day with exciting 'Road Hunting' – still allowable in the Dakotas. I have tried to interweave a few stories that do not center on upland hunting episodes, but they are connected in one way or another. I hope you will find them meaningful and interesting as well.

There is nothing better than real life experiences, in my opinion. Overall, I have done my best to create a book that abounds with the tremendous joy and excitement we all experience when we seek that wily bird, especially in the freedom found in the Dakotas and parts of Iowa.

Foreword

Dr. Joel C. Tate

Dr. Tate is a Professor of Social Sciences at Germanna Community College, Virginia. For many years he has used Ed McGaa's books, especially *Mother Earth Spirituality* and *Native Wisdom* in Anthropology, Humanities, and Sociology classes. Ed has conducted Sioux Indian workshops at Germanna and on Joel's farm nearby.

> Author's note: The last chapter, chapter 11, includes Dr. Tate's detailed description of the Conservation Reserve Program (CRP), and how it has enhanced pheasant populations and the environmental quality of large segments of South Dakota and neighboring states. The next to last chapter is his alone as well, wherein he affords us a lively account of out-in-the-field happenings of two seasonal hunts punctuated occasionally with a good bit of southern humor.

I had hunted quail as a boy and young man in the hill country of Middle Tennessee, but prior to hunting with Ed in November 2006, my pheasant hunting background was limited to a single trip to the Chamberlain, South Dakota area a few years ago with my quail-hunting partner, Larry Shrader, his older brother, and a community college dean. We drove a long way in Larry's large diesel pickup, loaded down with our Beretta, Franchi, and Browning 12-gauges, lots of outdoor gear, a perky, young Brittany Spaniel and my German Shorthair. The Brittany had pointed grouse in the Southwest Virginia Mountains and the Shorthair had been trained on tamed birds. Neither dog had ever seen a ringneck in its natural setting, and four "bird-starved" Virginia wingshooters were just as inexperienced as pheasant hunters.

Larry was one of my best friends and former community college teaching colleague. He and I spent a lot of Friday afternoons, and all-day Saturdays hunting cut-over pulpwood timberland, and lapwood gullies after deer season ended in mid-January. Larry was quite an athlete in "his day" as they say. He always seemed to walk a little faster, and shoot a bit quicker and more accurately than I did, but both of us brought a lot of birds home in those days. We walked across beaver dams, waded streams, and marveled at the sight of quail gullets literally filled with Poke berries growing on Poke bushes surrounding the old sawdust piles of vanished lumber mills. My Tennessee heritage had taught me that the shoots and leaves of young "poke salad" were very good for breakfast if properly prepared with hog brains and scrambled eggs in my mom's kitchen, but that the berries were "paisin" (poison) for humans and other animals if consumed at the wrong time. However, my own eyes were telling me that Virginia quail really ate those Poke berries in the winter time when quail food was scarce.

The Virginia and Tennessee boys in our group were decent wing shots, but we worked very hard for our three-day pheasant limits on a few hundred acres of prime South Dakota farm and pheasant country. We paid the farm owners a reasonable daily access fee and flushed a good number of birds. But, the dogs were virtually green and almost worthless with the exception of a few "dead-bird" finds, and in our concerted back-East opinions, early flushing pheasants did not hold as well as Virginia Highlands grouse or Virginia/Tennessee bob-whites. Fortunately, we were introduced to a few pheasant hunting techniques such as blocking at the end of long rows of corn, separating hens from roosters, and recognizing the type of cover where ringnecks were likely to explode in flight. We had also learned to observe and help "tackle" a few uncontrollable "way out" dogs (as Ed would say) who had left whistling and yelling hunters to pursue pheasants on dog terms rather than man terms. We loaded up our dogs, our gear, and our much-deserved dressed birds and headed back to Virginia, vowing to return one day to South Dakota pheasant country with or without canine companions. One of our Virginia hunting buddies has since passed away, and although two of our group have hunted elk and mule deer in Montana and Colorado, I believe that I am the only one of our Virginia contingency lucky enough to return to South Dakota for more pheasants. This time around, I was most fortunate to have two very experienced and knowledgeable pheasant hunting instructors-a two-legged Ed and his four-legged Golden Retriever sidekick companion, answering affectionately to the name of "Puppy."

Arrival at Sioux Falls, South Dakota

Ed had agreed to meet me at the airport in Sioux Falls and drive me to our destination at Blacks' Hunting Fields near Estelline, South Daktoa He had also volunteered to loan me a shotgun since I wanted to avoid buying an expensive gun case or being hassled by airport security as a would-be pheasant terrorist. I have a smooth-shooting 26" Beretta semi-auto 12-gauge which I purchased for my earlier pheasant trip to South Dakota, and since quail are almost extinct in my neck-of-the woods, it stays locked in a closet most of the time. My borrowed Benelli was a real field-tested 24" barreled, 12-gauge semi-auto outfitted with a shoulder strap and a rather extended orange front sight. Its synthetic stock came up to my shoulder as if it were customized for me, and my "shooting-with-a-borrowed-gun-missing excuse" silently vanished. Ed also furnished an assortment of lead, two-and-three-fourths-inch 5's and 6's lead shot shells, and some "three-incher" steel 2's and 4's for what he called early flushers and high flyers.

Over the next few days I would learn a lot from Ed about mixing my loads for different shooting distances, and the effective use of a great-shooting, short-barreled Benelli.

I had expected Ed to come to pick me up in a Toyota, Chevy, or Ford pickup with dog, dog box, guns, shells, and, of course, lots of dog and man food and drink. All of these items were present except the pickup truck and dog box. In lieu of a gun-racked four-wheel drive truck, Ed was driving a dark blue, 1989 Cadillac "Pheasant Mobile" whose backseat was occupied (ruled over?) by "Puppy." Puppy had taken the place of an aging Rex, another Golden Retriever that Ed had shot many birds over in the past. Actually, the name Rex was most appropriate because "Puppy" was restfully ensconced upon a raised, padded carpet throne just behind Ed in the driver's seat. I threw my gear in the backseat next to Puppy's throne, took a quick look at "my" Benelli, assorted shells, and hunting clothes, got into the "Pheasant Mobile," and headed north. Ed and I engaged in immediate dialogue on any and all domestic and foreign issues, and we were on our way to South Dakota corn and CRP hunting territory.

Three Skunk Night and Arrival at Blacks

As we drove down a country road near our three-day destination at Blacks' we saw three large skunks gently crossing the road ahead of us. We had just been talking about pheasants and their predators such as owls, coyotes, and fox. I thought "pheasant egg eaters," recalling my childhood trapping experiences in Tennessee when what we called "polecats" were often found sucking eggs in a Rhode Island Red hen's nest. Our "save-the-pheasants-for-us" instincts kicked in, and for the next two nights we pursued our pheasant competition. Lucky for me, that we did not capture our quarry because Ed said that he would have to give me the Indian name for "Three Skunk Boy" if we had been successful in our skunk quest. At the age of 65 plus, I have been called a lot of things, but something about that name really stinks! At least he could have said, "Three Skunk Man." Oh, well. By the time we checked into our cozy hunt cabin, "Puppy" and I had become good hunt buddies, and he spent the night at the foot of my bed.

Hunt Day One – Flushing Pheasants: Lessons from Ed and "Puppy"

The morning of Hunt Day One was frosty and crisp, but not the Midwestern cold that I had anticipated. A beautiful light frost was on the recently-harvested corn stalk remnants, trees, and CRP cover crop grasses. We had hunting access to approximately one square mile, and as we drove down the road with coffee in hand, we saw a few pheasants flying across the road ahead of us. A large beautiful rooster ringneck sailed from left to right just ahead of us. Ed quickly said, "Mark where he lands, and get your gun ready." I felt as if I were a student rather than a professor, and that two knowledgeable pheasant hunters, Ed and Puppy, were getting ready to teach this old two-legged dog some new tricks. I was instructed to get out, walk into the cover just off the road below the fence post mark where the pheasant had landed, and wait for Ed and Puppy to try to flush the bird toward me. Ed took his "Pheasant Mobile" and Puppy about 50 yards up the road and parked. Ed was talking to Puppy constantly from the time we had seen the huge bird until they came toward me "Easy Puppy. Go easy, easy now. Get ready Joel. Easy Puppy, easy." Although I had been using a shotgun for 50 plus years, I was a bit nervous in the presence of my new teachers who obviously knew their subject matter. There I stood under perfect conditions-a wonderful sunny morning, very light breeze with my finger on the safety of the Benelli, eagerly anticipating my pheasant-hunting pretest. Though nervous, confidence and relaxation came at just the right time in my teachable moment. Puppy moved cautiously straight ahead of me, turned slightly clockwise to my right, and the big rooster erupted at three o'clock. I pushed the safety, gun swinging right, and dropped the bird with a good clean, dead shot. Puppy, with wagging tail, retrieved the pheasant to Ed, and Ed put it in my hunting vest. Perfect morning, perfect pheasant find, perfect dog-master communication, perfect flush, perfect shot and perfect retrieve. Pretest passed with flying colors. The rest of our hunt would not be all perfection for me shooting-wise, but I will never forget *this* morning and *this* shot as a peak hunting experience to be played over and over again in my memories.

After missing a couple of straightaway shots which may have included a wounded bird which got away (most pheasant hunters hate this occurrence!), I was able to get my limit of two more by early afternoon. Puppy worked good and close, and, as I recall, Ed got his limit-1, 2, 3-without a miss. My early morning observations regarding the expertise of my four and two-legged hunting instructors were confirmed on Day One, and I then knew that my brief pheasant sojourn in South Dakota was to be a very rewarding experience.

Introduction

I am a South Dakotan; a Marine Corps combat veteran who served in Korea and Vietnam. Of my era veterans, I am probably a bit unusual in that I still have 'my legs' and yet have the ability to hunt the wily Ringneck pheasant. Pure Dakota bird hunting demands a degree of physical fitness. Resort hunting can be a bit easier and I highly recommend our resorts for a goodly number of the older generation, my age and younger, who have 'paid their dues' tramping about in much tougher conditions. The younger hunter also can get a great deal of excitement and fine hunting at our resorts, especially those who will let you get out on your own. Many Dakota resorts will give you that sort of experience if you simply ask for it.

Land is becoming harder and harder to 'get on' and the hunting resort is becoming the answer to productive and bountiful hunting. Besides our many resorts, the Dakotas offer abundant public lands that are loaded with heavy foliaged sloughs as well. A thick slough with no other means but to plow through it is a fairly apt example of demanding stalking. Some combat veterans of the Vietnam era will almost think they are back in the war zone when they have to bust some heavy broom grass, canary grass and cattails or that thick Iowa snake weed along the banks of the drainage ditches. If you have a dog that loves to root around in that stuff, you will have it much easier as you stand at the water's edge and watch him work a cluster of cattails. You will surely get some extra shooting that many hunters never see. It isn't any wonder why Wily Q. Ringneck loves to hide out in it. My suggestion is that some of those tougher spots will pay off with some fairly exciting shooting, providing that your dog will stay in there.

I never believed in Fairy Tales and have no pictures of John Wayne hanging on my walls. I was a Marine Fighter pilot and flew 110 combat missions of which I am stand-up proud. I even volunteered for a combat tour prior to my enrollment into law school. The Dean of the Law School at South Dakota set my enrollment back a year so that I could join my Phantom squadron for Vietnam. It was the same squadron, VMFA 115 (Silver Eagles) that our famous South Dakota Governor was in during World War II. Governor Joe Foss, a World War II Marine ace was an avid pheasant hunter and of course I was proud to be in his old squadron.

I have had a few thrills in my life and not all pertaining to hunting. I strapped on a Brahma Bull for our college rodeo and that caught my attention. I was one, darn proud 17-year-old when I got my P.F.C. stripe from Marine Boot Camp.

That was back in the days, 'pre-Drill Instructor Sgt. McKeon'* when the D.I. could tap on you a bit physically if you needed it. Over a decade later, when I soloed that big monster F4B Phantom, (a single seater Re: pilot controls) that was a real high. Probably my most memorable accomplishment was when the check pilot gave me a big 'Up' mark on the squadron pilot's board after a solo check ride. Now, at that very moment I was no longer the unofficial outsider. I was now an official member of a Marine Phantom Squadron: quite a thrill in my book.

The Marine Phantom has but one set of controls unlike the two sets of controls the Air Force version had. Your check pilot in the back seat has no way to help you out once you start doing the various maneuvers, loops, spins, slow flight and touch and go landings required for your check out. On to Vietnam, I cut a French church in two pieces with my external, Hughes two-barrel Gatling gun, resulting in explosions due to the Viet Cong storing their ammunition there. That mission was under heavy gunfire from their 37mms. I had a serene sense of accomplishment on that one even if it was a church. That ammunition would have killed our Marines and no structure is worth sparing when it is used to endanger our troops.

> *Sgt McKeon, was responsible for the drowning of several Marine Recruits at Parris Island Recruit Training Camp in South Carolina some years after I attended Boot Camp. Prior to that happening, Marine Drill Instructors were allowed to 'physically correct' a recruit which meant a slap on the back of the head most usually, or if you were wearing a helmet or helmet liner, a sharp wrap from the Drill Instructor's swagger stick got your attention rather quickly or made you remember what, when or how you were supposed to do something. It also speeded up your correction powers regarding errant behavior such as one would find on the drill field. Such teaching or instructing methodology severely improved one's concentration or focusing powers. The Marine Corps deals with real life and death issues. Focus is a key prerequisite when engaged in the depth of battle. Personally, I was never touched in my three months of Boot Camp. If one kept one's mouth shut, paid attention and simply did what the D.I.s told you to do, one rarely got smacked, my opinion. It was simple as that.

The Pheasant

In Dakota, that wily ringneck is the true King of birds despite what some writers tout, giving that title to the ruffed grouse or the southern quail. Come to South Dakota on opening day and see who the real King is. A Dakota town, Mitchell, will be an exemplary example wherein all of its many motels have been sold out for years come opening day. From throughout the nation, hunters flock to the Dakotas and leave quite satisfied. In any Dakota town with pheasants at its outskirts on opening weekend, you are going to find it almost impossible to get a motel room unless you book far in advance. Hunters and Anglers spend up to $1 million per day in South Dakota, according to a report by the Congressional Sportsmen's Foundation. Out of a population of about three fourths of a million South Dakota citizens, almost 20 percent are resident hunters. The primary quarry is the rooster pheasant.[1]

I mentioned earlier that 'Wily,' the pheasant, will cackle away in a split second, exploding unscathed into the sun, while you send a barrage of ammunition after him. Indeed it is a bit of pressure when you have another situation and become a 'Blocker' with almost a dozen fellow hunters driving out in front of you and here comes a burly rooster out ahead of their shooting range. This author hunts with an 'Opener' Dakota group, just east of Mitchell, and has been for years. They begin with hitting the cornfields. That time of year, the corn is still mostly standing in northern country, the Dakotas and combines are busy doing their best to alter the landscape.

"Yes, and here it comes, gaining altitude as it bores on right in your direction because you just happen to be a lucky key blocker where the birds have decided to fly toward. He (the rooster) is getting closer, the wind is helping him along and every one approaching the edge of the drive is watching. You line him up; put that sight not too far in front of him as he closes. Nowadays, that 1400 fps, two-and-three-fourths, #6 lead shot doesn't take as much lead (leed) compared to the 1200 fps of yesterday. Fifteen hundred to 1550 fps is less lead yet. You have much more time to get nervous compared to the usual surprising burst of wing beats coming up beside, behind or in front of you while with the walking crowd. You pull the trigger, hoping against hope that he will crumple and fall, but he keeps on coming and passes to your left. You open up again and one more time with a three-inch shell this third try, thank God someone invented 1500 fps or 1550 fps for this shell – a steel four, as he is going away and you breathe a quick sigh of relief as he goes down and your dog is on him. Now that is sheer, pure excitement that I have never found in deer hunting, elk hunting or any of those type of so called 'big game' shoots. If you have been a 'blocker' in Dakota land, more than likely you have had a similar experience, have you not?"

A Few Years of Hunting

I can still walk miles yet and do so every season, for close to some 40 years now. I do not know exactly how many years I have made the Dakota Opener, usually the third weekend in October. I never bothered to sit down and attempt to make an accurate supposition and do not intend to. I base my rough estimate on the fact that I have had four Golden Retrievers as hunting companions. You are lucky if you can get ten to twelve years out of a heavily hunted Lab or 'Golden,' so I have come up with my estimate as around 40 years. One dog did not live long but I hunted before I had these four but not as intensely.

I am very fortunate to be allowed to hunt with a group of 'Good Ol Boys' out of Emery, South Dakota on Opening Day for several decades now. I should include a 'blueprint' drawing of the hunting party garage they have there which has been designed especially for our annual gathering. It has every practical feature and facility for the processing of pheasants and the following party after shooting hours. Likewise I have another wonderful group down in Iowa, Eagle Grove, that I am so fortunate to hunt with the following October weekend at the Iowa Opener. Their gathering spot is an equally equipped and comfortable facility within walking distance of a productive deep drainage ditch with heavy cover on each side that extends a mile each way where many a bird has leaped out from.

I also am fortunate to hunt at a Dakota resort where my dog helps out as a guide occasionally. Since he can not answer a phone or drive, I get called on as well but it is him that they really want to employ and not me.

"Not 'dummy' birds, but explosive, high-quality true ringnecks, nationally known and used to compliment native hunting."[3] Chris Dorsey's book relates a resort's advertisement that appeared in a national hunting periodical. I readily admit that the pheasants you now find at most resorts are indeed as action packed and responsive as any of the wild birds which they soon move in with and flock with. In the Dakotas my experience is that the large resorts have an abundant wild stock already built in to their land holdings. That wild population often makes up the majority of the bird population and the released birds adapt quite readily. Where I hunt, every bird comes up like a rocket and there are quite a few three and four year old birds which proves their adaptability.

In this book, I have left out specific chapters on guns and dogs, various models and actions, various dog breeds, different choices. I certainly do not want to argue over dogs. No way! My four dogs could just as well have been Labs, Weimaraners, Springers or German Short hairs or Wire hairs. I started out with one particular breed and like most hunters never switched. This will not be a book pitting one breed against the other. A few breeds, I have seen in the field have characteristics that are not for me and there are quite a few hunters who won't approve of what I seem to prefer. A common complaint about Golden Retrievers is that their long coat picks up burrs. The simple solution to that admitted problem is as I stated earlier; get your dog clipped or do it yourself. He will look like a Golden Lab but that 'Hunting Close' characteristic and Blood Hound nose will be right there. I don't care to be punching shock collar buttons when I am hunting. Most all dogs can be great is my opinion and a lot of them, including Goldens, can not be so great and even worthless, whiny 'Way-outs.' Whatever you lack in a particular dog, in my opinion, it is the owner that lacks in the training perspective and most generally the dog is not to blame. It is the training in the dog that I will continually tout that can make him great. Some dogs just 'do not have it' however, and like military flight school, some will just have to 'wash out.' Unfortunately too many of these types are still brought out into the field and can make your hunt a bit unpleasant, to say it mildly. Owners of these types seem to never admit they have such a dog that usually gets 'way out' there, out of gun range. They would do us all a big favor by training a new dog and leaving their 'way out' home. An important chapter is about picking out your pup and a very common sense method to help you select the right one.

Guns and dogs are like a man's choice on women. What one guy would jump off a cliff over, others would scratch their head as they look down at the broken body and say, "Darn Fool, jumped because of that one particular woman. What he saw in her... beats me."

I intend to fill you in a bit in an early chapter as to my background with the wily ringneck starting way back on a Dakota farm when two and three plow rated tractors were the most common. My venture into this writing will not be an academic fashioned hunting tryst based on snobby principles that seem to permeate most hunting books of similar subject material. Maybe the term, 'Upland Game' has caused more than one writer to get a bit uppity. Instead I will simply try to make it a bit interesting with genuine hunting stories, most of which have been gleaned down through the years.

Snobbery reminds me of a pleasant, innocent conversation with an Englishman on an airline bound back to the States after a book signing in England. I queried the man about pheasant hunting there as I had seen some wild birds in the countryside. His eyes lit up as we broached the subject. He belonged to an English hunting club that held to staid and fast rules regarding their hunts. Hunters are hunters however, and we began to trade a few stories. He had that aristocratic air about him which seems common to many English. I discovered from him that they even dressed a bit fancier for their organized hunts than we Americans would ever think of. Being a Native American, at least partly, I have a natural tendency to respect culture and customs of most people. In some of their hunting forays some members will even have another person carry their 'piece' (gun) as they call it. 'Hmmm, interesting.' I thought. I wondered what they did when a bird simply leaped up in front of them without having a dog point it out or the time to have the gun errh...unhh ..I mean ...'piece'...passed, but decided such a thought would be a bit impolite to ask.

The English are polite, no question about that. All the times I have been in the British Isles, including Scotland and Wales, I was in a few Pubs and never saw a fight or witnessed an argument. When I told him that observation he just laughed merrily and warned me that I had happened to be in the 'wrong' pubs. I didn't openly disagree but secretly held to my belief that they indeed are what you would call 'extra polite.'

When I mentioned how I loved my Benelli automatic and its reliability he wrinkled up his nose and waved his hand. "Oh no, never in England would that type be allowed." He drew in his breath and pronounced a following "Never!" with utmost disdain. For a moment I felt as though I had committed some kind of mortal sin or somehow insulted his wife by my admission. "How about pumps?" I tried to back out innocently. He brushed my question aside with the wave of his hand not needing to answer otherwise. "Over and unders and side by sides?" I queried. His eyes lit up and he beamed a smile. "Ahh yes." He replied. "Your

Yank guns, that Benelli one. That would never be allowed in any English hunting club." I never mentioned that the Benelli was Italian made. I thought I may as well get agreeable; it was a long flight back home. "I used to shoot a Charles Daly over and under. Nice gun. Was a 20 gauge, improved cylinder and modified." I left off that it was also three-inch capable and that I had got many a bird with it when I was quite a bit faster... and younger. I figured they just might have a rule against the three-inch shell improvement as well. I almost muttered to myself. "Darn good thing I never brought up road hunting!" I left the conversation with, "Yes, pheasant hunting. Indeed it is a most enjoyable sport." No sense ruffling anymore feathers. I had nothing to prove.

South Dakota and North Dakota are both unusual states for these modern times we live in. We Dakotans still have plenty of room and are the fewest of the few that are not rushing pell mell to increase our populations. Our wildlife still flourishes and in many cases wild fowl habitat has been increased and improved mainly through the CRP system (Conservation Reserve Program). We will spend an entire chapter on this wonderful method to preserve our wildlife that unfortunately is becoming endangered due to the high price the corn bushel brings due to needed Ethanol production. Many farmers are enticed to pull out of the habitat provisioning CRP program.

This book will attempt to be direct and to the point although my stories will have a natural tendency to ramble some. I seem to have gotten by with this characteristic within my writings for eight other books so may as well avoid any spectacular change in this, my last one. They are true happenings however. Some 'Dakota' stories, happenings and viewpoints are not purely pheasant hunting material but they will be related in some degree, in most cases. Beyond all – I didn't want to write some mechanical – 'How to Book on Pheasants.' Not that I fear that I lack the experience to write thusly nor lack the confidence to spell out a few tidbits of possible useful information. I think one can 'teach' to a merited degree through mere description from experiences. We will go into some detail regarding various phases of dog training in a latter chapter.

I live in South Dakota; born there. Being Dakota born and on top of that acknowledgement, I throw back at the Mayflower claimant folks that my ancestors were here to meet them whenever they start spouting their lineage roots. I am also part Sioux, a Teton Oglala, born on the Pine Ridge Sioux reservation. My people were here a bit early, the Oglalas crossed the Missouri River along with our close sister allies, the Teton Sichangu, back when the American Nation was just beginning in 1776. The state is named for those of my lineage – Dakota/Lakota which means allies or friends.

I use the term Sioux, every now and then, as does my tribal council and the rest of the tribal councils in the state, despite the ever meddling Academics who are doing their darnedest to change our official title back to Lakota or Dakota. Nadouesssiox (pronounced Nadooh ess sux) is a corruption of the French Chippewa term for enemies. My take on that term is that we were very efficient enemies, especially against the U.S. Cavalry who suffered severely for over several decades in our encounters with them under our great chiefs; Red Cloud and later Chiefs Sitting Bull and Crazy Horse, who defeated Colonel George Armstrong Custer quite handily at the Battle of the Little Big Horn. We were also significant enemies against other tribes that dared to confront us as well. Eventually we were overwhelmed by sheer Army numbers but we left our mark as being extremely formidable 'Enemies' that made you pay a very dear price for meddling with us. Since those glory days of riding our mounts with both hands free (equestrian style) and making the handicapped cavalry (only one hand free due to the reins required for the cavalry horse) pay dearly, we also had conditioned horses far more used to gun fire from the buffalo hunting. Army horses were confined considerably in stockades and never were used for daily hunting. Army scouts provided their meat. Indian youth rode our warrior's horses daily to keep them in superb fighting condition. Plain old common sense dictates as to who had the better horses and of course which equates to winning in the field. The Native Americans also have the highest enlisted and volunteer ratio of any nationality to fight in our country's wars, beginning in World War I up to the present Mid-east conflicts.[2] Our people are extremely patriotic and not just in words only. We enlist, we join; we serve!

Consider the above as a brief 'Dakota' history lesson. I have been hunting those beautiful birds before I could carry a shot gun. Hmmm. That must sound a bit strange and downright illegal, doesn't it? Those are good starting credentials. Rural South Dakotans and our northern cousins, as well, see birds along the roadside practically every day. They are as much a part of our scenery as our cattle, fence posts, jack rabbits and John Deeres. Most of us expect our limit when we go out for opening day.

Bird hunting is akin to religion or politics, however. Somewhat like the Englishman, some folks are not going to give up on how they were culturally raised. That full choked 28-inch or 30-inch Remington 870 pump will never be exchanged for a Benelli or the Englishman's expensive over and under stamped, 2¾ only. "This 870 (pronounced eight seven tee) belonged to my Dad!" More than one 20 gauger is never going to be shooting 12's. "Them 12's. Too much lead to pick out of the bird," was one stubborn retort I heard.

Lastly, it is the dog that is the heart of pheasant hunting, my opinion. You can pay an extraordinary fee for a dog and foolishly expect him to perform with little or no training. It won't happen. The more birds a dog is exposed to, the more he is trained around them, the more he will perform and become the obedient and resourceful four legged friend you want to admire and appreciate. I hope to prove this point as we read onward.

Watching from a Pickup Box

Flying into the Sun

So many wonderful experiences you will have with that four legged specimen called the Upland Hunting Dog regardless of his or her species. Two of my 'four great dogs' were not Upland dogs, however, yet I have to tell about them. Even a missed bird can lead you to a unique experience with those beautiful animals. I tell this episode because therein lies some important hunting points which we will come back to later, in case you initially miss them.

It was just this past season that I have had the oft repeated episode. Just as we started road hunting, a rooster we spotted, lifted up and went straight into the dusky sun. He was a 'sure thing,' when my pal Joel and I had watched him earlier but such was not the outcome.

We were sitting in the resort's older pickup which they loaned to us. The truck is a nice blue four-wheel drive, and a thrill to return to once you have had to give up yours due to the gas prices, city parking spaces and just plain old less need. Evening was approaching and we were deciding where to go for some 'road hunting.' Our legs were tired and we were enjoying a good sit in the pickup, which was a welcome respite while we contemplated and weighed over a local map as to which of the different hunting spots nearby we would be covering. Resting one's tired body, especially your legs, is a practical reason why the late afternoon switch to 'Road Hunting' makes it so popular. My Golden (Golden Retriever) was standing in the pickup box waiting anxiously for us to make up our minds. He wasn't tethered or kenneled. He never is and doesn't need to be …and never will be.

The majority of hunting dogs are kenneled, I am well aware, but I never was much of a crowd follower nor a crowd pleaser. I had no problems following a couple decades mostly of Marine life with its required disciplines and demands but on into my civilian life I usually march to my own drummer.

Our 'answer' walked right across the highway which passed by the resort. We spotted him nonchalantly strolling in our direction on our side of a gently banked paved road. I am sure that 'Puppy' in back saw him as well but was too experienced by then, despite his name, to leap from the pickup box and give chase as many an inexperienced dog would. 'Pup' is too well trained, seen too many birds close up or maybe he is just too intelligent dog-wise to attempt such a shenanigan. Yes, I know, … he indeed has a strange name. His professional reaction to the strolling pheasant was commendable, in my view, despite his name.

I backed our pickup purposely from the rooster, possibly less than a one-year-old; we call them first termers. The real late hatches, the red color is yet a bit weak, but this guy was fairly red and cautiously went back away from us, disappearing across the road. The younger ones in the fall come in at about the same size and weight as a hen (under three-pounds). This was what I wanted as they are quite tender. A three year old rooster may go four-pounds and the rare four-year-old may possibly reach five pounds. Some, according to a retired game warden interview make it to five years. I took my Benelli out of the truck and let my dog quietly out of the back who was, as I figured, watching from his perch as well. I was careful to not clang the pick up gate and purposely did not shut the pickup door. Less noise the better. I gave my Golden a very pronounced 'pat-the-ground signal' which he understands as …'this is road hunting and we now have new rules.' Number one rule is: Stay back!

I don't have to kennel my dogs in a pickup or anywhere else and I certainly do not have to leash one when I am going to sneak up on a spotted bird. If I have to cross a busy highway, I simply take him by the collar and walk up, checking left to right. If it is clear, we cross the road. One nice feature about Dakota highways, except for the freeways, the Interstates, they most often have a much lower incidence of approaching traffic. The farther one is out away from the state's major towns the less the traffic. In way out rural Dakota, passing vehicles are scarce. The Golden had obviously spotted the rooster but didn't boldly, or I should say uncontrollably, jump from the box and bolt after him being that close as many a hunting dog would do. How you can train a dog for just that situation we will get into later.

I had told Joel in the pickup earlier to come over the top of the road to the rooster's left when I did. The nice high concealing bank with an easy incline was perfect for both of us. I advance to the right and Joel to the left was our strategy, because once he went back across the road there was no guarantee he would squat down and sit and wait for us. He could also decide to keep on walking away from the road. I brought my dog up close to me as we crept forward with a simple hand signal and when he approached the incline he hesitated in order to pick up a bird's trail that would take him to my right, and back at the bottom of the incline. I thought this was fine and let him follow it, figuring he would come up as soon as we fired. I would also have to give an instant check for cars as well and didn't want him immediately close beside me in case the rooster bolted and flew. In the case of a car coming I'd have kept my dog next to me holding on to his collar or give him the stay sign with a loud accompanying yell to 'Stee-aaa-yyy,' which he always has obeyed – rooster flying up or no rooster flying up. The dog is a helluva lot more important than any rooster.

Danger

When you get to the edge of a field this situation often happens. A car is speeding down the gravel road toward you and about that time running birds ahead are about to leap across the road. The loud 'Stee-aaa-yyy,' call can save your dog and it is probably the most important call to practice. I have seen a black Labrador killed that way when a rooster bolted and also another dog meet his end similarly by an approaching truck. That fatality we didn't see because we were all approaching the field's edge below a much higher incline with tree and bush cover when several birds rose across the gravel above, but we all certainly heard the sickening thud.

I was relieved to see my dog engrossed with his tracking away from us and to our right when I came up onto the road and no cars in sight or the rooster either. With my eyes riveted to the grass at the edge of the pavement ahead, I called for my dog and a 'come here' slap of my leg and then sent him across the pavement where he began to pick up scent. We were a bit off to the right of where the rooster had crossed back over and I should have realized that this scent might be another bird. A rooster burst out of range to the west and it must have been this rooster whose scent he had picked up on because he pursued in that direction away from the pavement and then chased up a few hens within range. I crossed down into the opposite ditch, crossed out of it going west following my dog. One more hen came up out of the end of the concealing grass where the rooster had leaped. Further west was picked bean field which even a well camouflaged hen cannot hide in. I called the dog and returned toward Joel standing on the road.

A few steps and up burst the rooster right back into the sun. In no-wind conditions he can hit 35 to 40 mph. With the wind; more. I had to be still thinking about those hens, because that rooster into the sun…well – I could not tell for sure and I damn well was not going to drop a hen. I wish he would have given me an identifying cackle but no such gift. It was the end of the day and we had walked miles. Fatigue had set in as well at my age. I just was not that sharp to discern and I can't blame my eyes. They are still miraculously at 20/20 – good enough to strap on an airplane yet but I just couldn't or wouldn't pull that trigger. Joel held back purposely. He had already taken his limit and he said later, "I thought it was such a sure thing for you that I just let it go. No sense in the both of us filling it full of lead."

Well, that is the wily bird. Straight into that sun even a young rooster seems to go. Or he will spin your pursuing dog round and round in the thick heavy grass, especially an older one, and usually gets away if the cover is that good. Your dog will be on a 'sure point' and old Wily will slowly slip back out. You knock him down and he falls in thin cover and your dog saw him fall and is heading at full speed his way. It is a sure find, you think. Over and over you have met this situation with elated success. Your dog will track him down if he runs no matter if he's gone ten minutes or so but he will come back with the bird bobbing in his mouth. But you look and look for this one and he is gone – simply vanished. Your experienced dog is frantically making expanded search squares in the fairly clean cornfield or lightly scattered weeds. Yes, that is what my latest one does and I never taught him how. Basically because I wouldn't know how to teach him that maneuver, to be honest. It has to be sheer instinct. If you check a bit more thoroughly – a badger hole, coyote or fox or just a hole holds your bird. He is gone and you are not going to retrieve him.

I hope the reader grasped a few principles regarding the watching dog in the pickup box and the concern for his safety crossing the road and the tragic outcome of the two other dogs mentioned. How many hunting dogs, completely free, under no immediate voice command and untethered, have you seen that could be so relaxed as to not bolt out of the box at first sight of the approaching rooster?

I forgot to mention that in that pickup were also five untouched roosters at his feet, (untouched by the dog) once we placed them there earlier, up in back of the truck's cab. Once you have taken it from his mouth and placed it in the back of your carrying vest and then on into your vehicle usually right beside where he is usually stationed, he ignores those birds. Two birds were wet as can be and one of those had a goodly crust of mud. He had pointed and flushed three of those ringnecks out of thick cattails and found two later, hiding in a shelter belt for a double. One went into the lake close by and I took a picture while he was closing in on the floating bird. One bird he had run down after it landed fairly well intact but with a broken wing. One of the cattail birds lifted and went into an adjoining set of cattails on its way down after being hit by a set of 6's. We waited a good ten minutes for that one. The dog had seen him go down and charged off at full speed. I was about to call to him and there he was, emerging beside the fluffy pollen bearing water weeds with a wet, muddy rooster in his mouth. Another good picture I took of him after yelling "Stee-ayyy," to keep him standing in the water with the rooster and running toward him with my camera. While working the thick, resistant cattails, he flushed up hens, four times the amount of roosters he drove out. He was a busy worker and a very effective dog.

The methodology of how this dog came to arrive at his present state will slowly unfold as we turn the pages. Basically, it is repeated exposure to the ring-neck that most often makes a good dog great.

☰ 2 ☰

Early Hunting

    I believe I started hunting the ring necks back when I was about 12 or so. I was laying on a snow bank on a moon lit winter night in almost blizzard conditions with a single shot Winchester .22 caliber rifle. No! It wasn't a shot gun. A heavy squall unloading snow on the eastern Dakotas had rolled in and I was outside with my sister's and brother-in-law's dog, Cedric. South Dakota is divided in two sections about equal in size by the ambling Missouri River. One side is West River and the other is East River. East River has more crop land and although West River also has crop land, it is more noted for its wide expanses of cattle country and has more wide open space. Close to the Missouri, West River, the Gregory/Burke area, probably has the most concentrated area for pheasants. Both sides of Dakota are excellent areas for pheasants.

    My brother-in-law, Mark, was a former Prisoner-of-War flying out of England in B-24's. He was shot down over France and interned in a German prison camp for the war. His father was a farmer in heavy pheasant country in East River and Mark took up farming after returning and marrying my sister. I enjoyed working and helping out on the farm in the summers and occasional winter visits and especially enjoyed the company of Cedric, the family dog who was part Golden Retriever and German Shepherd. He was a bit broader and taller than the average size of both breeds. I dearly loved that dog and I think he loved me also. We were almost inseparable except for at night. He would guard the front room door that led to a closed-in porch due to the harsh winters.

My sister was partially crippled and Cedric just took it upon himself that she just might need some extra protection. One night when my brother-in-law went into town and she was alone, an intruder left his car out on the main gravel road and sneaked into the front porch. Fortunately the front door just inside the porch was locked and the man tried to force the door. Cedric was on the inside barking ferociously and the man was trying to break down the door, despite the dog attacking the door from the inside. My sister said she was sitting on the front room couch with a loaded Ithaca 12-gauge, her finger on the trigger. When the door latch finally gave out the intruder met his match and was viciously attacked by Cedric. My sister, although crippled, was quite attractive and the man surely had to be desperate (besides crazy) to face a vicious big dog. He never made it inside the living room. His blood was all over the front porch and he retreated straight through the screen door with Cedric attacking him all the way back to his car where bits and pieces of his bloodied overalls were scattered. It was a wet night and you could see the mud where Cedric knocked him down at least twice. My sister had hobbled into the bedroom to retrieve Mark's always loaded shot gun and regrets she did not use it while Cedric was mauling the intruder on the floor of the front porch but she was too afraid she would have hit her dog.

He was one tough farm dog and useful in other ways as well. We had milk cows in those days and he would bring them in for evening milking. A cantankerous (and dangerous) bull found out the hard way just how forceful Cedric could be. The bull was named 'Fence Jumper' and belonged to the neighbor. It was always getting out and hence his name. The bull came into the front yard from the road out in front and charged at Cedric. The dog leaped right at the bull's nose and hung on viciously while the bull flung him to and fro. Cedric had a Golden's coloring and had that big Golden/Shepherd mouth which bit in hard, drawing blood. The bull started bawling and stopped his flailing. Cedric let go and came around to his back hind legs and bit him several times, sending the Holstein back out to the road on a fast run. It was a daring sight that I will never forget. Besides the bull, other farm dogs gave our farm a wide birth.

One remembrance I have of that dear friend was when he was older and I was a young Marine home on leave and about to ship out for Korea at the age of 17. My sister needed one crutch to walk down to the barn to gather her eggs. Cedric would always escort her on her morning journey. By that time the milk bull had been replaced by an enormous Brahma Bull. Unlike the wandering Holstein, this bull was as tame as a kitten. He belonged to my brother-in-law's friend who had to find him an inside stall for the frigid Dakota winters. Brahmas just do not winter well in northern climes since they came from India and do well in the southern states like Texas and Florida. That is why you rarely see them in the Dakotas. They are rather docile and quite contrary to the mean-like image which we see in the rodeos. This big humped Brahma with the saggy neck skin had a stall that he could retire into on the south side of the barn where his body heat and thick straw bedding kept him comfortable. Well, the Brahma became quite friendly with all of us and would saunter out of his stall when my sister opened the yard gate and he too would escort her with Cedric down to the barn. Cedric on one side, great big humped Brahma on the other and my pretty sister hobbling in the middle. That is one unusual sight! Obviously Cedric did not sense any danger from the bull as they ambled on down toward the barn. Despite the mean Holstein, old Fence Jumper, Cedric just had good old common dog sense. Not all Bulls were mean his opinion obviously.

In the summer, the Brahma took it upon himself to guard and rule the milk cows. Occasionally in those days, bulls would stray away from their own herds and come looking for new cows. Here came 'Fence Jumper' again. Cedric must have gone into town with my sister as normally the Holstein would take the far side of the road up close to the fence when he would come by and run as fast as he could when he would come abreast of the farm. This time he jumped the fence and came onto the Brahma's herd. It was no match. The Brahma butted him back to the fence and simply picked up the wandering bull with his oversized horns and threw him over the fence.

Cedric was probably part everything but the Golden Retriever part gave him his orange color and for size and fighting ability he had a lot of police dog in him. His Golden nose spotted many a pheasant for me when I would go down to the farm near Mitchell, South Dakota from my Black Hills home. I was a bit small and mainly too skinny yet for a 12-gauge shotgun, but I made do with the .22 rifle, which, for a kid with a lot more time at his disposal, is much more effective. I was about as illegal as can be that particular bright moon lit night and completely oblivious to the State of South Dakota game laws when the pheasants flew out of the snow and into the tree above the dog below. The clouds were thin as the squall lightened and the full moon gave them a luminescent glow, allowing me to sight in with a degree of accuracy.

Like most farm boy South Dakotans in my age bracket, we got more pheasants with our .22 rifles than we ever did with a shot gun. Ask an elderly South Dakotan who was raised on a farm in abundant pheasant country. Most will admit that they did not hunt much different than I did. And we ate every bird that we took. In our hunting code, it was unheard of to shoot the bird just for the thrill of killing it. You field cleaned it with a pocket knife and turned it over to the nearest adult who would cook it. Cotton tail rabbits were the same.

Our method of hunting pheasants was pretty simple. Mind you, I no doubt have a whole pheasant abundant, state load of elderly folks to back up what I am trying to tell you. We would spot a pheasant in the distance, usually toward evening when they would be emerging out of the corn and grain fields and on toward the gravel roads to get their gravel for their craws. When we spotted one, Cedric and I would take cover. I'd pat him with a sit signal and he would take position sort of like a 'spotter' that the Marine sniper teams employed except he generally remained sitting. For a young boy, he indeed was one heckuva great companion! As long as we kept our distance, the pheasant seemed to pay little heed to us. I would take the prone position, draw in my breath like my World War II combat Marine brother Mick (Tarawa, Saipan, Marshall Islands and the Gilberts) had taught me and slowly let half of it out. (In my imaginative kid mind, I would often imagine myself as a Marine sneaking up on a Jap garrison with the new M-1 rifle.) In those days, Japs were the enemy and that was what everyone called them including ministers, priests, news people, Congressmen and our Moms and Dads, most of whom had a son or two fighting them or the Germans across the Atlantic. There was no such thing as political correctness way back then. I could sing the Marine Corps Hymn on my way to grade school during the height of the war – all three verses. I was destined to be a Marine but never dreamed I would culminate my active duty career as an actual, real, combat experienced Marine Fighter pilot.

I would commence then to take a steady aim on the bird. At first I would go for the body of the bird but eventually I got fairly accurate and made mostly head shots. That long barreled rifle and my 'kid' steadiness became deadly. As soon as I fired and it was a single shot anyway, Cedric would be up and running. We were quite a team. We never over did our 'poaching;' I guess you would legally have to call it that although the term (which I was unaware of) never entered my mind. We had to clean the bird, at least field clean it, so I never racked up big numbers. Field cleaning is removing its innards but leaving the feathers and feet on. It is fairly easy to do on pheasants once you do it a few times. They are way easier than cleaning ducks or geese. There was always abundant grass to wipe your hands off on. One bird was enough usually because you knew you had to clean it. Once in awhile another rooster would be taken. Mark always told me to never shoot a hen. They were always less bold to come out of seclusion anyway. If another rooster was dumb enough to stand there and watch his buddy flop around then he became fair game too. The big and older roosters nearby always leaped airborne at the sound of the distant rifle shot. It wasn't all that loud because we were at a distance but they had little problem remembering the previous season and may have sported a few pellets embedded as serious reminders. They usually vacated the vicinity rather quickly.

Cedric would pick up the flopping bird and bring it back and, due to his gifted nose, if I just wounded the bird, he would most usually return with it after disappearing in a cornfield for some time, often up to 15 minutes or more but back he would come with the bird in his mouth more often than not. Later, in the Marines I wound up with an expert shooting badge. Maybe this early shooting experience played its role for me.

I am adamant against lying and over-exaggeration. My Indian spirituality is strongly against such type of bad conduct. In our belief system, the Benevolent Creator is All Truth. If we lie and tell false stories (other than mythology or humoristic) than we believe that we are going away from Creator who to us… is All Truth, as I said. In our concept of the Spirit World beyond, we maintain that those who lie and are untruthful in their lives here on Mother Earth… well, they will have to be with their own kind in the Beyond. Those who are truthful and lived their lives, according to plain common sense morals, ethics and Creator's Truth…they will be with each other. In real life here, this practice is most people's choice… in reality. Rest assured however, I do not intend to convert anyone to our Sioux beliefs, especially the white man who is fairly well locked into his own belief system. Like the Jewish people, we just do not proselytize but I only reference my belief system to explain why I mention sometimes, material I probably should 'politically' leave out. What happened however and what I did in my past in relationship to the subject area of this book, I just cannot 'cover up,' so to speak, regardless if some extreme legalism bound types or 'score card' types who will no doubt take exception to what I project, when they read this book. One blizzard night, which I will also honestly relate, Cedric and I did a number on some birds in a spruce tree as well. I imagine that will really rankle a few feathers (from certain of the purist types). It happened. We did it. Take it or leave, is our attitude. I am sure, or at least betting, that Cedric shares my opinion.

Cedric was the all-around type farm dog and I consider him a great dog. He deserves a place in any book I write regarding his particular species. It just wouldn't be respectful if I left him out. After all, he was my first bird dog. The ringnecks were so abundant then; we got our share. I didn't over do my hunting of them. There were too many more exciting targets like the rats and mice in the granary and corn cribs. The rats were the most exciting, especially one particular summer when I was a year older. They were way more exciting than shooting the pheasants which you avoided come summers, even the roosters. Hens were off-limits and not knowing biology much at that age, I just assumed that the roosters were too.

One big rat I shot came up in the crib toward me. I about fell out of my high perch on the rafters, such was my fear. I always carried several rounds in my teeth on those sojourns and managed a quick reload to dispatch him. He was about as big as a cat and it was a real scary situation. Actually, as an after thought, I do not think he was coming at me, as my later experience with those creatures was that they avoid humans as much as possible. He must not have seen my location and was simply trying to avoid whatever was inflicting his sudden wound down below. He just happened to come my way. One never knows, I guess, but he certainly gave me a shiver. Can you imagine a big rat the size of a cat coming at you?

My second summer on the farm, the rats would come out en masse come evening, usually down by the hog yard where they would feed on spilled grain and no doubt the undigested corn from the cattle and hog droppings. They are practically extinct on most Dakota farms now due mainly to the effective warfarin anti-coagulant poison. Back then, these rats were getting a bit numerous as my single shot could not keep up with their reproduction. Maybe they belonged to one of those certain religious groups that zealously believes we humans need to over-populate our planet. The more I shot at them, the more cunning they became. The slightest movement from the house toward evening and they would scatter back under the foundation of the storage structures. I had grown a bit by my second year there at the farm and my brother-in-law suggested that I try out his Ithaca pump 12-gauge, Model 37 with a lighter load shell than the normal pheasant load. It didn't seem to kick as hard as I expected when we first tried it out. He had me fire in succession several times, working the pump which was quite a first time thrill for me. It was sort of like when he had me drive the hand clutch John Deere tractor for the first time. I admit that *that* was a much bigger thrill.

This time I had to sneak up on them and had to leave Cedric in the house which was situated between the west and north shelter belt and faced east toward the farm structures. The rats lived under the granary, mostly. It was the first building you passed when you came into the driveway from the newly paved blacktop road east of the farm. It was the first time I heard Cedric whine with disappointment as I closed the back door with my Ithaca pump in hand. My brother-in-law always kept that gun loaded. He had left the low powered skeet shells in it; I noticed when I checked it. I cocked it open and rammed a shell into the chamber. I took a shell out of my pocket and placed that into the tube. I checked the safe and headed north, crouching low. I had sneaked out the back door so that the now educated rats would not see me. I sneaked back through the north shelter belt and then east into the farm structures from the north and on toward the east side of the last building, a machine shed before the granary where the rats would be feeding and we had earlier spilled a little extra corn purposely on the south side. I pushed the gun's safe off.

Around the corner I flew, my pump gun blazing at the first sign of the rats. Big ones and little ones went scurrying. I wounded quite a few was my guess but only three were shot outright dead. Some hopped and jumped but made it back to their dwelling. If I would have had Cedric, I figured I would have got at least a few more as he would always run in after a .22 long shot and finish off a wounded one.

For several days there were no rats. Mark said eventually, if I kept at them, they would move to another farm. Mark didn't waste words but when he did speak he was usually always right. He sure was smart to give me those lower powered shells. I was a skinny little thing when I was that age. I had another brother-in-law that would load you up with a high-powered shell just to have a good laugh when it kicked hell out of you. It was good for a young kid to have such a thoughtful adult around while he was growing up. Especially one that would turn you loose on a tractor after some careful instruction. John Deere developed my motor skills early. Maybe that is why I had few problems learning to fly in flight school, especially formation flying and eventually stepping into the top fighter of our times – the Phantom F4B. It had so much power that you could climb straight up with it.

Once Mark told me about a lone P-51 pilot that saved their lives. He said they were returning to England all shot up and crippled, a B-24. On the way back a group of Messershmidts ganged up and formed an attack formation. They line up abreast on a crippled bomber and then flick in one by one on the attack. Just as they were about formed up a lone P-51 showed up and without hesitation attacked the flock of German fighters, breaking them up from attacking their bomber. He said they had no idea what happened to that 51 pilot but it was the bravest act he saw in the war. What ever happened to that American pilot we will never know until we reach the Spirit World where my religion believes all acts are recorded – good and bad. That pilot should be honored. Maybe then and there I wanted to be a pilot someday or at least try. I never dreamed I would be one let alone a combat one.

As I said, Mark was usually pretty right about a lot of things but I was hoping that he could be wrong regarding the rats' leaving, however. They were much more thrilling to stalk and shoot than the silly pocket gophers that also were fairly numerous. In a day or two after their seclusion, the rats returned. While the animals were hiding, I worked with Cedric to obey silent commands. I wanted to get more rats and Cedric figured in my plans. No one taught me how to do it and I had no book to read. I just did it out of sheer common sense and Cedric responded out of his sheer dog common sense, like he already knew what the heck I was up to. I still train my dogs that way, which, if you continue to read onward, you will find out.

We repeated the sneak up procedure with him at my rear. I'd signal him to stay (sit) with hand signals and with words initially and then advance when I motioned to him with a come-on gesture. Never would I let him get ahead of me, although he would come up beside me and I would give him a pet and tell him how smart he was. Maybe, way back then, I was cultivating my own teaching skills. Dogs love to know that they are being appreciated. Soon he was doing a good job with my no-word training. I never hit Cedric or yelled at him or was otherwise mean to him. At my age and size, it would have been quite foolhardy. To this day that is my motto or official 'modus operandi.' You do not hit a Golden! Be surprised how quickly they learn when they are totally relaxed in your training presence. I don't like arguing with humans. Why should I argue with my four legged hunting companion? Since I never attempted to intimidate him, he thusly always responded in a confident and willing-to-please manner. A relaxed atmosphere certainly speeds up the learning process. I follow that procedure to this day in the training of my Goldens and have had abundant success with them.

I do hope that some of you readers pay serious heed to what I have just related. Mind you, I have little experience with the other breeds of dogs. I cannot speak for their effective training methods.

I took the shot gun way out into the slough, about a half section (half mile) from the house and the rats. The slough had a pond that was home to ducks and those funny little skitter things we called coots or Grebes. It was summer and full of various birds. Some roosters lifted as I approached. A momma duck with her little ones following behind went quacking away into the cattails. I never gave them a thought, since I was so intense on my dog training. Cedric was happily out front sniffing away. I called him to me and we went through our stalking procedure as we drew closer to the pond. Before we got to some cattails, I had him stay. I advanced slowly and just as I came closer to the open water, I put on a burst of speed and opened up with a couple rounds into the clear water. I figured I was far enough away so as not to disturb my main quarry – the rats. Cedric needed no signal with the burst of gunfire. He was right there immediately after I fired and went into the water to retrieve whatever I had fired at. He swam around searching futilely for a minute then came back to shake water on me when he came ashore. Maybe he was telling me to hit something when I fired.

We employed our technique the next evening. Later in life, several decades in fact, I would be employing this same successful technique road hunting with my Golden Retrievers. Then, it would be wily roosters as our quarry. It worked. Cedric killed or finished off a few wounded rats each time we attacked them; at least for a while.

I think that the rats eventually employed 'scout rats' for they seemed to be always resourceful. Soon they would vanish when we sprang around the corner. We tried coming around the west side and that worked a couple times but then they had a sentry out on that side too. I noticed that we were affecting their population, however, on those two successful encounters.

Next we crept down to the hog house for a frontal assault and I had to pretend I was a John Wayne Marine when we had to crawl over hog poop. Cedric didn't appreciate this stint but he stayed with me and didn't go back to the house. I bore sighted them that time after a careful and long crawl with Cedric patiently crawling behind. We had a convenient hole in the wooden slated hog fence. I hammered my final rounds into them as they fled under the granary.

With that encounter, every last one of them departed. The farmer near by complained to my brother in law that he suddenly had a noticeable jump in his rat population. Mice hunting just wasn't fun any more compared to the rats. They never bunched up and Cedric wouldn't think of picking one up after I had dispatched it. It is strange to admit but we both dearly regretted the departure of the rats.

I can't remember exactly why I was playing around outside that particular winter night when we shot the pheasants. Kids don't have to have reasons for going out in the snow with the family dog, especially with such a companion as Cedric.

I remember walking near some Spruce trees and Cedric was ahead of me. The short lived squall blizzard snow was beating down heavily upon us. All of a sudden the snow burst open beside Cedric and a pheasant had flown out of the snow and into the upper branches of the tree. Cedric stuck his nose into the snow and several more pheasants burst out and since the snow was falling so heavy with the wind, they conveniently remained in the tree branches safe from the dog below. I called to Cedric and we ran to the farm house for the single shot .22. When we returned, we could see the pheasants bobbing in the upper branches. I took a prone position at a distance while Cedric ran to the tree sending a few more up and barking at the birds. Several more burst out of the snow and joined their companions above. I took aim at the bobbing blots with the snow swirling in my eyes. The whiteness all around allowed me adequate vision to fulfill my task. I hit one and it began to fall to a lower branch. I shot at it again and it fluttered down low enough for the leaping dog to grab. We repeated the procedure several times. Cedric would bark down below and leap up high when the tumbling bird came within his reach. After about a half dozen or more birds, the flock fled out into the blizzard night while we retrieved our pheasants, which we ate in due time.

The next day, under a bright morning sun, I found one more bird that I had shot that had flown for about a hundred yards and expired. Like I said, we didn't waste game. That bird 'went into the pot.' My sister read this passage recently on that wonderful long departed animal and asked me, "Don't you remember when you two came in with your pheasants that night? Cedric had one in his mouth." She looked back into time and her eyes lit…her smile made her glow. "He was prancing in, …so proud of it."

"Oh yeah. I forgot all about that." I searched my mind and the long ago past.

My sis laughed loudly. "He put it down, and it came too and flew all over the house."

"I remember going under the cupboard to finally get a hold of it." I replied. I guess…way back then…with my first bunch of pheasants, at least seven or eight of them in total, I was bound to have some unusual experiences. I bet that's one of the few times any wild pheasant ever got loose in someone's house.

3

Four Great Dogs

Number I

They say a man has only one great or good dog. I beg to differ. I have been exposed to at least four, and a couple others were pretty close to being extra exceptional. Two of the great dogs were not pure bred hunting dogs. Cedric was not my dog, per se, but we spent a considerable amount of time together. And he was instrumental at my getting my first ringnecks. He has to be Number I.

Number II

Another dog was a brilliant and beautiful German shepherd that seemed to be part wolf as he was so large and strong and he had nothing to do with the ringneck.

I was a young Marine pilot then and drove a Kharman Ghia convertible. With the top down, Perpsie, would ride in the small back, standing up like a statue as we drove around. He was a smart one and you could get him to do anything. We dressed him up as an old grandmother, complete with metal framed 'Granny' glasses and a 'Granny' night cap. Of course some elastic bands helped to keep them secure upon the dog. I worked with him for a couple days prior to the big costume party at the officer's club getting him used to his paraphernalia. Like I said, you could get him to do almost anything. We even fashioned a sort of lace night gown for him. My attractive wife went as Little Red Riding Hood complete with a red cape and the going-to-see-grandmother little basket and of course Perpsie went as 'Grandmother' dressed in wolf's clothing or vice versa. It brought the house down, so to speak, at the party. Even the base General and his wife had to come over and personally complement us. A pilot friend borrowed my warbonnet and part of my Indian dance regalia and won first place along with my wife. Perpsie is a rather strange name, I know. But like I will probably repeat several times: real life (and real hunting) just is not like the movies.

Once we moved into a new neighborhood near a Marine base, a North Carolina town. We had a rented dwelling on a circle of similar houses. Behind the circle a small creek coursed behind the house. I was a new pilot fresh out of flight school with my pretty wife and in a squadron. Life was good. We were not there long before a large pit bull bulled his way down into the back of our yard and on out toward the circle. I found out that this was his customary walk and all and any dogs in the vicinity promptly disappeared from view. A neighbor hated that dog mainly because he claimed that he was the one that had killed a chained up female German shepherd near by.

Perpsie was one big German shepherd with a big head, actually oversized, which gave him the advantage of quite a large sized mouth. He had been in a few successful fights that large dogs seem to always encounter sooner or later since he had always accompanied the paper boy at our last location. Naturally the paper boy dearly loved the amiable and a bit overly friendly dog. Well, here came the pit bull and I was relieved that they did not fight, but Perpsie followed that Pit Bull right up tight to his skin in escorting him through the yard. It was sort of like 'One move Buster and we are going to tangle,' as my German Shepherd leaned into that shorter but heavier monster while escorting him on. I was scared to death as I looked on as I had heard that pit bulls never lose in a fight with other breeds. I hardly noticed that the pit bull seemed rather anxious to get the hell out of our yard with that oversized, younger and in his prime German Shepherd breathing down his neck. After that semi-encounter the Pit Bull never came back and the neighborhood kids who loved to play with my amiable dog all hailed, "Perpsie, Perpsie! King of the Circle." Perpsie loved to chase and retrieve balls which the kids enjoyed. "Perpsie, Perpsie! King of the Circle," they would chant.

It must have bothered the pit bull woman upstream from our circle because eventually she came down for a brief visit or actually a warning. She was simply a slob is about the only way I can accurately describe her. I think she resented that I was an officer and a pilot, with a good looking, trim wife on top of that and probably the kids having a good time with my dog every evening, with no more interference from her Pit Bull scaring off the kids' dogs whom Perpsie played well with. "I want to give you fair warning." She said. "My dog kills German Shepherds. So be careful he doesn't wander up our way."

I replied that I was well aware that her dog had killed the female German Shepherd and would keep an eye on Perpsie.

Well eventually, curiosity got the best of me. I just couldn't believe my dog was about to lose to a dog, which was a bit older and decidedly not in much physical shape compared to my big wolf like guy who was constantly in action, especially with the kids on the circle. I guess the fact that the so called 'killer beast' had anxiously wanted to get the hell away from my dog was too much of an incentive. I was also moved by just not liking the bully S.O.B in the first place and, of course, what he did to the female.

What next is to transpire may not belong in a so called hunting book but I recall it; say, as a tribute to all the good dogs that the criminal Michael Vick no doubt threw into his Pit Bulls just for sheer practice. No doubt many were good and fine hunting dogs who rarely fight: gobbled up and cruelly broken by his G.D. Pit Bulls.

I was on my bicycle and Perpsie was out in back. The very shallow, small, sandy Carolina creeks are firm enough to ride in and before long I was up behind 'Pit Bull Momma's' house. Suddenly, two half breed pit bulls came bursting out of the back of the adjoining house and came running and barking down toward us. Perpsie spotted them and I honestly didn't fear for him at that moment. 'Two half-brothers,' I guessed. I figured that they would soon put their brakes on and stop and run back as they were a bit smaller than their obvious predecessor. They kept on coming down the long yard though, to my surprise. The lead one bravely charged into my dog while the second one waited briefly to make his move. Out of the corner of my eye I caught a shadow open the back door of the adjoining house – Pit Bull Momma! ... and out came the bruiser. So this is how they operated. I picked up my bicycle to stop or slow down the main killer, ready to slam it into him. Perpsie met the first dog and immediately broke its leg with a decided crunch. A high yelp emitted from the lead attacker and then the Shepherd turned on the smaller one, shaking him and sending him flying like a rat. Both wanted no more from this newcomer and ran back to their house. Meanwhile 'Killer' had such a head of steam up that he couldn't stop and didn't realize he would be fighting now...all alone. When he did realize he had no help he started to turn but Perpsie was so mad that he grabbed him by the back of his neck and those big Wolf jaws went to work. He growled madly is the only way I can describe him as he attacked and it wasn't a fear growl it was utter, P.O. madness! He certainly was mad for those brief moments as if he completely understood what they were up to and how they had played their unfair and vicious game.

The next day, 'Killer' died of wounds and no one came down to complain. All the neighborhood was happier and willing to testify that it was three on one after I told a few what happened. Big Momma never showed. Ever since, I have never liked Pit Bulls. The Englishman on the airplane told me that Pit Bulls were banned in the British Isles, after our conversation drifted toward dogs and various breeds. I imagine the infamous dog fighting promoter, Michael Vick, in his jail cell wishes they would have been banned over here.

Number III

My third 'Great Dog' is Old Rex. Old Rex became his 'nomer' after the young one came along.

I never dreamed that I would have a better hunter than Rex III. Oh, he had his faults as just about every dog with a personality has. But in my opinion, what faults he had, they were not that overwhelming to be seriously detrimental to his hunting. If I wanted to be picky, I'd complain that I didn't like it when he spotted the waiting pickup as we returned. Usually you walk the ditch back up to your vehicle which often can serve as an efficient blocker for any birds you happen to be fortunate enough to be driving ahead of you. Mostly there are no existing birds but once in a while you get lucky. Rex, would almost quit hunting once you got within 50 yards of the truck or car. I tried to break him of this habit by purposely walking on past the truck but to no avail. He would head for the truck.

What he did for me however, on one wintry day, made any and all faults immaterial, insignificant and out and out unimportant.

My new son-in-law from Queens, New York of all places, was on his first Dakota pheasant hunt. A big storm was about to roll in and he had to leave early and get back to his new job in western Dakota. I always like to hunt with him because if there is such a thing as 'luck,' (which I honestly do not believe in) then he certainly brings it for me. I simply have uncanny shots when he is close by. So much that he foolishly thinks that I am one hot shot bird hunter. The ground beneath me never crumbles just as I pull the trigger, no roosters lift into the sun, the dog seems to point more and flushes up easier shots more often, fewer hens rise for me in comparison to roosters and I even manage to rarely fumble with getting that safe off. The gun never jams either. I hated to see him leave.

Well, the winter storm rolled in early. We were still in to October and most often that close to Opening day we are in our T-shirts even. The guys I hunt with near Mitchell were comfortably playing cards in the Hunting Birds Garage.

I was fortunate to know a group of 'locals' from Emery, South Dakota, just east of Mitchell that I wound up hunting with for years. I had Rex II way back then and he was a good pheasant finder. One day I came across a group of local hunters while out solo. Two of their group were nephews of my brother-in-law and they were having a bit of trouble getting out some downed roosters hiding in tunnel grass. Rex II found a couple birds for them and I have been hunting with them ever since. It pays to have a good dog.

While they were all crunched around the table playing cards, I went out to a restaurant and ate some lunch, waiting for the weather to lift. By mid-afternoon I was a bit bored and decided that I would go out to some public land and see what I could scare up while the wind howled. It wasn't a very bright decision and several told me to stay put, but to no avail. Rex was waiting in my van and his wagging tail coaxed me into thinking I had made the right decision. I had a five day out-of-state license and wanted to make the most of it. I had left my native state for Minnesota and hence was now an out-of-stater.

We started out east of Emery. I parked at a public hunting site after passing a white house with a fairly large barn. The public land was loaded with sloughs barely frozen over and mostly slushy ice at that, enough so that you could not cross them. I walked into the area which was loaded with ponds. It was a waiting trap.

Rex got a rooster up right off the bat, to make my situation worse. I downed it and another got up and dropped farther into the area away from our van. I felt pretty good about my shooting and watched Rex get up some hens. Farther we went into the slough which was actually several sloughs and ponds. The snow swirled down heavily and weirdly above me sheet lightning rumbled. I looked up at the swirling grey and the sky seemed like it wanted to crack open with the blue grey sheet lightning rumbling. I thought how a swimmer must feel when a Great White, man-eating shark would be circling him. All of a sudden things went one dimensional. I had a stupid thought. I imagined a great big shark coming down out of that grey, ominous, swirling sky. I even held up my Benelli to dispense with such foolish wandering of one's mind. I thought how odd it was for thunder to accompany a snow storm. Maybe it was the powerful roaring of the thunder that was leading me to such foolish and actually idiotic fantasy. It certainly was not a boring situation that was for sure.

The snow pelted down and it wasn't long before I was completely turned around and disoriented. It was getting late and sundown was coming earlier every day. When I realized I didn't know where I was I looked every which way and I seemed to be blocked by water. Visibility was down; I could barely see the cattails at the pond edges. The sun was getting lower. I stupidly had no matches or a compass. Had I had matches or a lighter, I would have tried to wade across a pond as most are shallow and started breaking down tree branches from a shelter belt, especially the fallen ones or dead ones. 'Build a fire and sit out the night,' would have been my strategy. That is what most lost deer hunters who wisely have matches or a lighter do. But what pheasant hunter expects to get lost? Find a fence and it will usually lead you to a road or a dwelling. But swamps don't have fences. I was beginning to get myself into one helluva predicament. I almost started to panic. I had some degree of panic or muffled thinking because I failed to realize that the storm was coming in from the northwest. My left side was being covered by snow. If I turned slightly right, I'd be facing north toward the highway that ran past the swamp, running east/west. I was too muddled to realize that, however; such was the overpowering enrapture with my disorientation that brought me to near panic. I was flat lost!

I did have sense enough to 'get lighter.' I threw my two roosters out of my vest. The second one was still warm so I put that one back into the front part of my vest. My glove had frozen wet and I threw that away for the temporary warmth of the pheasant. I started to empty all the ammunition I was carrying. I thought about leaving my Benelli as well and if it were not for its sling, I would have. I didn't eject its shells. Keep calm, I told myself as the sun started to shrink. I remembered back when I was crashing a Phantom. Concentrate, concentrate I told myself and did the right procedure to save most of the airplane and myself along with it. I wasn't cited for any pilot error.

Something made me think of my tracks. 'Your Tracks. Your Tracks,' sang through my mind. Rex came over and rolled on the snow playfully as to reinforce the newfound phrase. 'Your Tracks. Your Tracks.' Sang out. I looked down. Rexie rolled. I walked on, getting colder by the minute. Then I suddenly stopped and called to my dog. "Rex!" I yelled against the storm. "Let go home, Rex. Find the Car, Rex. Find the Car." Rex put his nose down to our fresh tracks. I started to back track to encourage him and kept on going while the swirling snow was rapidly covering them. He started out ahead of me and kept on even after they had faded from my vision. It looked like we were heading back. Then, all of a sudden as we approached the edge of a pond, a car slowly drove by. I damned near jerked my shotgun out from my shoulder and blew a hole in the car's back end to get it to stop. It was just across the pond; that close! I jerked on my Benelli and as I did so the wind let up and to my right at the edge of the pond, my side of the highway, I spotted a fence line. We turned and at the fence line crossed over to the road. To our left, west, where we had parked our van, there was the more conspicuous barn and the white house, vaguely in the distance. Rex had gotten me out. I shivered almost uncontrollably when I started the van.

Lost Again

Up in the north woods of Minnesota, Rex repeated what he had done for me in Dakota. That time, my son-in-law and I went out for some grouse, what we call Prairie Chickens. I am not a big fan of trying to shoot around trees as a straight shot out of a cornfield is tough enough for me but my son-in-law talked me into grouse so off we went. I remember back in my college days when my roommate, John Nordlum, from International Falls, Minnesota, the nation's cold spot, took me out after some Spring season walleyes. Nearby Rainy Lake was loaded with that delicious fish, back then. We used to feast on those delicious Walleyes and feasted also on Ruffed Grouse. Up there they are referred to as 'Spruce Hens.' We took them with rocks or a .22 pistol; you could get so close to them. Not so, the Sage Hen or Prairie Chicken which are much larger. In the North Country, we had a goodly plot of land to hunt on from one of the hockey player's Dad, Jim Gehrke. I had taken his son, Chris, with my last son Kyle, both hockey defensemen, out on a prairie dog/Dakota rattle snake excursion and his land offer was a form of reciprocation. His son came back all aglow from the excitement of shooting, cooking and eating his first rattlesnake besides firing a brick of shells at the elusive and grass consuming prairie dogs.

Rex III was still my dog back then and again pulled both of us out of danger when we managed to get briefly lost in those big woods. We started out in a circle out from the cabin and got up a few grouse. The highway was about a mile away to our south but in those dense woods it seemed a bit farther. We started out southwest from the cabin and took a few birds and then started our circle back. We were about a half mile from the highway and you could hear occasional traffic. Evening was approaching and after we started on our return orbit, we over shot the cabin and came up against a large swamp. We were fortunate to know that behind us was the highway and you could still barely hear the passing traffic. I told Rex to once again, "Go find the car, Rex. Let's go home, Rex. Find the car." Rex turned around and took us straight to the cabin which was behind us and a bit farther in within our circle. We would have been able to see the glow of lights from the distant passing cars eventually and been able to find our way to the highway but this was another example of Rex III's ability to get us back safely.

It hasn't been that long since this great one's passing, Rex III. I will save his hunting exploits and input for blending in with the bulk of the hunting stories yet to come.

The Gehrke cabin is where Rex III and I trained my last dog with ten pheasants which will appear in the Training Your Dog chapter. It is so much easier and more productive if your older dog is still around to help train the young successor that is up and coming. The older dog usually is not too fond of this new intruder into his exclusive domain but when it comes to training with dead or live birds and then real hunting, all jealousy and intolerance toward the beginner is most often thrown to the winds by the older, experienced dog, such was the case when Rex III trained the younger one.

Number IV

My present Golden Retriever… "Puppy." I guess I should have called him Rex after his predecessor passed on but I just never got around to it. The exceptional way he hunts for me and others as well, we really don't care what his name is, anymore, to be truthful. Like Cedric, he just doesn't need a fancy name. Mind you, there are much better dogs than mine, were we ever to be challenged in a field trial. But for an over all companion, I am more than satisfied with that little bundle of fur I picked up one March day near St. Cloud, Minnesota.

Unlike the rescuing ability of old Rex however, the following is a related episode that I believe is worth mentioning, regarding Puppy and I. Yes, Pheasant hunting can be outright dangerous, not just from weather alone. One does take a risk, especially out hunting by yourself.. Maybe it is the old fighter pilot that still lurks within me but even after the following, I still go out there with just my dog. Puppy did an almost unintentional fatal number on me when he was less than two years old. One dog had saved my life, the next one almost took it.

We were hunting down in Iowa during the holiday season and that time of year, my hunting companions were too tied up in the usual season's social events to go out with me hunting on that particular day. Right beside my motel, which was at the edge of the city limits. (It is a small town with only one motel.) A shallow drainage ditch courses through the northern edge of the town running west to east. I frequently stay at this particular motel and had always noticed an abundance of birds going in and out of it about 100 yards from the highway crossing less than a block from the motel. Being by myself, I thought that this was as good a place to hunt as any.

I had hunted the week before with my local hunting friends beginning at a bridge farther upstream from the motel, just outside the city limits so I walked on the frozen ice at the bottom of the fairly deep drainage ditch to the bridge crossing for the gravel road farther west and began hunting. The depression of the ditch was about eight to ten feet, enough to hide a walking man and almost immediately we got up a flock of hens lifting from the gentler sloping sides of the ditch in comparison to the usual sharper slant of most Iowa drainage ditches I have experienced. As we walked, the narrow frozen stream spread out to frozen pools. Nothing but hens seemed to be rising as we walked along. Finally a rooster got up just out of range and since that area's slope was easily accessed, we probed the thick grass for a possible extra rooster. After awhile, I went back to the bottom of the ditch and headed upstream. I usually stay with my dog when he is poking around searching but the area just did not look productive and I figured the dog would soon join me.

A couple hens bursting out of shallow cover were the reason why he had stayed yet I kept on walking. Finally after I began to cross a larger frozen pool, I turned and called to my dog and added a beckoning pat of my knee to join back up with me. With this signal, Puppy leaped with his young energy and started to run toward me. Mind you, this was a frozen over pool that separated us. I had but a few yards left to go to the edge of the pool and turned and kept walking. This was a very big mistake. All of a sudden, my world turned into a half somersault. Up into the air I went heels high up over my head which went crashing onto the ice and fortunate was I wearing my very winter-ish, Mongolian Marine cold weather hat which is pictured on the back of this book. Despite the fur padding, I went into darkness with my dog licking my face when I woke up. How long I was lying there I had no idea. My Benelli was lying on the ice about ten yards away. My neck was sore and my head hurt and I was staring up at my dog who kept licking my face. I do love my dog…all of them, but at that moment I remember saying slowly, very slowly, out of my stupor… "Puppy… you…Son…of…a…Bitch!"

I wasn't angry at the dog. It wasn't his fault. But I still said it.

What had happened was when he hit the ice at full speed, he could not stop. He went sliding, crashing into me and with his size hit me right at the back of my knees with almost 80 pounds of fast moving force and up into the air I went. I was thoroughly checked as if he was a hockey defenseman. For a long moment as I laid there, (I think the word 'laid' is a much more applicable word for description and to hell with the Academics!) (Ain't is also a handy writing word at times.) I wondered if my body was still working. My neck was darn sore and my head was throbbing. Still in my stupor, I started to panic. This was a very poor place to be paralyzed, I began to think. For that matter, any place is a helluva place to so be restricted. Slowly, as I began to focus, I began to be afraid to even try and find out if I was okay or not. My arms did not want to move it seemed. Slowly I went to my legs and wondered fearfully if I could feel my toes wiggling. What a relief. Then I could move my legs. What another bunch of relief. I could imagine myself lying at the bottom of this drainage ditch and no one would find you, not until it was way too late. I tried to move my shoulders and they moved. And then my fingers and hands could move. It was one scary experience. I rose slowly to my knees and crawled toward my Benelli and began walking after I retrieved it, downstream this time, back to the motel.

Like Rex III, 'Puppy' will stand out within the many stories about to come. One example is when we were all getting assembled for a cornfield walk and it was a genteel resort crowd, sixties and upwards, and mostly over and unders. Those experienced folks don't miss many shots. While the dogs were being let out of their kennels, Puppy, who always rides free in the client bus ambled over to some heavy weeds by the nearby cornfield obviously drawn by the fresh scent from a bird deciding to exit the bus parking spot when we drove up. I never saw him leave but there he was, standing among the startled and exclaiming hunters looking for me with a live rooster in his mouth. All the rest of my memories are very positive about this dog who turned out to be the most outstanding hunting dog I ever had despite his defenseman-like ability to knock you down on the ice. It could have been a pretty tough situation back then… but I sure as heck hate to do my passing on…in an old folk's home. I plan to keep on hunting, and often with just the dog and I, as long as I can! Hopefully I can avoid what so much of America winds up in… the old folk's homes. Get out and hunt and keep that body moving…is my advice.

Puppy does have a good friend, an elderly lady that lives next door to him. Her name is Helen Neitzel. Every dog owner should be so fortunate to have such a neighbor. She fell in love with Rex III when he was but a pup and mourned his loss right along with the rest of us when he passed. She insisted that she pay for half of his veterinarian bill including the cremation. He is buried by the lake in back of the house. Pup goes to visit her often and at times stays overnight sleeping at the foot of her bed as did Rex. His picture and Rex III grace her night stand. He also has the run of her land that borders the lake in back. Incidentally that lake is loaded with ducks and geese that come up to her backyard bird feeder that often holds corn as well for the larger birds. Both my dogs got rather used to them and learned to tolerate their presence especially when the big Canadians stood their ground come Spring when their young arrived.

4

Picking Your Pup

This simple, practical method, for picking out your young dog, that I will bring out eventually, I have never found in the few hunting books I have read.

Most hunters will randomly select their dog out of a litter. Most often, the largest male goes first and so on down the line. We always hear the term, 'Pick of the litter,' or 'He was the runt of the litter, the last pick.'

My last three dogs have come from a certain line that caters to field dog classification versus show dog classification. The show dogs bring a higher price but no way do I want a show dog over a field dog bred line regardless of how pretty they are. I personally feel sorry for the show dogs, just my admittedly biased opinion. The hunting dog (field line) is bred to do just that…to Hunt! The show dog's instincts have been curtailed to the extreme and most, actually practically all… will never have a bird in their mouths. This subject reminds me of how sad it was for the old Sioux warriors who had to eventually come into the federal Indian reservation system and would no longer hunt the buffalo… the deer and the elk as well. Eventually, the Sioux warriors would even have their ponies taken from them. They were such effective fighters against the United States Cavalry, that the government, the politicians and lobbyists mainly, came up with the idea that they should lose their mounts as well. It all brought chaos and despair to a proud people who had a respected record as great buffalo hunters and had held the United States Army down for over a decade, mainly under three courageous and able leaders, first Chief Red Cloud and then later, Chiefs Sitting Bull and Crazy Horse.

Over-population and Predators

The hunting world is actually rapidly beginning to experience a portion of what the old warriors suffered. We are now witnessing the steady erosion and loss of hunting privileges and opportunity. The NRA (National Rifle Association) membership is steadily declining. I blame over-population mainly and hunting experts much more knowledgeable than I in this matter have a long list of the major reasons why. The core of the loss however is still directly traceable to more people and less available land. What land is left, greed has taken out the fence lines, drainage has removed the wet lands, and essential cover has disappeared. Dakota still has room and the farmers and ranchers still do not 'plow up to the middle of the highway,' so to speak. There still exists such things called ditches along our gravel roads which are not mowed until after the Spring chicks are more mobile, and hopefully some Game, Fish & Parks Department egghead (DNR (Department of Natural Resources in other states) will not change this law. We South Dakotans are allowed to keep a loaded rifle in open view within our vehicles uncased for predator control. (No shell in the chamber, of course.) Yes, this is a very true South Dakota allowance. I know that this is a bit difficult to believe, such are the ever increasing gun control laws. We do not have to call the G,F&P (Game, Fish & Parks Department) either, for permission to shoot a predator – skunk, raccoon, possum, fox, feral cat or coyote. Most states use the term DNR for their wildlife/habitat department. Hawks and owls are protected federally however; even though they take their toll of ring necks. Again, I hope some Game, Fish & Parks egghead does not get the state ruling regarding predator control altered or changed. We had one egghead claim that 'Predators do not harm the pheasant crop.' Thank someone who allowed this person to retire early. I will repeat my protective philosophy in favor of hunting throughout this writing, so be forewarned.

Turkeys?

As I mentioned earlier, I am wondering if I should add 'Turkeys' to the Dakota predator list except for the Black Hills area which is fairly devoid of ring necks. We have numerous pheasant hunters visit from the south. They recall their early days when quail were abundant. Like Southern Iowa, the quail are gone. Northern Iowa is quite abundant with pheasants at the time of this writing and I have yet to encounter turkeys in that portion of the state. I remember going to Southern Iowa a while back with Rex number II and getting my introduction to the thrill of quail hunting. They are mostly all gone now as it is in the south as well. So far, the Game, Fish & Parks (DNR) administration is not a bit worried in regard to my 'imagined' danger of turkeys. I saw my first turkeys in eastern Dakota this past season and was shocked. I shot one of those things down in Iowa a while back. The farmer asked me to get one for him back on his land. He had a license for one but was a bit crippled up. My dog wouldn't pick it up, just sniffed it. It turned out to be far from being a butter ball when we butchered it out in his barn. You know, the 'Butter-ball' types we buy in the stores for Thanksgiving. Turkey adherents tell me that the gobblers do not eat pheasant eggs and won't move hatching hens off their nests. How they get this information beats me. As I said, I was shocked this past season to find a flock of turkeys in Eastern South Dakota. A turkey is much larger than a hen peasant and food is food out there in the wild. I hope I will find out otherwise from the Game, Fish & Parks folks relative to my 'Sky is falling' supposition but my concern for our pheasant population is worth some scrutiny be it real or imagined. I guess the comparison between Northern and once abundant Southern Iowa is worth looking into.

Agricultural Practice

The 'differing farming practice' alibi doesn't hold up because Northern Iowa farming is the same as the Southern farming. Southern Iowa is loaded with Turkeys however and Northern is not. Southern Iowa is not loaded with Pheasants however and Northern is. Before the Turkeys, Southern Iowa was once abundant with ring necks. To me, this glaring evidence makes me a bit wary of the immigration of Tom Turkey into fertile pheasant grounds. It might be easier sitting all bound up like some kind of mummy in a camouflaged burka making a bunch of cackling and rasping sounds but I prefer walking the miles, the repeated excitement along with the repeated adrenaline rush and getting off a few more rounds to get my type of bird. I just hope that the administrative scrutiny by the upper level Game, Fish & Parks echelon will at least be perked and that they take notice. I am all for Turkey hunting away from pheasant habitat like our Black Hills offers although for me, at least, a bit boring in my opinion compared to the wily ringneck.

Finding Your Pup

Let us move on to picking out one's pup.

This subject could easily be summed up by three words. Those words are... Bring a Pheasant! That is how I picked my last dog who was so cute as a puppy (Are not they all?) Eventually, we simply named him just that... 'Puppy.'

I keep several roosters frozen from the previous season. I field clean them prior to their placement in the freezer. Field cleaning is just that. You remove the insides and leave the feathers and feet on the bird. Often this is done, 'in the field' without the benefit of running water, so hence the term. A pheasant is the easiest animal to clean. The skin simply peels off and you can cut off the feet easily with a strong pair of scissors and likewise at the wing and thigh joints. A couple frozen roosters, completely intact wrapped up in a plastic grocery sack, except for their innards, takes up a bit of room in the freezer but that is life. Even when I have a brand new pup, I put away several roosters every fall for 'contingency' purposes. You never know how the pup will work out or a friend may want to train a dog or worst of all fates, one could lose one's dog to illness or accident – usually being run over by a car.

Another fate which I have seen befall some bad luck hunters is that some dogs just will not get over being gun shy and eventually after repeated trial and procedures, the dog will have to be given away or kept as purely a house pet – No Hunting – status. We will discuss my technique for countering gun shyness later. I happened to lose my first golden to a car since I rarely kennel my dog and they are raised as house dogs besides their usual run as a hunting companion. That first one was unneutered, which gives them a tendency to wander. My last dog simply refuses to go into a kennel – even at the pheasant resort where he is quite welcome by the owner to roam free. He poses before the hunters for their pictures most often in front of a goodly stack of birds. He looks straight into the camera by the birds and hunters all standing behind him. Maybe that is why he is granted such favored status. Possibly, he just might be the most photographed hunting dog in Dakota or at least a major contender for that title.

Rex III was getting older, about 11, and the next season would be his last was my estimate. Larger hunting dogs just do not have long lives in comparison to the smaller dogs, it seems. If you can get 13 years or more out of a dog that hunts often, you are lucky. They will hunt right up to the end, such is their desire and it is an oft repeated sad, very sad experience one has to go through with good hunting dogs – taking the dog to a Vet to be gracefully and humanely put down. Rex had lymphatic trouble and I hoped he could make it at least into the summer to help me train a new pup.

I drove to a Minnesota town about eighty miles north of Minneapolis near my undergraduate college, which has a more respectful title as a University to be a bit more on the political correct side. I received a biology degree there and afterwards went into the Marines. My alma mater was situated 'out in the woods' so to speak, and that part of the state is fairly well wooded and covered as well with many lakes. Ducks and geese abound within that 100 mile area and some pheasants are among the limited corn fields in comparison to the larger tracts of grain fields found in the Dakotas. My future dog had a beautiful home for a hunting dog. The house with an adjoining, spacious kennel was situated on a peninsula of a small lake covered heavily with cattails and slough grass at its edges. I could see the male dog in the kennel as I drove up. Adjacent to his kennel was the female and I could see some small heads bobbing up and down in the third kennel. As I got out of my car, the owner came out of his home to introduce himself. I had called him earlier for a 9:00 a.m. appointment, the same time that another prospective buyer, a lady was going to arrive. I was about fifteen minutes early. I purposely wanted to be ahead of the other buyer when he mentioned her and the time to arrive. My early arrival alibi was that I came from the Minneapolis suburb area and had once attended the college nearby. I said I had planned to drive by the school briefly for old time's sake but changed my plans and would do that on the way back. He told me he had only three pups left, a female and two males.

I pulled out Rex III's lineage papers and asked him if he could verify any relationship once again, which we had spoken of in our conversation earlier when I found his ad in the Minneapolis paper. A friend I had hunted with claimed that his dog's line was related to my dog. I am not much of a lineage tracer when it comes to dogs but I took my friend's advice for what it was worth. An important point here is that if you neuter your hunting dog and the dog becomes a worthy hunter, naturally an owner will want to find that line again to obtain his next hunting dog with the hope that the new one will be as good as and even better than the forerunner. I suggest that you keep your papers on your dog even though he or she becomes neutered. Personally, I have found the neutered dog to be an effective hunter, I have had three very good hunting dogs, all neutered to verify from where I speak. My major reason however, why I neuter my dogs is to keep them alive longer – to put it bluntly. I have lost two unneutered dogs to cars. An unneutered dog throws ordinary common sense caution to the winds when he smells a certain female dog in the area and doesn't look normally where he is going when it comes to crossing a road. Rex #1 was unneutered and I did not get a chance to hunt with him long enough to make a more accurate judgment call regarding his hunting abilities, which more often then not, takes a few seasons to merit an accurate analysis.

We talked for awhile about lineage and, of course hunting experiences with his dogs, the pup's parents. Golden Retrievers are notably more pheasant or upland game dogs than they are ducks and geese retrievers in comparison to the more popular and admittedly hardier Labradors. I do not intend for this book to become a championship contest on which dog is a better breed for upland game in particular. By sheer numbers, the Labrador, be it golden Lab, black Lab or otherwise, far outnumbers the 'Golden' in the pheasant fields and duck blinds, as that breed also outnumbers the wire hairs and the rest of the Pointers combined for bird hunting popularity's sake. I have seen great Labs and I have also experienced some sheer runners ('way outs' is a common term) getting up birds too far away while the owner furiously is blowing whistles, calling angrily, and pressing the shock collar button. Often the dog is so far out that he is immune to the range of the shock collar and is having a gay old time spooking up birds. Likewise I have seen great Goldens and some real horse manure ones – to put it bluntly. I sum it up with all hunting dogs – well most all of them – it is the training provided for a dog that makes a major difference. (In most cases.) The more birds the dog is exposed to and the more experience he or she is provided, the better that dog will become. We shall cover this aspect later but first let me explain why I would bring a once frozen pheasant which I had thawed out prior to my trip.

By now it was a bit past nine and the owner looked at his watch. He glanced down the driveway to the adjoining highway and seeing no approaching traffic, he motioned toward the kennel. He had mentioned earlier that he had three pups left, a female and two males. When he asked if I was planning to neuter he seemed relieved when I answered affirmatively and that I preferred a male. I admitted that I had lost two unneutered males to cars and that was the major reason. I asked his opinion regarding neutering affecting hunting ability. He briefly touted his male's non-neutered abilities as we drew closer to the puppy cage and did not fully answer my question.

I took a good look at the parents who were both more blonde in color compared to the usual redder or red orange-ish, or golden orange color of most Goldens. I explained to him that I liked the blonde trait, due to my recent experience shooting snow geese both in the fall and mainly in the spring shooting season. I offered my appreciation that the lighter colored Golden blended in a bit more concealing with the high canary grass we were hiding in. One male was more blond and the other male was slightly orange as in Little Orphan Annie's dog, 'Sandy,' if the reader is old enough to remember some of those comic strips we used to read. Little Orphan Annie had the rich Daddy named Warbucks. Oliver Warbucks, wasn't it? Seems an appropriate name for some politicians nowadays, wouldn't you think? Ahh yes, and Turban wearing Punjab was the big guy with the long knife, and of course there was that real cunning guy – the Asp. I hope this clarifies the comic strip a bit more clearly.

The owner let the puppies out of their kennel gate wherein they began playing at my feet. His wife came out of the house at the moment and told him he had a phone call. I was left alone with the puppies playing. They wandered around toward the back side of the kennel. While they did so, I went back to my car. Besides my pheasant, I also wanted my camera to take pictures of the parents. When I returned with my camera and the pheasant still in its plastic grocery sack, I snapped pictures of the parents in their kennels.

The threesome of puppy fur rolled and tumbled about near my feet. I placed the camera on top of a vacant kennel before taking the pheasant out of the sack and studied the cattails for any sign of wind. I looked down at the pups, marveling at the blonde colored male, thinking that he was going to be Rex IV and what a great life he was going to have. I hardly noticed 'Sandy,' the darker one, whom I had now dubbed. I took the pheasant and threw it upwind. The pups continued to play at my feet so I moved toward the pheasant which was now lying in a small weed patch. Goldens seem to have a penchant for wanting to be close to their owners – so it has seemed with ones I have owned. If you are typing away, as I am now doing, there they are at your feet. You go to a different room to watch TV and again they are at your side. These little rascals seemed to have that trait at their early age. When I moved they moved with me even though they seemed oblivious to any other interest but tumbling upon each other. As I drew closer to the weed patch, all of a sudden 'Sandy' stiffened. It was as if something strangely was subduing him.

Again I will bring up past media for an example. Do you remember Lon Chaney, the actor in the Frankenstein movies, and Boris Karloff as well? Well, Lon Chaney would transform into this scary and hideous wolf man character and as kids watching Saturday matinees, this would frighten the hell out of us. Frankenstein we figured we could run away from as he appeared to walk pretty slow, we reasoned as we walked home from those movies... but... this wolf man character we figured was not very slow and a bit harder to elude. Anyway, 'Sandy's' transformation at that very moment reminded me of a bit of weird 'transformation' that suddenly changed his playful character totally. The little pup bristled as he sniffed seriously in the direction of the weed patch. He even lifted up a front foot as he stood there. All manner of play was behind him as his sister and brother continued to frolic with each other. Then 'Sandy' slowly stepped toward the waiting bird. His steps were guarded but he continued to advance. When he entered the weed patch, he jumped back at first sight of the bird. He stood there rigid, but instinct made him advance in again. This time he made it all the way to the ring neck. He made a peck at it once and jumped back with a feather in his mouth. I reached down and picked him up and returned him to his litter mates.

By this time the owner came out and informed me that the lady was going to arrive soon. "I told her I had a pheasant hunter here looking at them. She said that she didn't care much for hunting but liked Goldens because they were great house pets. She asked if they were all the same color? When I told her she said that she liked the blonde color. Said she seen one on a calendar once."

By this time the pups were playing at his feet, including 'Sandy.' I told him I had initially wanted the blonde male at first sight due to the snow geese hunting and blending with the slough and canary grass, but first I had to make another experiment. I motioned toward the weed patch and pointed down toward 'Sandy.' "This darker one is getting the inside track, however." I said as I walked toward the weed patch to retrieve the thawed out bird and returned toward the puppies. He looked at me oddly. Holding the bird behind me I turned and threw it a shorter distance upwind toward the weeds again. "I'll be damned!" He uttered with an awed tone. I motioned for him to move toward the bird and the playing puppies followed. "Never seen anyone pick a dog like this before," he muttered. It wasn't long before 'Sandy' again stiffened, going though his 'Transformation.' All play was again forgotten. This time he walked at a swifter and more assured pace toward the pheasant. I nodded my head and said, "You know,

I don't really care about hunting snow geese all that much in comparison to those Dakota birds (meaning pheasants)." He understood. I picked up 'Sandy' and said; "C'mon little feller, you are going to have one helluva great life."

Strangely, the name 'Sandy' just didn't stick. My kids all started calling him 'Puppy' and that name stuck. He hunted so well as a so-called 'teen-aged puppy' before he was a year old that I never felt embarrassed about his name among my hunting friends when he started in with more experienced and older dogs. He is in his prime now and fairly well known and respected by my hunting peers. Fortunately or unfortunately, however you wish to call it, now as a full grown, handsome hunting male whose record is numerous, numerous birds retrieved, pointed, flushed, chased down and found, and who even does his duty helping out at a Dakota resort.. alas alack…he is still called 'Puppy.

I do laugh and call him 'Sandy' for awhile when we have him clipped for the new season. Most often we do it earlier for the summer heat. They always act more comfortable with less hair upon them at that time of the year. Before hunting season he gets a new clip. He doesn't seem to mind. A clipped Golden can easily pass for a golden or yellow Lab once he comes away from a good shearing. If you are a serious hunter and hunt your dog a lot, you'll learn to clip your Goldens for the cockle burrs mostly. A heavy growth of cockle burrs can stop a long haired dog in his or her tracks. Let his hair grow out for the approaching cold weather and it doesn't take long for him or her to look like a Golden again.

5

Training Your Dog

Gun Shyness, Signals, Retrieval, Road Hunting, Staying Close and Field Feeding

Ideally, for gun training, the shooting of a cap gun, if you can ever find one and rolls of caps of course, works best. More than likely you will never find one and have to resort to a .22 rifle which half the people in South Dakota seem to possess, or more conveniently a .22 pistol. Forget about some magnum cannon. Go down to a hardware store and buy a box of short .22 rounds if they have them. Bird shot rounds are also a good round to start out with. You want noise, but for starting out, a minimum amount of it is desired. When your dog is eating his morning or evening meal, crank a few rounds off into a pail of sand as faraway as you can within your household if he or she is an inside dog, which mine are. The basement may be a good place to start out with your gunfire. Have someone report his reactions upstairs, if any, while you are so engaged. If he is an outside kennel type, then use the garage with the door down or bring the dog into your basement for his or her meals.

If the dog seems like he doesn't mind, bring your sand bucket and pistol a bit closer. If this does not work and he gets edgy, you will have to go out into the country. Throwing clay pigeons has worked for me every time that I have tried this method. But you have to have quite a few folks involved. Two or three clay pigeon shooters are needed. One will have to throw or run the mechanical thrower. Twenty-gauges or 410's are better to start out with than the louder 12's.

More than likely 12-gauges will be all you have available so that means you use quieter, low brass skeet shot which are much less loud than the heavier hunting artillery. Dog raising and hunting is an expensive process for most folks, so expect to spend a few coins on your training. It will be much cheaper in the long run than turning your dog over to a professional trainer. If you are 'well heeled,' then by all means seek a professional.

Drop your dog off a goodly distance away from where the clay pigeon helpers are setting up. Your shooting group may as well be having a good time and not worry about the dog as they bang away with enjoyment. The person you drop your dog off with should be someone the dog is fairly close to. He will think he is out on a nice walk which every dog seems to love. Ahead of the dog who is being led in the direction of the skeet shooters will be a person, usually you, who has just placed a fully feathered pheasant, thawed out from the freezer, and dragged across the dog's path which is leading toward the skeet shooters. Two to three thawed birds, at least, you should utilize, which as a pheasant hunter, a wise one, you have saved from the past season. You may want to repeat this process as you draw closer to the shooters so give your dog a goodly distance to walk when you first let him or her and the handler out.

The dog is most often oblivious to the distant shooting and is enjoying his walk. When he comes up on the first pheasant trail he will immediately start tracking. He should be removed from any leash by that time. The bird has been dragged but a short distance and he should be heaped with praise and even given a small treat when he finds it. If he has had birds trailed before and was praised all the better. As you start in again toward the skeet shooters he will discover a few more positioned birds and you may as well give a few extra tests like skipping your bird a few times, lifting it over a log or obstacle, etc. and zig zagging a bit. The dog never seems to notice the rope I drag with. I leave my dragging rope or twine on it when I drop it for him or her to find. He has found a bird and, rope or no rope, he gets quite excited. This all may take up some distance from the shooters, but in the end he should wind up right under the shooters and by then is completely oblivious to the noise.

The wild smell of that bird is like opium to a drug addict. It makes him or her oblivious to what is going on in the immediate outside world around them. I failed to do this for my last dog and wound up using ten purchased live birds and lucked out with success mainly because I had an older dog involved. I should add that if you do not have any thawed pheasants for dragging a scent, then dead pigeons, which are considerably cheaper, will work. Any good, big pet store should have training books that may have training methods wherein you do not have access to live or dead birds or skeet shooting areas. I find this last method (clay pigeons) almost sure fire effective however.

Number one rule against the possibility of gun shyness: Never blast a shot gun over his head for his first time out. He may run under the car and stay there. I never had much of a problem gun training until my last one.

My table saw is loud so I would feed him as a growing puppy in the garage and turn it on. He never seemed to mind. One day I got a bucket of sand and took my .22 pistol out there, and closed the garage door, (I lived in pristine, rules bound suburbia of a large city) and as he ate, turned on the saw and in one rear corner of the garage I fired my pistol into a sand bucket. He jumped and quit eating. Ever since then he got nervous when he saw the pistol and I turned on the saw. So out to the woods we went. I had my stewardess friend take him and he was nervous when he saw the pistol. Earlier, I made the mistake of taking him duck hunting with some friends and since I am not too much of a duck hunting enthusiast I made it more of a training mission while my friends banged away at a distance. I kept him way back and came up slowly as they – the duck hunters – were shooting Passovers, about the only time you can do this as usually they are out in the duck blinds, but he pulled back. He just didn't like shot guns. I thought, "Oh Damn! I got a loser," despite his earlier demonstrated tracking ability out in wild country or with the dragging and hiding method.

Out in the woods, I had trailed some pheasants I thawed out from the previous years hunting and dragged them in the woods and left them. He proved to be good at tracking and was happily on a steadily improving course until I began firing the pistol. He continued tracking when I started firing at a distance and sort of got used to it. The stewardess helped as he was more attached to her than me in his early stage. He just didn't like it however, showing no 'jump-up–and–down' enthusiasm when I brought a gun out or the pistol.

Next I bought ten pheasants (live) at a bargain ($7.50 each) from a grower and had those out in the woods in a loaned box from the pheasant supplier with a spring shutting trap door to reach in and grab one. My old dog, Rex III was still alive and had been through this before. I mentioned the Gehrke cabin earlier and about Rex III finding our way back to it. I had been told by the Gehrke's about the pheasant raising farm near by and they told me to use their cabin property for dog training. I left the dogs in the car and took out my birds and carried them about a 100-yards from the cabin. We had plenty of privacy in secluded acreage containing an old hollowed out, fallen birch log and an oak tree about 30 to 40 yards distant from the hollow log.

I took the two dogs out of the car at a distance from the log and oak tree. We will call this the staging area, to use a Marine Corps term. This same area was where my bird pen was placed; say about 50-yards away from the log. I told the dogs to "Stee-ayy" at the staging area and then I took a thawed out bird and dragged it from the oak tree which I will call Point 'A' and on to the log. Since the bird was on a short rope, I lifted the bird up and threw it away from the log as far as I could so as not to confuse the dogs when they arrived at the log. There was nothing secretive about what I was doing. The dogs curiously watched what I was up do to as they sat obediently to my last command–Stee-aayyy.

I took a bird out of the latched box and spun it round and round to make it dizzy. You tuck the head under the wing and after about 20 to 30 seconds of spin, it drops off to sleep or passes out. Odd, I know, but it works every time. I walked down to the log with it and placed it back into a hollowed space at the end of the large fallen birch. The opening was the mouth of a tunnel back into the log which ran about ten yards before coming to an opening at the top of the log, large enough for the bird to escape from in case he was being pursued. Remember, I had already dragged a dead bird from Point A about 50-yards away at the base of the oak to Point B. I called Point B the mouth of the birch log, and Point C would be the bird's flyaway spot. Then I walked back to where I told my two dogs to sit beside the box of birds. Old Rex had been through this before and calmly waited.

The pup waited curiously beside the older dog, staring at the birds in the pen. When I tell my dogs to sit–they sit, despite a live pheasant you are holding in front of them or a box of birds in front of them within a slatted cage and the birds within, clearly visible. The older dog had seen so many ring necks in his life time that he just took everything going on as a 'matter of business,' so to speak. I then took them to the Point A spot where Rex immediately began to track to where the live one had come alive from its brief sleep. I am also carrying a 20-gauge over and under with the lightest 8's I could fine. I was not firing a loud cannon. If 'Puppy,' at his young age, didn't pass this test, I would have a house dog only.

Be sure to wait a good five minutes after you place the sleeping pheasant (or pigeon) far enough where the dog cannot grab him. While the bird is in his deep coma you return to the staging area and release your dogs to follow you to Point A. At Point A, both Puppy and Rex smell the scent of the dragged bird to Point B and immediately get hot on this trail. By this time the sleeping pheasant has awakened. The pheasant sees the dog's nose, hears him and smells him and probably thinks, 'Oh Damn!' He turns and goes the opposite way down the tunnel. He sure as heck is not going to come out at the dog and try and finagle his way out of the predicament. No way!!

About 30 feet down the line in the hollow log is an opening where you stand waiting with your shot gun. Up hops the bird. He sees you and leaps skyward. You let him get out there with seven and a half shot or eight shot. You want to wing him if possible and not blow him the heck away. Skeet shot might be best for this position. 'Boom'; pheasant usually drops down and best if it is a runner and the dog chases. 'Boom' again, if you have to and usually the bird will go down. Well, Puppy did not like that shot gun but Rex could care less and was having a heckuva good time. Easiest birds he had ever come across. Puppy cringed a bit on the first bird but there was nowhere to run away to except the woods, so he hung in there obviously wanting to remain in our company. After six pheasants and my deepening exasperation, "I paid $400 for this guy!" Plus going through all the puppy raising stuff and the peeing and poohing in your house and 'chew every damn thing up' stage (which lasts for quite some time). Moral: Buy many, many 'chewies.' LO! This particular portion of the training phase is becoming extremely important and I was beginning to worry. My $400 investment was only a few birds away from depreciating into a full fledged house dog.

Bird #1 came out. I shot with my light shell and Puppy cowered. He had followed Rex in the tracking who was smart enough to know that we were going to go through the whole procedure again by the third bird. The fourth, fifth and sixth birds brought the same lack of enthusiasm from the young dog. A couple birds took an extra round but all came down for retrieve eventually and luckily over half of them were runners. The second bird was kind of funny. I opened the holding box the wrong way and that one was up front instead of way back with the rest of the birds trying to avoid my grasp. Out he went and off into the woods; all seven dollars and fifty cents worth of him. Rex was having a gay, old time besides receiving a heap of praise. Puppy tried to get in on the praise as Rex would bring the bird up to me. I brushed him aside, ignoring him completely and this response he was not used to.

A light bulb finally clicked on when the seventh bird escaped down the hollow log tunnel. Out of sheer jealousy of Rex getting emphatic praise over each bird chased and retrieved, Puppy flat got mad and chased after #7 bird which fortunately was a runner after I broke its wing. He did not know what to do with it once he caught it. He had trailed and picked up many a dragged dead one but this baby was alive! He just pinned it down with his paws and when Rex got close he'd pick it up and run with it. On the next three birds he got the idea. Been doing great ever since.

My other dogs never gave me this much trouble but they never got near a shot gun until much exposure to a cap gun, then short .22's, and then finally gradually walking up to shot guns being fired at clays and having treats as we got closer, and about three dragged pheasants to find several times over as we got real close. Rex went along as a pup on a hockey player's prairie dog expedition and heard so many .22 rounds (about two thousand) in three days that shotguns never bothered him. With clay pigeon procedure my dogs never heard the shotguns, figuratively, as they were so excited over the birds and the praise to go with it. Some dogs however, remain scared of guns and run under the car. Puppy was almost that and would have been a flop had I not had Rex. Puppy evolved to becoming a great dog, at least for my hunting needs and did bloom unexpectedly at an unusual early age but then he has had a wealth of experience and it was old Rex who brought him past this critical stage. Over and over we went out and he did blossom, but first he had to get past the gun stage. What a nose! I have an

Autumn picture of him bringing back a bird across a ploughed field at less than a year old after a long search and chase up an Iowa dry creek. He sees a gun now and like any good hunting dog, wags his tail with excitement.

Training To Retrieve

This is a most important requirement for the hunting dog. Fortunately most of the breeds have this trait built into them. I have come across a few hunters who have had dogs that would not retrieve and yet seemed to be satisfied with them. I wondered about what they did when they wounded a bird and it simply took off into heavy cover. I guess they had to shrug their shoulders and just keep on hunting. What else would you do with a dog that doesn't retrieve?

When your dog is emerging from the puppy stage he will want you to play with him and that means throwing him a ball which he will chase endlessly. At first he will want to play around with it and keep it from you when you try and take it from his mouth to throw again. Relax and let him enjoy himself. It won't take him long to figure out that he has to let it go if you are ever to throw it again for him. Simply have patience. It may take several days before he gets used to the fact that he needs you to throw him the ball. A tennis ball works fine because it can bounce so well and its elusive bounce will soon be a fun challenge for him. The more you play with him at this game, the more he will do what you want him to do eventually bring you the ball. Eventually, he will let go of it upon command and stand and wait for you to throw it again. With my big Goldens, I don't mind giving them a gentle, light kneeing in the chest when they are reluctant to release the ball and are standing on their back legs or sitting with it tight in their mouth. This seems to get them the message that I want the ball, and before long they are letting go of it at will and want you to throw it again. The more you throw that ball for him, the sooner he will bring that bird for you, especially if you drag a previous season's kill a goodly many times and hide it while someone holds him or he has reached the state where he understands 'Stee-aaayy.'

Most hunters use the 'old sock trick' with a growing pup. You take a pheasant wing or two and wrap it up in a stocking. You can pad the sock with another pair of socks if need be. After it is all tied up firmly, it is ready for throwing and retrieving. In the field he will pick up on the real thing when he sees the older dogs returning with downed birds in their mouth. It has been a natural for my young dogs to become a bit jealous of the other dogs retrieving and soon they are racing to get to that bird first. After a few hunts, retrieving simply becomes mechanical for them and now you have what you have always wanted a darn good retriever.

I really don't know where this term, 'Does he have a soft mouth?' came from. Maybe the guys I hunt with are like me and just way out in the woods on that one but we never mention whether our dogs have soft or hard mouths. The young dog latches on to that bird and after being spurred a few times, they soon learn to pin that bird down and the larger mouth that they have, the better. I have a neat scar on my right wrist from a spurring. I personally wonder, with all those feathers on that bird, that it has to be a bit difficult for a good dog to sink his fangs way down into the meat of the rooster. If you will notice how a dog, especially the big jawed breeds which I naturally prefer, the big Labs, Goldens etc. roll that bird somewhat to keep those spurs away from them before bringing it to you. How often have you seen a dog bring you a bird (I don't use that snobby term – 'bring to hand') carrying it belly up, its jaws (and fangs) sunk deep into the breast with the roosters spurs ready to claw into his face? Natural protective instinct demonstrates that the dog keeps himself protected from being injured.

The pheasants I have always seen brought up to us are firmly being held in the dog's jaws and their spurs are reduced to a position where they can do the least damage, if any. A large dog most often will do himself a favor before 'bringing it to hand.' He will clamp down on the bird, let it go momentarily, and clamp down again, positioning the bird to minimize the bird's ability to spur. Often I see my dog clamp down tighter in this process and I suspicion they are forcing the air out of the bird's lungs somewhat and thus sending the rooster off to dream land for a short spell. When the rooster does come to, he always seems to be in a complacent state if, of course, he happens to still be alive when first found. Every time I have experienced a live bird brought up to me by a large mouthed dog, the bird's head, will be bobbing around, but it always seems so complacent, like it is enjoying the ride and never is wildly attempting to spur and claw its captor. As I said earlier, regarding the 'soft/hard mouth' term: I have yet to see a pair of canine fang holes in any pheasant's breast that I have had retrieved for me, yet I know those big Goldens and Labs and related sizable canines which I prefer for hunting, well, they are clamping down hard to keep that bird but there is a goodly degree of feathers protecting that bird.

I am reminded of a dog, and it was part Golden. It wasn't papered and was one of those 'bargain kind.' Well, this dog could hunt and retrieve birds to a reasonable degree, but it loved to chew on anything that was brought down. We took a goodly amount of snow geese one day as Canada wanted this particular species reduced in population because their grazing habits were seriously destroying the Caribou's grazing habitat. A very high number in limit was allowed.

Left alone in the pickup with a dozen or so downed snows and blues, the 'bargain dog' left us with neat red patches on their breasts where he bit into almost every one of them. When we found the same infliction on our pheasants, that dog went out to an early pasture. Maybe he would qualify with that soft/hard mouth terminology. In summary, I have been satisfied with the retrieval of every downed bird brought to me by a number of dogs and some not my own.

When you down a rooster and your dog prances about proudly with it and refuses to 'Give,' I find this, 'holding on' is a fairly common trait or characteristic if it is one of the first birds of the season. My heavily experienced dog does it every time on opening day and usually the next day too. After that he gets down to business. The more birds he gets into his mouth, the more businesslike he will become. Get him real busy and he eventually will not take time for you to take it from his mouth. Soon he will be bringing your freshly shot bird up to you, dropping it on the run and spinning around and looking when he hears another shot being fired. More than once on a multiple shoot I have had my dogs do this procedure. At one shoot I was in an open bean field, last position downwind from the main body of hunters. A blocker named Jim, a darn good shooter, was at my edge of the bare field, freshly picked. The drivers were into a shelter belt of weeds and stunted trees and kicking out bird after bird that kept sailing over me or Jim. My luck bearing son-in-law was off to my upwind right. Jim's shots dropped birds in the open field as did mine. Rex III simply stacked two separate piles of them while he waited for more business to fall from the skies. Rex was an outstanding dog.

On his first triple as a young pup under a year, Puppy burst out of the grass high above the road where our pickup was parked with the old dog in it and looking on at our action through the window. The pup bore down on me out of that thick grass where the bird had dropped; #2 bird was in his mouth. I had just miraculously stepped on my #1 bird, which was still alive, and was keeping my eyes focused where #3 had my last round into him and gone down. I pinned the rooster with my foot and reached down to take him. He was all business and didn't prance or strut one bit. I dropped my Benelli and reached out to Puppy with my free hand as Puppy came bursting over to me with his bird. Four shells had just been fired and excitement was still heavy in the air. He quickly let go of #2 as I reached for it and as I began wringing its neck, my dog started searching the grass up ahead. I kept my focus on where I thought #3 went down and managed to grab #1 with my free hand and wring its life out after #2 had met his fate. That done I managed to get two shells into my 12-gauge whose safe was still off, such was the excitement of the moment. It was an empty gun when I dropped it in the grass but I pushed the safe back on, out of habit after reloading. I like the Benelli mechanism that allows the ejecting bolt to remain open for a quick reload of dropping a round into the open chamber and hurriedly slamming a shell into the magazine tube just in case the wounded bird would get back up again from under the dog's nose. The third was a cagey bird however, and after the minutes ticked by; it looked like the young pup just was not going to find him. I was about to lose my coveted triple title even though I knocked him down, but he wasn't found and therefore not within my hunting vest.

Pheasants do get super exciting at times. I rose with my half empty gun and both birds in the grass to take off my orange colored hat and throw it out ahead of me to establish a crude mark where I thought, not far behind my hat, #3 had gone down. I dug my heels into the ground and pulled a couple long shafts of grass to lay them pointing from my position on toward my hat. It is very easy to get disoriented when your immediate surroundings are all the same. Puppy was busy searching while I was setting up my marking system. "Damn!" I thought. I sure did want this triple. I stuffed both birds away in my vest and walked to the edge of the banked incline and looked down at old Rex who was on his last legs while the young dog was searching futilely. Old Rex was a seasoned finder and had searched out many a bird. I thought I had worked the old dog too hard earlier and gave him a deserved and needed rest when a pair of hens had flown out of the ditch and up ahead of us about a quarter of an hour earlier. One hen went high to the grass above us and a rooster rose just high enough for us to see and then back down when she had landed close to him. That had started the whole episode and the catalyst to why we were standing there and searching for a third bird. Triples don't come often and you hate to lose the third once you knocked it down.

Just a few minutes before all this concentrated action and not having the faintest idea we would be seeing such action as a triple possibility, I thought the young pup was ready to tackle a situation where a rooster would be right in front of us as we came over the rise, and he would have his first bird, unassisted, providing I would do my part. Looking down at Rex, I re-checked my safe on my Benelli and went back down to the pickup. We retraced our path we had come up on to return to the truck and I noted a pretty little pool which I had ignored seeing when we had made our initial apprehensive climb from the bottom of the ditch, and the adrenaline beginning to flow. All I could think of as we had crossed the trickle of a stream feeding the pool was that one rooster's rise and what we would do when we got to the crest. We re-crossed the trickle of water feeding the miniature pool and climbed up a lesser incline to the gravel road and the pickup.

My best chance, I figured, to recoup a possible 'Triple' was to utilize the old dog – maybe for his last time – for we would be heading back soon. His spreading lymphoma was getting worse, his neck so swollen that I had removed his collar and you could tell he was losing his strength. Right away we should be leaving as we had enough birds and if we found #3 we would be on our way for sure. Rex was calmly waiting for us. I threw the two birds into the box and opened the door for him. He stiffly got out but his tail was wagging. We ascended back up the incline, passing by the pool and he went to work like the old efficient veteran that he was. One thing about Iowa, a Dakotan notes, is that they certainly have more water. Their drainage ditches are often actually good sized creeks. I started Rex out beyond my hat and he picked up the scent. Strangely, within a short search he returned back down the path we had rose up on. Talk about a back tracking rooster! It had either followed us, or more than likely left ahead of us and the pup missed it on the way back. I was wondering if Rex was telling me he just didn't have it anymore and wanted to return to the truck but his nose was down to the ground and that low approach with his tail wagging was always his signal that he was onto something. Back down the incline we went. All of a sudden, there was movement just as we came down toward the little pool. A splash, and a rooster with a spent wing started to skitter across the water. Puppy was on it in a flash and had it pinned just as it got to the other side. We had our triple. It was bittersweet however, for it was old Rex's last find. He never ventured out again and died soon after.

You deeply appreciate Retrieval when you drop a bird into the water and your dog swims out after it. I have more than one camera shot of this episode. The dog and rooster in the water. I often carry a camera ready to go while I am hunting. It is right there, hanging from my neck and clanging at times against my barrel. I have shot enough birds to be satisfied, and rarely has it cost me that many shots. I do have several camera shots where I have caught a rising rooster or hen in my lens. It has taken several escaped roosters to get these pictures, I have to admit. My absolute best camera's shot is a blurring hen right up in front of me, which Joel took.

Retrieval Signals

When you drop a bird across a creek on the opposite side and your dog starts after it, you quickly realize the value of your retriever. In this case, you will appreciate the value of hand signals when he needs a bit of direction from you after he reaches the other side, and especially if the bird has revived and has decided to get up from where it has fallen.

Hand signals are simply body language to your dog. When you are playing ball with him, occasionally throw the ball off away where he is not looking. You can fake a throw to your left and he will turn and run or face in that direction and when you do let go of the ball, try and have it in the opposite direction he is facing. As he moves out and turns to look at you, use your body language, with over emphasized arm and hand signals directing him toward where the ball has fallen. You can also fake a throw and after he has turned to run and taken a few steps, call to him and hold up the ball. Then make a pushing out movement with your arms and step forward toward him; even take a few steps with your 'pushing back' signal for emphasis. This is your indication for him to move backwards. Once he takes a few steps, throw the ball behind him. When he happens to be searching for a ball, call to him and give him your exaggerated signals toward where you know the ball is and begin walking in that direction and continue giving him these signals. All this should be done in a playful and enjoyable manner and you will be surprised how quickly they catch on when you make it enjoyable and keep it a pleasant experience. Never, never lose your temper and scold a dog simply over what really is just a game. This is the manner in which I train my dogs.

I remember one time with Rex III, and our hunting party of mostly Emery, South Dakota, 'Good-Ol-Boys' and their descendants, who return annually from all parts of the country. We were all in a line, pickups, SUVs and vans, east of Emery. We were in the process of moving from one field to the next. A combine was working a field to our right and next to the road. To our left, close to the road, about a third the size of a football field and about half as narrow, was a pond. The lead truck knew the farmer and stopped to chat with him. As they approached the combine a pair of roosters burst out of the fence line. The farmer said he had seen quite a few birds running back into the corner and just a few passes were remaining to clean the field. He suggested that on the last pass we would probably have a few birds to shoot at.

On that last pass, a flock of roosters and hens crossed high over the road, right to left for our caravan and several were bagged. One rooster was winged and sailed across the pond next to us and adjacent to the road. It landed in the cattails at the opposite side of the pond. Several dogs had seen the rooster go down, including Rex, and were anxiously standing at the waters edge, perplexed as to what to do. I yelled at Rex and gave him a waving push with my arm toward the water. I did this several times and he entered the pond in the direction of where the rooster had hit the cattails. He was on his way and I figured if that rooster was dead he would soon be swimming back with it. While Rex was in the water however, the rooster came out the back side of the cattails and was exposed by a clearing of short grass and then disappeared in a clump of weeds higher up by the fence line.

The whole caravan was watching our pheasant drama by now and everyone started yelling with excitement. Rex reached the shore line and was unaware that the bird had moved. The bird had now crept from a weed based fence post and ran several posts to our left as we faced the water. Every one again yelled in excitement. By this time Rex was out of the cattails and looking back quizzically at me. I 'pushed' him back toward the fence line with my signals. He kept his eye on me, backing up as I kept giving him my signals and then I steered him to our left with my left signal. When he reached the fence line he picked up the roosters scent and every one cheered as he bore down on the rooster's hiding place. Out popped the rooster with a drooping wing and the race was on with every one cheering. It wasn't long before Rex was swimming back to us triumphantly with the rooster in his mouth. That episode was a result of hand signals and makes you fairly proud of your dog when 'the whole pheasant world – to us – on that day' was watching.

I didn't know who had shot the bird and didn't care. It joined the rest of the pile of roosters in the back of a pickup. We would clean them later and have a grand Dakota Saturday night pheasant party. Tales would be told and Rex would be one of those legends. This is a grand happening clear across the state on that particular Saturday night as it is in Northern Iowa where I often hunt with a similar group. I had never raised my gun at those particular combine birds. I figured we had enough shooters to do the job when the combine bore down toward us upon that last pass. The success of my dog doing his job was far more pleasing and rewarding than had I shot a couple birds.

One Iowa Day when Puppy Came of Age

The old guy had passed away that first Fall of my young dog's life and now Puppy was on his own at less than a year old. Most dogs would still be in serious training at that age and not out on their own, but I had no choice. I didn't expect much, but I thought he could at least find the ones he saw go down close by and possibly get a few up for me, such was the easy numbers in Iowa that season. Well, I only hunted a day and a half – too wet and cold – down in Iowa. I had a book I was finishing up and mainly wanted to briefly get back out just to remember old Rex a bit more by visiting a few of his haunts. I hunted on the way back and wound up with six birds, my limit for two days, so couldn't complain.

'Los Poo-peay,' (Puppy) was picking up some new nick names and we were seriously thinking of changing his name. With Rex's death so recent I just felt a bit strange to start calling him Rex. My son and my flight attendant friend had their own suggestions and since none of us could reach agreement, Puppy still remained Puppy and which he indeed still was, at not quite a year. On that first solo trip out for him, he did well for his age. He was no Rex III, not by a long shot but he was pleasingly coming along. He was fairly adept at getting birds up for me but finding a cripple in heavy grass or weeds, he was lacking.

A rooster was in the middle of the road as I approached a slight rise by an old abandoned Iowa farm to my left. I stopped well short and got my empty Benelli out of its case. (Those are Iowa rules; cased and empty gun which cost me an $80 fine the year before.) I loaded it and got out quietly as the rise of the road was keeping me covered. Puppy got out from the back seat of the Cadillac. My pickup needed some maintenance so thought I would ease the driving with a smooth running comfort car for long drives that has a portion of the back seat made into a platform and flat for the dog's comfort. He lounges on a double folded blanket, as well. As I said earlier, I don't kennel my dogs. My Iowa buddies all have pickups we use anyhow, once I get there.

The rooster got nervous and went back toward the abandoned homestead from where he came. Thankfully, I had given my young dog some road hunting training earlier and he stayed beside me as we approached from the concealing ditch. Two roosters and a couple hens came up as we came over the rise. I got off some rounds and knocked one rooster down but he was a runner. He ran for the creek below us to our right and hid in an old fence line where Puppy tracked him. I saw feathers where he went through the woven wire fence and put Puppy on them. The dog tensed, pointing at the post and the bird leaped up just as we were searching the grass. It looked like he came straight up the fence post but went right back down on the opposite side as Puppy was pointing at him and went upstream in a narrow tunnel of grass and dry creek, toward a heavy concentration of grass, cattails and weeds. The fence was woven wire and held Puppy back momentarily, giving the rooster a big lead. I lifted him up and over rather easily for he had yet to reach his full size. It was like a wide open track for the rooster and he did everything but fly, but a young pup approaching maturity can almost fly as well. Once the fence was cleared both were pell-mell down that tunnel of overhanging grass and creek puddles. Puppy chased him for a long ways, immediately going out of sight as the dry creek wound out and away. I wasn't worried about losing my dog but when he disappeared for several minutes I did get a bit nervous. A half mile or so the stream bent to a busy highway and I didn't want my dog chasing a rooster that close to deadly traffic.

I now had cause for serious worry. I left my gun on a fence post allowing me to legally enter land after a wounded bird. I got out on an adjoining plowed field so I could see up this winding brook size stream when it held water. Dry Fall it was just heavy weed and a few puddles. After a long ten minutes or more, way in the distance at the edge of a plowed field, I could see movement and I was about to call Puppy back. He was so far away I couldn't tell if he had anything in his mouth or not. That is way, far away, when you cannot see if he has anything in his mouth; probably a third of a mile at least, maybe more. I called to him and he acted like he dropped something from his mouth when he reacted to my call. He turned quickly with his head down back into the covering grass and cattails. "Damn," I thought. "He had the rooster and I may have caused him to lose it." I had sense to get my camera out and did snap a picture when he came back out of the cover again. He was but a mere dot in that picture. I certainly did not expect him to come back with that rooster but it did look like something in his mouth as he trotted back in the clearing alongside the cattails and dry creek cover. As he got closer, 'Lo! It was the rooster!' What excitement and pride at that very moment: one's young, very young dog, strutting home with his prize! "That is a dog!" I thought as he came closer across the plowed field and I snapped his picture. That really made my day. He had turned in quite a performance and proved he had the old bloodhound lineage nose, customary to Goldens. Looks like he may become an apt replacement for old Rex after all.

Road Hunting

First: Pheasant Road Hunting is a unique South Dakota experience that many of the good visitors we have from out of state miss out on come October 'Pheasant Opener.' This Dakota custom is a truly exciting upland game hunting experience. Those who hunt at the many hunting resorts also miss out as well. Most often before noon these hunters have filled out or limited out on that opening weekend such has been the abundance of birds. The hunting has been so good lately in this new century, that most hunters are starting to 'fill' (get their limit), by the time the birds begin to leave their abundant cornfields in late afternoon to pick up bits of gravel for their digestive system. One of the first discoveries you make in relation to chickens in your high school biology class is that chickens (which the wily ringneck is related to) need to find small pebbles or stones/gravel for their gizzards to utilize for the initial digestive process. These stones are stored in the bird's gizzard; they are the miniature grinding mill for the hard corn, soy beans and all manner of weed seeds consumed during the day's foraging. There would not be much road hunting if the ring neck had no need for a grinding mill and roadside stones/pebbles.

In many states Road Hunting is outlawed; not so South Dakota or, as of this writing, Iowa. Road hunting is exactly what the name implies. You drive miles on the Dakota gravel roads looking for your quarry instead of walking the many miles you have in the earlier part of the day trying to stir him out of his cover and feeding areas. Often you will see the birds crossing a ways up in front of you. I have never had the experience yet, but I have talked to a few hunters who have spotted birds behind them in their rear view mirror. After a full morning's hunt and on into the afternoon, it is a welcome respite to sit back and drive a bit to stalk your quarry. In the group hunts I am associated with, we usually break up and wander off in pairs several hours before sundown. We bring our birds back to a communal cleaning session and the party begins where it left off the evening before. Iowa usually ends its hunting hours at 4:00 p.m. South Dakota let you hunt until sun down, so in the earlier months, South Dakota gives you the edge for road hunting. This is a historical Dakota custom as celebrated as the old John Deeres, Farmalls, Cases and Allis Chalmers, cowboy hats, and Mt. Rushmore and Crazy Horse Mt. thrown in. It is sheer fun and pure excitement when the birds are there.

Normally, when you see a pheasant at a distance on the road, you usually drop a hunter off early. He will wait until you drive past the quarry and also will have exited your vehicle some distance away before he advances and closes in. It is an odd experience, it seems, to drive close by them after you have left your partner out, but they are used to passing cars as long as the vehicle keeps on moving by. If you foolishly stop beside a fence line and a road side pheasant, instead up it goes long before you have time to emerge from your vehicle to get a shot off. Every one has their own technique but mine is to go past the ringnecks. 'Mark mentally' their position as you pass by in relation to the nearest telephone/electrical pole, shrub, fence posts or any form of item you can mark their position from. 'Three-and-a-half poles down from corner' or 'fifth fence post from gate,' etc. Check what significant marker reference is on the opposite side of the road as well. With two people hunting, you drop your partner off a goodly distance away so as not to 'spook' the roadside birds, then drive past them, and after some distance you get out and then the two of you close in on your quarry. When I am by myself, I usually follow the same procedure somewhat. Naturally, two persons closing in from opposite ends have the advantage. Often the quarry will hear one hunter or become suspicious and move toward the opposite hunter and afford him a closer shot.

Another version is to have your partner get out quietly and tag along beside the car, hiding on the opposite side as you move toward your quarry, then immediately crossing over after your moving vehicle passes the birds. This method allows only one shooter and the birds may have moved, one way or the other, maybe even out of range, either to the hunter's left or right and most generally away from where the car stopped to let the hunter out. I favor the pincer movement, as usually one or the other will get in a decent shot or two. With a good dog for retrieving that stays behind until the last moment, often you will come up with a bird or two.

I had a short termed friend I regretfully wasted a hunting trip with. He was a former classmate and insisted that we stop beside any roadside bird and leap out as quick as you can. His technique was far from effective but he was too bull headed to accept any other procedure. Ideally, if the road where you spot your pheasants has a concealing ditch opposite to the side where the pheasants are on, that is a perfect situation to have. I have successfully used the concealing ditch many times. Do not rule out passing the birds twice if a concealing ditch affords you that opportunity and if stopping your car when you first discover them just might spook them into an early exodus.

Once, near Burke, South Dakota, I was returning from a Nebraska prairie chicken/pheasant trip. You cannot road hunt in Nebraska and I was anxious to cross the state line the next day to South Dakota where, as I said before, Road Hunting is a favorite and exciting pastime. I had been fortunate the day before near Gordon, Nebraska to come up with a 'triple' in a shelter belt with my new son-in-law from Queens, New York who was getting in some memorable hunting in what to them (New Yorkers) is still the 'Wild West.' The shelter belt triple was just a fortunate set of circumstances. I was going to block for my son-in-law at an open space midway between two shelter belts and the birds came right at me. Not far into South Dakota, I drove past a flock of roosters on my right, picking their gravel for the evening. To my left was a nice deep ditch, adequate for approaching concealment. I parked further down the road after taking note of a stand of shrubs growing close to the fence line by the half dozen birds.

Another ideal situation for road hunting is to have a dog that minds and is not some over-excited hyper 'Runner' or 'Bolter,' in this type of situation. The perfect 'Road Dog' is one that can be let out of your vehicle and he will stay behind or beside the closing-in hunter with no verbal commands. Damn few dogs can do that, has been my experience, and those dogs that can't will get left in the kennel or truck. I don't know of any dog training schools that include that 'sneaking up' training in their repertoire. I recall on my 'Triple' near Burke, my old dog Rex was a good 'Sneak-up Dog as 'Puppy' is too. Nice trait about a well hunted and experienced Golden is they usually do not get too hyper. A good dog that has had a lot of birds in his mouth can get out of the vehicle in a dramatic situation; to him at least, and he knows you are road hunting where the excitement is a bit more intense and yet he remains fairly calm. Both Rex and Puppy had this trait. Long ago my training as a young boy of Cedric, the farm dog, would pay off many times. I like a good dog that you can keep in the vehicle with you or free in your pick up box, one that doesn't whine or jump out when you stop; one that stays there only until you open the back tail gate or open the door for him."

I put a harsh expression on my face and made a pat down toward the ground in a hard manner. Being a bit over-emphatic never hurts when it comes to hunting. Then I hit the side of my thigh several times and patted emphatically backwards. This is my signal to stay behind me or 'Heel.' The dog stays behind as we advance down the ditch on toward the quarry. If I am alone and get to where I have estimated the birds to be, I give my dog the go ahead signal and we both race toward the top of the ditch or toward their estimated concealment. This is what we did for the 'Burke Triple.' Normally you do not have to depend on any 'Rush' signal. A good dog knows what is happening and he will move as soon as you do. Yes, with a good, experienced non-hyper dog, often some signals are just not needed.

Rex and I crested the road out of the ditch after I could see the top of the shrubs. The birds leaped and I also had the advantage of nice firm 'road' footing. The first round took one down our side of the fence line. One sailed toward the corn going down and I needed two shots for one going high above the fence but he dropped hard and never moved. I was out of shells and my #1 bird was under the fence running away. Rex had the second bird in his mouth but dropped it to pursue the first bird. Before I could get a round into my gun, Rex was hot after it. By the time I was reloaded with a quick shell into the open chamber, the dog was too close behind it for a shot. I wanted that triple so bad that I kept guard on the one he had dropped and would have drilled it as I approached it in case it would have gotten up and started running. I slipped another shell into my tube as I walked up to it and took a hold of its limp neck. With Rex's return with his mouth full, I had gotten a triple back to back in two days. Birds do not out run Labs or Goldens and within a minute or so of my first shot, I had my triple.

Water and Food

October in South Dakota can get pretty warm. Carry a pint bottle of water, at least, with you in the field unless the sloughs or creeks have water but often you never know. Generally, Iowa in early fall you have no water worries, but Dakota can be different. Two gallons at least should be in your vehicle when dry conditions exist. A hard working dog puts away a lot of water. A big bowl of water is always waiting behind the pickup when we get back. Water, water, water. You can never have enough, especially when it is still T-shirt weather and you are not around a creek or a dam. Some real wise hunters with more than one dog in this kind of weather have a five-gallon jerry can full of water when they start out. Pour a pan full before you start out and the dogs will drink it dry when you get back. Food? I always promise the evening waitress a $5 extra tip if she can produce some good steak, prime rib or roast pork from the galley in a 'doggie' bag. You can also order a bigger steak or prime rib than you can eat. I cut that up with my cleaning scissors and mix in with his dry high protein ration. I feed my dog plenty of meat with his dry. During the canned dog food scare I went out and bought beef heart, which surprisingly is not all that costly per pound. It is as rich in protein as any part of the steer or cow. I cooked up several pounds of that and cut it up into convenient baggies before going out. I carried it in the cooler with ice. I have also traded many a bird for deer meat from willing deer hunters to supplement my dog's hunting diet.

Motels and Kennels

I feel sorry for those dogs peeking out of a kennel with a few tufts of straw under them on a cold morning. I have moved out of motels which have peed and moaned because my dog stayed in my room. I avoid motels where my dog is not welcome. Next morning after a good night's sleep he is ready to move out with zesto because of a comfortable night inside and not freezing in the back of some pickup. I do carry a couple sleeping bags and he goes into the pickup cab where I make a nice soft tent like structure in the back seat for him in case I have no choice at a motel. He has never had a shock collar on; never needed it. Some of the best hunting dogs I have seen wear them so I can't belittle them. In fact, many, if not most, of the real good trackers, flushers and retrievers will have them on.

I met one of the best hunting companions that I will ever meet through turning down a motel because they would not allow my dog in on one cold night. I was down in Northern Iowa and stopped at a motel. No dogs were allowed due to a recent incident wherein a pair of hunters left their two dogs in the room and went into town for supper. Well, those two dogs did such a job on that motel room that the two hunters almost had to buy the room. As a result, the manager issued a ban on all dogs. The manager sympathized for me but had to stand by his rules and did place a call to a motel about ten or so miles away. They were more hospitable – dog wise – and said it would cost $5 extra.

The next morning I walked into a restaurant for breakfast and ran into a group of hunters. Again it was my magic flight jacket. A retired Master Sergeant,

John Jacobson, owner of the best dog I have ever experienced, Angus, started up a conversation and we have been close friends ever since. I don't know how many times I have returned to the Sandman Motel in Eagle Grove, Iowa. They like me probably because I always give them a pheasant or two when I stay there. The first one I had to show them how to take off the feathers, cut it up and get it ready for the frying pan. I kept telling the manager that a pheasant is simply a chicken when it comes to cutting it up and cooking it but they seemed to be initially mystified by it.

A Dog's Feet

A woman named Diane sells those dog booties at the Oasis motel in Oacoma, South Dakota. She makes them from a very tough, resistant material with velcro holders. I have had good luck with them. No need to use duct tape to hold them on, either. The motel is right across the river from Chamberlain and has an efficient cleaning station. You need those booties though, for your dog walking some cornfields that have those wicked, dog stopping sand burrs. Many fields do. If his feet are not toughened up from gravel roads pre-season you will wish you had purchased those protecting booties. Be sure to take them off immediately after you leave the field, as your dog's feet will swell if you leave them on too long. For the majority of your hunting you will never need them, however.

Pheasant Camp – Hockey Camp: A Related Example

Kyle is my youngest son. Throughout grade school he excelled in just about any sport he entered into. It was such a joy to watch him participate. Just like some dogs you become fortunate to have, Kyle had a 'heart' so to speak, and with that determined 'heart' he also had what some call 'The Gift.' I had such enjoyment watching him compete in the normal sports kids play, such as soccer, baseball, football and basketball, that I even became a grade school affiliated 'coach' or 'coach's helper' of the various sports, if a more experienced volunteer coach could not be found. In Minnesota, hockey is a tough sport and needs to be prepared for early. Kyle was so immersed in the other sports including a later one, karate, that he got a late start for hockey which became the most suited endeavor for his talents. His love and interest for karate held him up for several of the early hockey years. He had won several tough contests in karate and his coaches were quite disappointed with his choice to try hockey, such was his heart and talent at battling karate opponents. He even fought in a higher weight class once and won the event.

He began to go to the numerous hockey rinks maintained complete with warming facilities, which are a trade mark of this particular suburb whose high school is noted for winning record championships. He missed a season of organized hockey when he first started in earnest but began learning the difficult skills. Soon he was playing with kids usually older than he was, but with his fast developing talent he was soon invited to join their pickup games. Often good players his age on organized teams would play in those games. Soon he was telling me what players he could compare his abilities to. He practically lived on those hockey rinks come weekends. The warming huts are not 'huts' at all, but are heated, spacious structures that have kept the suburb long into the state championship brackets by hatching early talent. This particular suburb has three indoor rinks. Most Minnesota towns are lucky to have one. I'd simply give him money to order pizza and pop which seemed to be the customary fare for the weekend hockey players who also spent all day at the rinks. The 'hut' was a handy baby sitter.

The following summer he went to a week long hockey camp which I thought would get him ready for fall try outs amongst his peers. That fall he tried out and was relegated to the Class C team, the lowest talented grouping. I didn't know much about hockey and expected a low rating for his ability since he was a relative unknown regarding the sport in a suburb loaded with talent. He enjoyed his teammates and became quite effective as a defenseman. This was also the first year that checking would be allowed at that level. His speed on the ice, ability to check and take a check, and his protection of the goalie in moving opponents away and around began his reputation. This year would bring a big change to these fledgling hockey players. 'Checking,' now would mean a player can hit another player forcefully if he wants to hold on to the puck. Some over-protective mothers would pull their offspring out of the sport over such a rough change. Toward the end of the season, the goalie's father and the coach urged me to send Kyle to hockey camps. Not just one hockey camp, but several. I have to add that when Kyle was not playing organized hockey he was back at the public ice rinks with his older friends playing pick up. Here he again played against his immediate peers and confidently related to me the ones that he estimated he just might have an edge on.

What does all of this have as pertaining to a good hunting dog? Let us go just a bit farther and my point will hopefully emerge.

The A tryouts came for an upper division. All summer Kyle was exposed to checking and liked it considerably, mainly because it brought back a portion of his old sport karate which he reluctantly had to leave for his new sport. He checked and received checks, but with his gift of speed he dealt out more than he received and certainly did not shy away from it. At the end of one game, one opponent coach became so incensed that he came out on to the ice and grabbed Kyle. Fortunately, a fight began at the same time at Kyle's goalie's position and the coach had to let go of him to run and break up the fight. Hockey can get a bit rough at times, even at the junior high level. Tempers get flared and that is life despite all the political correctness employed. Well, tryouts happened. The star player came out and shot a puck at Kyle. Kyle looked at the coach after the miss and at the coach's nod, he sped to the star and decked him. He made the A team. The coach remarked that was what he wanted to see for such a flagrant foul. Both players became friends eventually and still spent many hours at the public rinks honing their skills. Overall, despite the dramatics of his tryout, Kyle would have never made 'A's had he not become heavily involved in the hockey camps.

Like Hockey, Upland bird training is keenly advanced when the dog has plenty of experience, which means heavy covered land for the birds and, of course, numerous ringnecks. This is what upland bird hunting in Dakota is all about. It doesn't hurt to get your dog involved in 'hockey camps.' The more, the better for your eventual hunting experiences with him or her later down the hunting journey. But in the Dog's 'Pheasant Camp' it is you who will provide the primary role of Trainer, unless of course you have the means to have a professional trainer look after his educational needs. By all means, if you can manage it, have a professional trainer train him.

Whatever, no matter who conducts his training, if you live in the Dakotas or Iowa you will have little excuse for not bringing up a dog who can turn into a good dog and a real good, great dog if you give it your added touch. Of course there are exceptions and you may have to admit defeat on some dogs. Patience is a key virtue in dog training however. Had I bought five live pheasants instead of ten to train the best dog I have ever had – he would have wound up as my wife's lap dog and never enjoyed what he was bred for. Like I will say over and over, the more pheasants a dog becomes exposed to the less 'Hyper' and more assured that dog will be. That does not necessarily mean that these have to be birds brought down with shot. The vast majority that he is exposed to will merrily go on their way. There is no reason why your dog cannot sit in a pickup box and watch calmly as a rooster approaches in his direction and, with no one telling him verbally, to stay in that pickup box and not rush the bird! And he does not have to become a robot to react so calmly.

Training is basically simple. We have already talked about throwing a simple ball, yes, repetitively, over and over. The more you do it the better he will eventually retrieve. Kids are a real blessing for this training. That is a given. If you are too lazy or non-interested in this facet of simple yet needed training, you do not deserve a good or great dog. The throwing also builds up a close relationship bond between you and the dog. My dog thinks of me as one fun playmate; that is why he will practically do, or at least try to perform, almost any task that I can lead him into ...and his tail will usually be wagging while he is beginning to learn something new.

When he goes to relieve himself in the morning, I simply open the back sliding door that faces a large pond in the background with houses all surrounding. He walks outside in this pretty location in suburbia and does his duty. I shut the door and go back to what I am doing, never checking to see if he runs off or away. In the summers, the pond in back abounds with ducks and geese. He is a pheasant hunter and seems to care less about ducks and geese so they tolerate each other. He stares at them for a few moments and they stare at him but he'd much prefer chasing a squirrel up a tree than bother the big geese. He will retrieve anything brought down but his heart is far more into Upland. He also ignores other dogs unless they are hunters. He often will sit on the front step and watch the world go by and without an electronic fence to hold him in. He simply refuses to notice or 'sniff' those worthless little yappy things called dogs, or more precisely 'lap dogs,' when suburban women mostly, lead them by in front of the residence on their evening walks. I would be too embarrassed, to tell the truth, to ever have to walk one of those worthless things out in the public.

Within ten minutes or so after he does his usual sniff of nightly animal activity close by, he is looking into the glass of the sliding back window door and after about five minutes of patient waiting he will issue a few businesslike barks to get my attention to let him in for breakfast. In the evening it is also the same routine. Why doesn't he wander? My guess is that he is very content with our company and wants to get right back within his own 'pack'– even if they are humans instead of other dogs.

Lately I have become a re-resident of my home state, South Dakota, but I still spend time back in Minnesota in the fall and early winter. Occasionally, in the Minnesota winter, we will shortcut across the frozen pond to a larger lake nearby that borders a park where leashed dogs are often walked on a walkway. We have come across several Golden Retrievers with their owners. Once we met a couple with a handsome male retriever. "Your dog hunt?" I politely asked. The man put his head down with a shaking of his head while his wife responded as if I had asked if the dog had some particular disease. Right then I knew I had a Golden Retriever show dog in front of me. "We paid too much money to risk him to hunting." She replied bluntly while disdainfully eyeing Puppy who is not overly handsome, show dog wise, and was still growing out of the choppy haircut I had administered earlier to him. Her husband never met eye contact with me but yet I could detect a bit of agony within him when I had mentioned hunting. I like to avoid disharmony but I just had to inject a bit of a needle especially because of her superiority attitude. "My dog hunts considerably, mostly in the Dakotas... and Iowa too." I petted Puppy at the moment and while releasing his 'walkway' leash, I added, "We have a good time, don't we Pup?" He responded by wagging his tail, probably more in response to the leash removal than my question. Besides a leash, their dog also had on one of those muzzle restrictors. No dog of mine will ever have one of those things on. Having nothing in common, we left the walkway and cut across some cattails bordering our frozen shortcut back to our dwelling and where he is free to sniff out the cattail borders to his heart's desire. Out on the ice, no one will come out and tell me to put his leash back on. I left them with, "Lot of birds this year out in the Dakotas and Iowa too. Pup here, he got his share." I though about the handsome dog they had and felt sincerely sorry for the animal. When we got out of ear shot I said to Puppy as he inspected a thick stand of cattails at the ice's edge, "Poor, pitiful, pretty, muzzled son of a bitch, Pup. That poor dog will never get to do what you do. No birds in the sky for him, Pup."

Let us get your dog out into a public land area before the pheasant season begins and when such training is permitted. Or if you are really serious, approach a resort and offer to pay them a fee to simply let you walk through their preserve or a part of it with your dog. A real large preserve isn't one bit worried that you will drive their birds away for they will usually pick up from one area and set in another area. When I ran back to the owner that I was worried I was driving his birds away he simply laughed and reassured me I was not doing him a bit of damage. I trained my dog so well on his land that now my dog will occasionally fill in for other dogs when their business is heavy. I also take clients out on that resort… solo, with my dog only. We get up 'tons' of wild birds, usually farther back in and within the more inaccessible places where vehicles just cannot penetrate. The owner often wants to go along with us when he has time simply because I think he enjoys our company.

Let us place your dog out in a field that is loaded with pheasants, and the little ones are no longer fledglings but are now of enough age that they can easily fly away from us. Always, it seems in this mechanized world, there are a few tire tracks in open grass fields. These car tracks are a godsend for training. Your dog will be ambling along into the wind so as to make it easier for him to track and the birds that do lift will be a bit closer and often will sit for him or her to test his flushing and pointing ability. You are off to the side and looking down one of these car tracks. Unseen to the human eye, a hen or rooster will be ahead of your dog and suddenly breaks out of the grass into the brief opening for you to now see it and like most animals, the bird will take the easier route even while thinking they are being pursued. The bird will choose to go either left or right. Rarely, if ever, do I see the bird go straight across the tire rut on into the grass. If you happen to be upwind from him, he will turn the opposite direction from you and scurry down his easier path crouched low, yet moving with exceptional speed. I have seen this happen many, many times while out training my dog.

Now your dog is but a few yards behind his quarry. When he comes to the corner where the bird turns, remember he is hot on pursuit and at this point in the chase, he is definitely going to be a bit in his 'Hyper' uncontrolled stage. When he comes onto the tire track where the pheasant's scent is severe and he starts to turn with the bird you yell emphatically – Ste-aaayyyyy!

Before you started out, back at your home, he will well know what this command means. He will be so pleased when you take him across the street and have him sit. You will give him an elementary Ste-aayyyy command as you back away from him or her with emphatic hand movements or body movements to remain where he is at. You will do this repeatedly until he starts to think he is some kind of dog genius getting a world of praise for some simple act of sitting on his behind while you fish in your pocket for some sort of treat to go with the lavish praise. This gets him used to the idea that the word Stay is not a bad word to be associated with at all. Even when a harsh emphatic tone for emphasis is used he begins to think that Ste-aaayyyy gets him some more attention or even a treat which dogs never seem to mind. In summary, the word Ste-ayyyyy becomes pleasantly programmed into his mind. I can yell 'Puppy' or 'Rex' at my dog ever so harshly and loud and he will sit there giving me his attention with a wag of his tail. He associates pleasantly with the word and never the harshness of the tone with it. If you ever have to save your dog with a loud harsh call of his name to get his attention while a dangerous vehicle is fast approaching at the end of a pheasant field you will understand my method.

So for teaching sake, let us return to the pheasant and the dog right behind it. Do not expect a miracle when he is hot behind a pheasant and in his early training. He just might ignore your Ste-ayyy and continue after the exiting bird. But sooner or later he will get used to the idea that he must stop and sit or remain stationary once you issue that command. If he bolts after the pheasant you simply bring him back and get him on the trail of a new bird. You might give him a bit of on-the-spot Ste-ayyy training and proceed with seeking a live bird. Eventually the light bulb within his brain will click, especially when he somewhat gets over the scenting of so many birds and he starts to become more methodical. I even use the term 'mechanical,' meaning that he has seen so many birds, scented them and seen them come up that he now begins a so-called more professional attitude toward them. Think of the dog in the pickup box and the advancing rooster. Now that, in my opinion, was one helluva professional attitude example.

How did he get that way? Did having endless pheasants out in front of him making observed tire track changes in direction have a bearing? I also would take that dog and his predecessor as well, and drive out into South Dakota preseason, even in the summer when the small ones needed to be protected and field training in their habitat is wisely not allowed. On a trout trip, I would stop beside some feeding pheasants, usually roosters who are mostly immune to any fear of passing vehicles or even motorists stopping at that time of year, as long as you remain in your car. I would stop slowly beside a couple of roosters near the road's fence line with my car windows open and my dog gazing silently out the window at them but a few feet away. This is indeed an odd sight: Hunting dog who has been led to learn Ste-aaayyy while looking out the window and pheasant looking up at the strange looking furred creature observing him while the pheasant is more interested in his feeding than worrying about us. Mind you this is not a reaction during hunting season but most Dakotans will vouch for how 'tame' they can become before the first shot is fired.

Naturally, the dog wants to jump through the open car window frame onto the curious bird, but he becomes more obedient to your command which you reinforce with a whispered Ste-aaayy repeatedly while both stare at each other. If you want, you can signal him to 'Get' the bird and he will leap through the open window and the rooster will cackle skyward. But overall, he thoroughly learns that powerful word in his vocabulary which will prove very fruitful come pheasant season. You now have accomplished a great deal in your dog training. I liken it to learning to land and solo an airplane for the fledgling pilot. You have a ways to go yet but a critical part is behind you.

Envision your dog out in the field and your dog is responding well while in a 'hot' field, birds are rising and he or she stays close enough to eventually give you a reasonable shot at flushing birds while the other guys are busily punching their shock collars on 'way-outs' and runners. You will start to realize the value of a good –'Stay Close' hunting dog who responds well to one simple command when it needs to be given. I guess that is why I most often like to hunt by myself or with a client and my dog only. The guys in Emery, South Dakota have the same view. Way-outs and Runners are forbidden.

6

Take a Boy Hunting:
Hammers and Safes

Chris Gehrke

Chris was fortunate to have a dad, Jim Gehrke, who took him hunting and fishing at an early age. Chris turned out to be quite a hunting enthusiast, and we have had some good pheasant and duck hunting experiences together and still do since those days when he was a junior high hockey player with my youngest son. Both were darn good defensemen, giving me a lot of excitement watching them. Jim Gehrke would have my son, Kyle, up at their cabin for family deer hunting and I would get both boys out for Dakota birds earlier in the fall. One year when I could not take them out, Jim took them prairie dog and rattlesnake hunting. I even helped train their young dog, Cash, a Golden Lab who had that built in wanting-to-please attitude, and was fairly easy to train. I took him out to Dakota pre-season, where he experienced a wealth of pheasants and was a good student with older Puppy who served as dog professor.

Although different breeds, they looked like two brothers as Puppy was cut down nice and short from his summer clipping. Be surprised how a Golden Retriever will resemble a Golden Lab when well clipped. Buy a set of electric dog clippers and 'Presto,' you have a "Lab" with close hunting genes, <u>if</u> you give him adequate training. As I said before and worth repeating for the dog's sake and comfort, a long haired dog is much cooler come summer and they seem to have an extra bounce of energy once they come off that clipping table in the hot summer season. Why people leave their dogs hot and shaggy…and uncomfortable…for the hot summers, beats me. Chris is now a semi-pro-hockey player which interferes with hunting season but when he is through with that career he vows that we will be hunting together more often. Our last hunt was recently in Iowa. He was home for Christmas. There is nothing more rewarding than to be blocking for a bunch that you once knew as young kids and now they are all grown men and the birds are leaping up for them and they are all having a good hunt. How rewarding! I remember vividly, it was just Chris and I, well into the pheasant season, dropping him off at a drainage ditch crossing down in Iowa. We were in a fairly heavy snow squall but driving his four-wheeler pickup, we were not worried.

The snow was coming down out of the northwest. He is one tough, big and strong defenseman and naturally in prime physical shape. Puppy has no problem hunting with Chris and without me. Cash and my Golden Retriever went off with Chris bucking the drifts north into the snow, walking the ridge of the drainage ditch which slanted down a good 30-feet to the frozen water. I drove on around to the next bridge crossing, a mile north. At least a half foot of snow was the average depth with higher drifts but Chris was insistent on getting some birds. Youth can be persistent but it would have been too much for me, especially for a solid mile in those wind-in-your-face conditions. I parked a mile north, eventually. We didn't have to worry about any car traffic on that day. With my back to the wind, which was blowing at times in strong gusts, I walked on down the drainage ditch ridge toward them for a few hundred yards. Without a dog I didn't expect to kick up any birds and kept my Benelli at sling. I could see Chris and dogs as three dots in the distance. He stopped, paused and up came his gun. A boom could barely be heard against the wind and the dogs went active; down in the ditch they dove. I could see him bending over to one of the dogs eventually, obviously picking up his bird. Twice more, he repeated the same procedure except that the second bird dropped out into the bare bean field to his right. He had his limit by the time he got to me. His determination paid off. Due to an injury, he will not be playing hockey this season and we are planning to do the South Dakota and Iowa Opener together. Cash and Puppy will be looking forward to our expedition. Cash picked up valuable experience this Spring, bringing in Spring Snows and Blues – over 100. Over 100 birds retrieved is very valuable experience for any dog. It will be a great time. In my later years I have many invitations to hunt with the young guys I helped start out and now are in their prime. What goes around, often comes around.

Mark and Todd

Two equally enthusiastic hunting (and sometimes fishing) partners were about 11 years old when we started out: my middle son, Mark, and his buddy, Todd. It was .22 rifles out on the Indian reservation shooting prairie dogs. Todd's Dad never took him hunting, but I filled that gap as I did for quite a few boys, especially with my 3rd son, mostly Minnesota hockey players. My oldest son and the youngest one were avid hunters as well.

Mark and Todd were fairly inseparable when it came to hunting and shooting. I can't remember when they first received their BB guns; much earlier than when most mothers would ever allow, no doubt. I remember how thrilled I was when I purchased my first 'Red Ryder,' lever action cocked, BB gun from my paper route money.

My sister had a significant spread of land on the Indian reservation I was born on. It was loaded with prairie dogs which take their toll on the grass and, of course, compete with the cattle. She and the surrounding ranchers did not mind a bit if we came out to relieve the land of some of the little rodents, who are a bit larger than a rat and close to cottontail size. When one goes out to shoot prairie dogs one does not enter upon the expedition with a couple boxes of shells totaling about 100 rounds. Instead, one does not leave without at least a 'brick' of at least 500 rounds. All of which will be expended against or at a live target. With their 'bricks,' I took this pair of boys out to the reservation as I had done with my oldest son and his excited friends and would do so later with my youngest son and his friends, who were also adept hockey players come winter. I hold to the concept – that if you participate with your kids and include even their friends, you will, most often, have a closer and a more positive bond with them than will those parents who essentially ignore their offspring. My concept has become highly rewarding for my later years. We still make these forays out to prairie dog land yet have not seemed to have made much of a dent in reducing the population all that much, despite the numerous 'bricks' of shells we have carried and expended out there. In these later years they no longer need me to make their trips which include enjoyable camping out besides exploring the isolation of that strange country, the Badlands.

Hammers and Safes

I started my oldest son, John, with a cute little lever action .22 that sported an exposed hammer and a tubular load. It was not the long barreled hammerless common to most 'prairie doggers' or a Ruger with a three-way clip which are far more efficient for the numerous dogs. I wanted safety and wanted to be able to look over at that rifle and see if the hammer was safely in a safe position and not cocked. Kid are kids and they can get excited and forget. It is only natural for them. I think that all young shooters should start out on a hammered rifle just for this very important fact – safety. To this day, out in the pheasant field after some birds get up and have been shot at, "Check your safes," I call out to the younger ones. In the excitement one can easily forget. With a hammer, on the prairie dog expedition, it is much easier to check.

I have since started out a young grandchild with a new hammered rifle. We broke one in shooting on the Cheyenne River at floating cottonwood bark that disintegrates when you hit it. He is also a hockey player and has been so successful that he has been raised up into a higher bracket after scoring numerous goals. He takes me back to my son's days at that age. I was watching him play and after the game all the parents went down to pick up their offspring. He came out of the locker room with those rubber clip-ons to their skates so they can walk off the ice. "Gran Pa," he said with a big smile and taking off his helmet. Heavy snot was packed all around his nose and his hair was a mass of hard working, determined sweat. His style reminds me of Joe Sakic of the Colorado Avalanche who never seems to quit. "Gran Pa. I got ten goals!" I laughed and remarked that seldom in hockey does a player ever get that many.

Before I go much further I have to elaborate for the benefit of any child psychologist, social workers, marriage counselors, therapists, juvenile advisors, priests, ministers, truant officers and such other related folks and professions: taking a boy hunting and/or fishing is almost a sure fire guarantee that the youth will most likely have a positive relationship with his father or the older adult who takes the time to simply see that the youth under his tutelage has a good, exciting time out in bounteous Nature and gets in some real shooting or fishing. Now, some decades later, I have a goodly number of grown men who have been in the Badlands and have camped out as young youth to a coyote's song and even ate some rattle snake while we were out there. As a result of what I was doing which I simply enjoyed as well, I am now invited to their hunting forays. There is that saying as I previously mentioned; 'What goes around comes around.' I find myself richly rewarded.

Sad Stories

I know of one relationship wherein a boy begged and begged his father to take him hunting and fishing but the Dad was too busy with ballroom dancing on weekends and ignored the boy's pleas. It is too bad that I never knew of this situation until well after the boy grew up and got into hunting big time on his own, as well as fishing. As I said earlier, I have taken many a boy out into Nature besides my own sons. Round and round the dance floor the father went during the hunting season and in the summers when the Minnesota walleyes and northern pike were biting. The boy grew up and married a woman who shared his interest in hunting and fishing. Thanksgiving came and the father was planning to spend it with his now newly married son. Wild game was to be served but the son told his father not to come because it made him angry when he recalled that his Dad had ignored his pleas. Even as time has gone on, the son is not close to his father and continues to hunt and fish on his own or with his spouse. That father paid a helluva price for 'Ooohhmm-pah-pah.' He lost his son through 'Ooohhmm-pah-pah, and around you go, dosey doe. Annn now vee have der valtz, and der shottisshh, der polka too. Come out to the floor and do der two-step. Get your partners. A one and a two.' It wasn't worth it, if your own son, someday, tells you to go to hell! Sorry, if I have to put it so bluntly, folks, but this Marine believes that you should play with and do things with your kids and especially... listen closely to their pleas. That is just where I am at... and always will be!

I have one more story to relate on this subject and feel that it is worth telling and worthwhile for the reader to remember and pass on to their offspring for the well being of our youth.

Juli G. was a gorgeous blonde and was a key marketing consultant for a Minneapolis advertising firm. My nickname for her was "Blonde Juli." My sisters all liked her and referred to her affectionately as "Blonde Juli" and never called her anything else. She was tall and striking with that long hair flowing as was her lone daughter who she raised in a one-parent family. Her former husband was too consumed into alcohol and was not a dutiful parent which obviously bothered the daughter, a very bright girl, like her mother. My brother, at least, redirected his life through AA. Juli's 'former' was beyond AA: Lost his driver's license, everything; yet managed to hold on to a girlfriend who chose to drink with him. He made a semblance of a living by managing motels wherein he did not need a driver's license to get by. Like Mom, the daughter was also tall and a gifted athlete and therefore was involved heavily into organized sports at a large suburban school. As time went by, Juli's daughter learned to cope with having but one parent to come to her many games of various sports she successfully competed in.

This was before my time, before I got to know "Blonde Juli," what I am about to relate. There was a nice looking guy that 'had everything,' so to speak, when it came to attracting or dating attractive women. He had a fancy car, a good paying job and knew how to conduct himself. Eventually, he and Juli started dating and naturally he wanted the relationship to keep going.

They were having dinner at an impressive restaurant in Minneapolis when Juli decided to do a bit of probing into the guy's life, an area that he had seemed to want to avoid. She asked him point blank about his previous marriage, centering mainly on his two young daughters who lived with their mother. "How often do you see your kids?" She asked bluntly after the waiter had brought them their drinks and they were studying the menu.

He hemmed and hawed and fidgeted nervously. He began by offering excuses as to his job making exceptional demands upon his time. "I don't see them as much as I probably should..." he began with and then went on, excusing himself with how much money he spent on them for gifts during Christmas and their birthdays. Juli is no Dummy however, and she can also be very persistent when she has to. "Don't tell me you only see them twice a year?"

"Ahh, ahh more than that," he weakly responded.

She told me that she put the menu down and leaned across the table. "Like how often a month? Tell me the exact truth, because I will find out sooner or later if I continue to see you and if you lie to me, it will damn well be all over with." I have a personal high respect for Juli; I for one would never lie to her, because you would pay dearly if you ever did.

Come to find out, the guy rarely saw his two daughters. Juli ended the relationship right there and then and made the guy take her home. At her door she cussed him out like a good Marine and told him to never call her again. Several months later, he had a friend who had a marketing relationship with Juli's company, come and plead for him. He wanted Juli to know that he was seeing his daughters considerably and wanted to get back together but she wouldn't budge. For what she had gone through with the same form of neglect that her own daughter had experienced, she said she just could not generate any romantic feeling for the person but wished him well and to keep on seeing his children.

I never neglected my daughters despite my many fishing and hunting expeditions with the younger set. I hit endless amounts of tennis balls to my daughters, primarily, who were heavy into tennis. I had a fairly high monthly winter indoor tennis bill for my girls, as I said earlier, which gave them a considerable edge on their competing peers. One made all-conference as a result of our activity and the younger middle one would have also made such an honor but she won a Rotarian scholarship to New Zealand for a year which was equally rewarding. My youngest, Karen, played on a college team. All that tennis and the related participation in several doubles leagues for myself that came with it has helped to give me the legs that I still have today for Dakota and Iowa pheasants.

In summary, take that boy hunting and his buddies too. Do things with your daughters as well. Be surprised how close they will 'bond' to you and have a better attitude to move on to the trials of life that are forthcoming. I have seen some great results from the boys I was associated with and have a close relationship with my sons and daughters as well who have also been at the end of a fishing pole, paddled a canoe and have fired a few guns.

After several summer .22 rifle forays, which also included shooting gar fish and carp in the Cheyenne and Missouri River shallows, it was time for the young hunters I groomed to move on into the light shot gun which they entered with relish. We threw quite a few clay pigeons for their 20-gauge pump guns and they became quite adept with the low brass firing and much less 'kick.' Kids learn swiftly at shooting has been my observation.

Their First Shoot

The Spinal Bifida program needed shooters for a game feed. Those days, you paid $100 to shoot for them, and they donated all the pheasants and ducks to a game feed. That fall I received an invite to shoot in the St. Paul, Minnesota Spinal Bifida charity shoot, which would be held at a fancy Wisconsin game resort. I knew the organizer and tacked on a couple years to the boys real age and requested that I be allowed to bring a couple of younger hunters who had fired thousands of rounds and had their gun school certificates which was a state requirement. I didn't volunteer that those 'thousands of rounds' were .22 shells. The first weekend we started the two youth out on a duck blind. They did well and were asked back for the pheasant shoot the following weekend. The hunt organizer had the same name as me – Ed. He also had two black Labs and heard that my dog was pretty good and probably the main reason why I received the invite. The hunt organizer would keep all birds shot which included our lunch, and to me, $100 for the three of us was a real bargain. It cost more than that just for an out-of-state license back in South Dakota without a shot fired. I was living in Edina, Minnesota then, a Minneapolis western suburb.

Well, the three of us drove up with Fat Rex, (Rex II) our Golden Retriever in the back seat. Entering the hunting lodge to sign in, trailed by my two half pint hunters, I don't think we made a positive impression. The shooters, all well dressed older guys with over and under 12's mostly, all except one, a guy we came to know as Ralph, looked down their noses at us. Later, when we unveiled our guns, my 20-gauge over and under sported a sling as did the two kid's pump guns of the same caliber as mine. This discovery almost made the smart crowd burp when I brought my slinged O/U out of the case. Slings are handy if you do a bit more than normal hunting: Rests my getting-old arms when you walk back to the car/pickup/van. My Benelli 12-gauge, darn well has a light sling on it.

Mile and Half Mile

Ed K., the guy who invited us, supplied his two dogs, two black Labs, whining anxiously from their kennels in his pickup box. They came to be known as 'Half Mile' and 'Mile.' He was enthusiastic to see me, especially since we had brought our dog and gave us a warm welcome.

We drove out to the starting point where the pheasants had been 'placed' earlier in a low growth, sweet corn field for easier shooting and off into prairie grass and some woods. The two Labs swept back and forth across the grass surrounding the parking lot rather impressively while old Fat Rex took an unimpressive dump in the weeds as the hunters assembled, about six of them standing close together. I think they were worried that some of them would be assigned by Ed to hunt with us. The two boys were oblivious to the obvious coldness directed at us and Fat Rex included. Ed, the organizer and shock collar handler for the two Labs, fiddled with his two shock boxes which he strapped to himself. I had never had much experience with those things, never had to, but I was curious and walked close to him for a look see.

Ed was a good guy, however. He invited us and never minded I had the two kids, which would be for several more forays that he directed. Each year he made a special effort to encourage us to come hunt and, of course he had the two Labs who never changed their hunting style. Rex was a Golden Retriever and did not know what the hell a shock collar, or a kennel was for that matter. Motels and a comfy back seat sleeping bag was what he was used to when traveling. He was a great hunting dog however, hunted close and could track a wounded bird in the thickest cattails or weeds. Thick, tall, huge cornfields and you never lose him as I have seen happen to other dogs – a couple permanently. Rex might be gone fifteen minutes but would most usually come back with your downed rooster in his mouth.

Well...we started out. The well heeled gathered purposely on the right side of the cornfield thus allowing us three sling bearers plenty of space. Two roosters bolted up for them and a series of shots rang out and the Labs dutifully brought them 'to hand' as bird snobs like to say. Three more birds went airborne before we fired a shot. A hail of shots and one kept sailing but the other two were being retrieved before old Rex swung into action and the two kids polished off our first two roosters. By this time the Labs were flying down the corn rows and pheasants were coming up in twos and threes, but too far out for effective shooting. Ed K was blowing on his whistle and punching buttons right and left but the two Labs by now were out of range of the shock collar and just flat out having the time of their lives. Todd and my son are now grown men in their 30's. This was back when shock collars had limited range; the Labs were simply out of range and could care less about responding to their owner's calls and whistle blowing. That is why I like Golden Retrievers. Oh, I have seen some bad Retrievers and have also seen some excellent tracking and retrieving Labs but over all, a trained Retriever, in my opinion, has a much stronger tendency to hunt close. The Lab ranges more and covers more territory and most Lab owners consider Goldens a bit lazy in comparison. Maybe that is the reason you see far more Labs in the field. I have to alibi for the Golden on this particular issue, however. My experience is that a Golden will not 'play out' on you or lose his stamina in that the Golden paces himself and you can hunt all day with him. A zippier dog that covers more territory will soon play himself out and that is why many experienced dog owners will put a new set of those types of dogs in the field to replace the earlier session. Their strategy pays off! That works out fine for them, but with my Goldens, I have never had to bother myself with extra dogs. All day long I hunt with a lone Golden or two, if we are training a pup and come road hunting time he is just as good as he was that morning.

I have another related theory regarding the point concerning a dog staying close and not ranging too far out. One raised in the household, be it Lab, Golden or what have you, and not outside kenneled, has a stronger bond to not want you out of his sight. That is why, when hunting, even on a hot trail, they have that tendency to stop momentarily, and look to see where in the hell you are at, before carrying on with the hunt. Even in a tall, thick cornfield, my retrievers usually will come back to me just to check where I am. All claims have their exceptions of course. The best hunting dog I was and still am privileged to hunt over, is a half black Lab and half Weimaraner called Angus. He belongs to John Jacobson of Eagle Grove, Iowa and with my dogs he rides free in the back of the truck and never has been in a truck kennel to my knowledge. He has quite a plush and open kennel at his home that even my dog has slept in. So there are always exceptions.

Ed's two labs got their names right there and then as the far out one was dubbed 'Mile' and the one a bit closer in became 'Half-mile.' We were polishing off birds Rex was getting up for us. The kids were deadly from their skeet training. Most went down and stayed down, giving Rex the edge wherein he could run down the ones with only broken wings. These birds were not the wild Dakota bird type. They were smaller and sat tight for a point. Often we did have to urge them to fly with a slight nudge of our boot; a bit hard to miss, I have to admit. That was all several decades ago. Times have changed indeed. The resort birds I have come to know now, in this decade, come up no slower than the wild ones. Where I hunt in Dakota, you cannot tell the difference.

Despite a bit of extra weight, old Rex had no problem outrunning roosters. We stopped to stack our birds in a pile because it made no sense to be carrying that many. By this time the crowd was drifting over to our side of the cornfield. I stopped stacking and as they came up I asked them what they were doing. They pointed way off to the black dots still raising a few pheasants. One spoke up rather sheepishly. "Our dogs are out of range...ahhh. We thought we could hunt with your dog."

"He sure seems to be a good dog," one chimed in rather friendly.

I shook my head. "You don't hunt over my dog!" I replied firmly and elaborated. "None of you people except one, spoke a damned word to us back at that club house. Now... all of a sudden we are buddies...huh?"

Ralph

The only friendly guy in the bunch, Ralph, from earlier said, "But you got a mighty nice dog there. I'd sure like to hunt over him." Then he added meekly, looking at the kids unloading their vests. "I haven't even got a bird yet."

"Looks are deceiving..." I growled. I pointed to him and replied in a changed tone. "You want to hunt with us?" The guy lit up, so I motioned him over.

I told the kids to keep going and we left the startled party with our stacked birds and new addition – Ralph. We allowed the new guy first shooting over Rex's points. I soon switched guns with him, loaning him my Charles Daly Miroku, short barreled, Over and Under with IC coming out and Modified, after he couldn't hit anything at first with his own piece. He was packing a 12-gauge pump, 30-inch barrel, full choke. I asked to see his shells and sure as hell, they were Premium, high Mag. 2' and 4's which gave him a pattern the size of a tennis ball, if he was lucky, close in. I asked jokingly if he had any BB's. "No," he responded innocently. "Is that what you guys are shooting?" as if it was our 'magic secret.' We were shooting two-and-three-fourths inch, seven and a half size shot and could have gotten by on 8's for our first round at modified for the two pumps. It was no wind and the birds were not breaking any speed records coming up. Number three and four shells in the tubes on the pumps were two–three-inch 6's for effective range. He had brought the wrong gun and ammunition for these tight sitting and easily flushed resort birds. I gave him a handful of 20-gauge, seven and a half lead, two-and-three-fourths, 1200 fps. A shell I wouldn't think of using in South Dakota on those heavier wild birds, resort or not, not even on opening day. A fall wind can come up out of nowhere and they would become even less reliable. I must point out that these particular birds then were far different than those larger and hardier rockets you will find nowadays on the resorts.

At first he missed with my short barreled over and under (24-inch barrel), partially because he was so damned excited. Eventually he calmed down and the kids held their fire to give him a chance. A couple birds, more than a few actually, we had to nudge with our boots so he knew they were definitely going to come up. It was as close to shooting fish in a barrel as you will get and he still missed a few of those. When he did fire, we lied like hell and claimed we missed and he had to have gotten it. He was so excited and happy, he believed us. I have seen kids get extra thrilled, especially on their very first birds, but this guy outdid anyone I had been exposed to. When Rex went on point and we purposely moved him on in, he'd be talking with utter amazement like the dog was some sort of magician or something. We got to where we'd simply send Old Rex in for the flush after his point and had the newcomer in position, but twice in a row the dog came up with the bird in his mouth and we'd have to throw it in the air. Those two… we had our newcomer get sole shooting rights to. One he drilled on his first shot and the other he missed completely, nary a feather lifted. "I never knew a dog could pick up a bird like that." He remarked. We looked at each other wondering if he had ever been pheasant hunting before. Some of these pen raised birds were real 'sitters.'

When we did get a double up, it was a sure win for him. With both birds down and Rex busy picking them up, we would ask which one he shot at. When he'd point we would all congratulate him because we would claim to high heaven it was the other bird we were pouring our lead at. Normally in life it is the adults who make kids happy; that fall day it was completely reversed. My two 'half-pints' kept him glowing from one bird to another.

By the end of the field, up came a bird and he missed and the kids opened up right after he fired his second round. The bird went down and we all yelled at him, what a great shot he made. By the end of the field he thought he had got five, maybe six, completely by himself, and was all aglow and made life miserable for the "smart crowd" with his innocent praise of Fat Rex when we went back in to eat at the club house. Geez, I thought he was going to get Rex entered into some kind of field trial, there for a while. We took him out again after lunch and made him think he got five more – by himself of course. The kids were good actors. When doubles came up, it was easy to lie as none of us ever shot at 'his' bird and indeed he did get some on his own. He was the happiest son of a bee I have ever seen hunting and praised old Fat Rex to high heaven again when we had a few drinks in the club house at the end and the kids sat drinking their pops, backing him up. I should have sold him my little 20-gauge, then and there, as age and Ducks and Spring Snow Geese has forced me on to the Benelli. I am no dead shot Dick as most hunters and especially 'hunter/authors' fancy themselves. I had those kids there for a reason. To cover my tail when a bird came up. At least I am honest. I hate people who tell me they 'never miss.'

The following season, of course, Half-mile and Mile didn't change much. Every year it was pretty much the same old story with those two dogs. Yet Ed thought he had a pretty good pair and kept buying more powerful shock collars. We kind of liked those two because we figured they were our guarantee that we'd always be welcome back. Our pheasant stack was always way more than theirs. A moral or teaching from this story is that you will find many a hunter who just will never admit he has a real loser of a dog and that is the one you want to avoid bringing out to Dakota or Iowa as that dog will really spoil your hunting for you. I am fortunate to hunt with my South Dakota opener group. You bring that type a dog out there and they won't hold back when they abruptly tell you to put that thing in a kennel and leave it there.

Todd went on to be one of Minnesota's best bird and predator guides, my opinion. He guides for a pheasant and snow goose resort in South Dakota as well. He takes me on many of his hunts. "You took me hunting as a kid. I never will forget it. Now I take you hunting." Because of Todd, I was led to the Dakota resort where I guide also. I go along in preseason without a gun of course and my new dog, Puppy and the Gehrke dog, Cash, where they have thousands of Dakota acres to hone their hunting skills. Bird after bird have gone up for what was once, early training. Before he was two-years-old Puppy was out at the resort, opening day, doing the job of a full fledged hunting dog, raising birds close and retrieving, and then picking up spring time snow geese that come in by the thousands. By then I could call him off a wounded Snow or Blue swimming right in front of him when a 'swirl' (flock of hundreds of Snows) would appear distantly and all retrieving dogs would have to come in quickly and hide immediately. Puppy was most obedient to my call. The owner recognized his ability and has asked him back ever since. Young Cash, the Golden Lab, has developed into an equally fine retriever.

Summary: Purposefully, this is a repeat of what I said before. In the beginning of this book, some readers may have wondered how a dog looking on from an open pickup box with no supervision could stand there and study a rooster approaching them without leaping out and bolting across a paved highway with some traffic, especially when the rooster turns and momentarily escapes back away from them. You can park beside a grazing rooster or several by a fence line as well with an open window between the dog and the bird down below and the dog will not leap out unless told to do so. Pre-hunting season roosters are often surprisingly docile before the hunting season's first shots are fired and will allow you this training opportunity. This conduct is all a part of the dog's training mainly because of being exposed to hundreds of ringnecks at close range and many during pre-season when nary a shot is fired. The more exposure the less 'Hyper' a dog becomes. It is all pretty simple as that.

As for Todd, we both benefited by 'taking a boy hunting.'

7

Five Days and Fifteen Birds

Dakota Opener

It was the worst pheasant year I have experienced. The earlier winter took its toll, especially in Eastern Dakota. The snow never let up and killed many pheasants. Western South Dakota seemed to fare better. Opening day I shot only three roosters and that was in a group with other hunters I have hunted with for years. Those birds were not packing my lead only. We had cornfields to hunt which have always produced many pheasants. The second day, by noon, I never fired a shot. After a few cornfields with few roosters on the second hunting day of the season, and none coming up in front of me except for hen after hen, I chose to head west, solo, when our group decided to break early for road hunting. I had seen quite a few birds earlier in the summer, out west of the Missouri, before the season opened while going on a couple Black Hills trout expeditions.

I was raised in the Black Hills when the streams were far more productive and much larger. Rapid Creek used to roar down through my home town of Rapid City. As kids, we not only fished in it, but swam in it as well, somehow being impervious to the cold mountain stream. Kids are kids, I guess, and it was our summer playground. I had a fly rod since I was ten and could cast a live grasshopper fairly effectively with out snapping him off the hook on the back cast and brought home my share of Brookies, Rainbows and Browns. It wasn't until I grew out of the kid stage when I started out on the imitation dry flies wherein you can make the much longer cast.

I stopped at a friend's farm nearby before starting out, a retired farmer's fields which were well known for their bird productivity and few people beyond his son are allowed to hunt there. It is quite a story why I am usually allowed on his choice, choice CRP land which the local group there call 'Don Smith's Nirvana.' I always visit with this retired farmer and his wife who happen to be of the same age group as my older sister and brother-in-law Mark and are close card playing friends. I happened to loan him a car of mine when he could not get a rent-a-car, because at the time he just refused to use 'one of those damn credit cards,' as he put it. Times change I know, but back then there were a few holdouts regarding credit cards and Don was one of them. He had flown into a large city where I happened to be working at its airport. He since has changed his mind about credit cards, but at that time he was in a bit of a pickle, and knew that the younger brother of his wife's best friend was somewhere in that town and had a staff position at the airport where the rent-a-car folks were refusing him service because he did not possess a credit card. I settled his problem with my extra car and wound up hunting his land ever since. Incidentally, he could have paid cash for a new car had he wanted to.

They usually pour me some generous glasses of their home made wine but this year I was spared that luxury. Instead they had one bottle of Mike's Lemonade which was quite a surprise. He said they knew I would show up eventually and had bought a six pack for me but liked it so well there was only one bottle left. It is only five percent alcohol and I never liked the real hard stuff most people drink. Not much alcohol in this one but it has a good taste in my opinion, so hence my satisfaction with a fairly weak drink. You can cut it with White Zinfandel wine, especially mixing the wine with the cranberry flavored Mike's. Not a bad drink; it's my favorite. Can you imagine getting to hunt pristine land all to yourself and drinking the owner's home made wine on top of it? Sometimes I do have a charmed life. Yes, I know, what most readers are thinking, but what would you do when folks want you to sit down and chat for awhile before running out and using their land that abounds with pheasants? It would be rather rude to turn them down, my opinion, and in my many appreciated sojourns hunting there, I haven't shot my dog yet. Not wanting to overdo their generous hospitality, I usually hunt by myself when I hunt there.

I had a brother who called me an 'alcoholic' when he discovered I didn't mind having a drink or two toward evenings, even though I drank the fairly weak Mike's. He was an AA (Alcoholics Anonymous) member, a real staunch one. Even his oldest kid had hit the booze pretty hard and lost his driving license. For myself, none of mine have had their licenses revoked, or me either, nor have I ever had a DWI (Driving While Under Influence). Maybe if I keep getting older, I can hang onto that record. I don't think he played as much with his kids as I did mine. You neglect your kids while they are growing up; you most often pay a price. As I said earlier, my kids did quite a bit of canoeing, fishing and hunting, besides other sports, including the girls and often with a friend of theirs or two. I don't know how many thousands of tennis balls that I hit to my girls. Backhands, forehands, lobs, serves and drill shots. One made all-conference and her younger sister would have too except for winning a Rotarian scholarship to New Zealand. A big advantage they gained by belonging to a group of indoor tennis clubs for the long Minnesota winters. I cannot take all the credit however. They also had an athletic step-mom who got all of us into tennis and spent a lot of her time with them. My monthly indoor Minnesota winter tennis bill was pretty high but it was all worth it: kept my legs in shape for pheasants as I also played a lot of doubles with athletic, aggressive and pretty step-mom; which may be the major reason why my legs are in such still solid shape for my seventies. I am quite proud of all my kids and the various sports were a blessing.

I now play a tennis indoor variant called Pikkal Ball for older folks but it is a fast game and we go at it for two to three hours and build up quite a sweat doing so. I also play volley ball. Often I am on one of the two courts six days a week, especially in the winter and non-hunting time.

Anyway, he (my brother) preached to me and hauled me away to one of those AA meetings. He was staunch in his belief that since we all had Indian blood in us that THAT was the main reason why Indians become alcoholics. (I since have adamantly disagreed with that crazy theory, much to the consternation of many an Academic besides my brother.) I believe it was Academia where that crazy theory was founded, as it is Academia that has issued many an off-the-wall type of theory about we Indians and of course, Hollywood has done its job of casting some really bad, false stereotypes. It was about time that 'Dances With Wolves' finally came out. Good movie – my opinion. There is a whole bunch of Academics who hold to this lineage/alcohol supposition. I guess we Indians have been endowed with different types of bodies and physiological functioning which I always thought the vast Creator has fairly well cooked up as all the same for all of us. Is not an Arctic/Alaskan wolf little different from his Siberian cousins? I felt like I was in some kind of church with all the confessions going on at that first meeting.

Well, not wanting to hurt anyone's feelings within that crowd of folks who were doing their darnedest to convince me how much happier they all were (and no doubt were). After some more coaching and prompting from my big brother, I got up and 'confessed.' I didn't have much of a 'horror story,' to tell the truth because basically I was pretty happy with myself and certainly not ashamed of my past. What? Coming out of a poor background and winding up flying that big Phantom and all the good hunting and fishing I'd seen besides raising good kids and getting to be a Marine officer too boot! My good looking, athletic wife who had brains besides, never complained adversely when I went hunting or fishing wherein my kids were well included. She would even go along too, at times and got all of us into tennis as I said earlier and introduced me to Golden Retrievers.

She was a great influence toward the positive way my kids turned out; not going on to college was not an option. They are all college graduates along with several Masters Degreed ones except for the two still in college who will graduate – no question. One of those speaks fluent Arabic and can type it as well. He just won a Master's Fellowship from a large University. An ex-hockey player, the Marine Corps could certainly use him.

I think my brother was a bit jealous of the good women I had chosen to go with down through my life, as he seemed to pick some genuine 'Lulus' right up to the end of his that were quite opposite from the women I went with. His last one was the Lulu of all Lulus earning him a nickname, 'Whipped.' He was bigger and much better looking than I; he certainly was not handicapped or inhibited but he went mostly for the 'bar-types' and in his later years they were 'AA' women. I was lucky, I guess. I never quite impressed the 'bar types' enough to wind up with one. Then he would get on some binges after they would apply some major screws to him – big time – until the AA program 'straightened' him out. So he claimed.

Smoking

'What the hell did I have to be so despondent about?' I asked myself before my 'confession.' I never did 'gurgle' down the booze like most of these guys had done, according to their stories. I am pretty sure though, that I let them down a bit there. My 'confession' story was fairly mild compared to theirs. He dragged me to one more meeting and I just didn't feel like I was much of an asset to them. I didn't like all the smoke either as I never smoked and detest it. As kids playing sports we were death on smoking and to this day I see old classmates who were early smokers carrying around those oxygen tanks and worse, a few who checked out early due to lung problems. It is a tough way to die. If you are a young kid, do not start smoking! It will be the dumbest thing you will ever do! I can't drink much coffee after breakfast. If I do, it seems to make it difficult to get to sleep come evening. They seemed to be happy as clams in their evening meeting heavy on cigarettes and coffee. I just didn't feel like I had an adequate enough background to contribute much. Fact was fact, I guess I must have reasoned and never went back.

In summary, I have my own theories. Most folks may not agree with me, especially the Academic types, but I still hold to the idea that Benevolent Creator gave us all the same make up. I happened to be a Marine Fighter Pilot and you just did not get too heavy into the booze. In combat flying you needed every bit of reflex and clear eyed thinking if you were to stay alive and more importantly protect the 'grunt' Marines down below you who had combat life far worse than you ever would. They are your primary duty and responsibility, especially in combat, and believe me, Marines do not shun combat encounters.

Gold Wings

You can't join up safely in a section (two aircraft) or division (four aircraft) at Mach speeds if you are high on drugs or booze. We drank at our 'O' Clubs and parties but you just did not over do it. If you got a reputation for being dependent on booze, you lost your wings because no one would fly with you… as simple as that. And who in the hell was dumb enough to give up their cherished gold wings over a bottle of booze… or for some woman for that matter? In our state of minds, flying was so dear to us that giving it up would be akin to having some nut ask you to shoot your favorite hunting dog. It doesn't happen. Period.

In my primitive theorizing regarding alcohol, I think that confidence and contentment have got a lot to do with whether or not you can handle it. Marine pilots are pretty damned confident, especially the combat experienced ones. And contented? How in the world could you not be contented; getting to drive that big beautiful monster? I'll leave it at that. Lastly, I do not intend to put down the AA programs as it has helped millions but I will hold fast to my contention that they can get a bit overly 'preachy' at times and a bit 'dictatorial.' I have had my experiences with missionaries on our reservations always attempting to tell us Indians who God exactly is. Yet they all disagreed with each other and always contended that their way was the only correct way. Sort of like the Christians and the Moslems making their dead fast claims. Personally, I do not want any limited human attempting to tell me about what I consider as 'Mystery' and save that area of wondering, speculating and postulating to my own experiences.

If I was so worried as to what my book sales would become or some newspaper's review, were I to be far more 'politically correct,' I would certainly not bring up certain subjects and definitely would 'pasteurize' this writing so as never to offend anyone. I would also remove all manner of Marine Corps swear words and description for the sake of any ten-year-old that could possibly read at that age. I will preach to that ten-year-old however, to never, never get into smoking and to be safe with a gun when they get older. He may also get deeper into the positive merits of hunting as a life building asset as well. I was greatly influenced as a young child by reading *Man Eaters of Kumaon* by James Corbett. Corbett greatly respected the tigers in India he had to hunt. The Chowgarah man-eater ate over 300 Indians in several years due to an injury wherein it could no longer hunt its normal fare of far more elusive deer and other wild animals. Most of the 'man-eaters' were reduced to human fare because of injuries inflicted by human hunters. This book greatly influenced me to always seek adventure and to appreciate the deeper meaning and merits of hunting and fishing.

In a later chapter, we will go into actual real live, death and capture combat and how we Marines converse at that time and which will continue on into Iraq or wherever. I will never doctor real live combat – no way – regardless of what some candy do-gooders and cowardly pretenders may cry out in rebuke. Sorry folks. I am not concerned about book sales or some slanted journalist (non-hunter) review. I simply want to basically talk about hunting and all related events that have their connections as is. My experiences are as they happened and deep down in, they reveal the solid, respectable character of combat Marines and Soldiers and later the Dakotans and Iowans I came to know. 'Take it or leave it,' I say to my detractors and newspapers critics who have never been where I have been.

Flight Jacket

Once in a while, when I would knock on a farmer's door, I would get invited in, and on more than one occasion, when my flight jacket was spied with its combat patches and pilot's wings, stamped leather name and rank plate, naturally the conversation would quickly turn to Vietnam, military service and fighter planes. Just about every farmer or rancher I have met has been extremely patriotic and before you know it, sometimes the farmer would pull out a bottle of bourbon or whiskey and offer you 'a shot.' Ninty-nine percent of them seemed to always prefer bourbon or whiskey. I always considered it a bit impolite to turn them down; after all there was usually a gorgeous slough out waiting on their land, or you had just seen a flock strolling somewhere on their property.

Hard Stuff

As I said, I do not care for the 'hard stuff' and never have liked it 'straight' but I would take a minimal 'swig' from the bottle which I preferred to drink from rather than a glass as they would generously pour in a bit much. I want to be honest. That flight jacket has inadvertently gotten me more than one 'free drink' which I was certainly not seeking. Some folks just seem to be mystified by aviation, especially if you have been a combat pilot. Also, often a family member had served in the military or sadly, was wounded or KIA (Killed in Action) and that was another reason why some farmers and ranchers have been so extra congenial, at least in my experience. I generally would ask if they didn't mind if I 'cut' mine a bit with water. If they were not looking, I'd drop some of a too generous offering into the sink while I ran my water. Straight hard stuff just does not taste all that good to me even if cut with water, but I had to be polite and appreciative, simple as that. I have had, on more than one occasion, a talkative farmer offer to drive my dog and me down to the opposite side of a slough or field and then park around the opposite side to save me a walk back to my car or truck besides providing a blocking service with his pickup for me. Like I said, these Dakotans are a different cut from a lot of people. They are extremely patriotic.

Four, Five and Six

Regarding Don Smith's land, I was told earlier by my fellow hunters that even this land was not very favorable this particular year as the farmer's son had gone out and got only one rooster opening day and the son's friend had only got one. I knew from experience that the friend's dog was an abject loser so that did not surprise me. So out I went, with the advice not to expect much as in earlier years. After driving to the edge of the shelter belt next to the gravel road, I parked beside an aging '51 Ford rusting away in the trees and a couple older stick shift 'pre-wars' rusting away, along with early post war combines the pull type. A couple pre-World War II skeletons were in that grove with trees growing through their floors and out the open windows. In one of Don's sheds a vintage, restored Model T Ford is stored for summer and celebrations.

With my dog, Rex III in his earlier years, I crossed the sagging barb wire and headed away from the gravel road, north and beyond the shelter belt with the abundance of old cars, and on up through the fairly thick CRP grass toward "Always Faithful" slough way back at the center of where four quarter sections of land meet, marked by a rock pile and the slough in the top corner of Nirvana. You can also dub this slough, 'Pheasant Nirvana.' I never made it to the promising place, as I promptly got my limit of three in six, maybe seven, criss-crossing passes, northwest into the wind. Rex brought them up close, one by one, with hens as well, coming out in ones and twos. We had hit a flock, bedding down and scattered out enough in the grass to not always rise at once. The wind helped as well, just enough to keep them sitting a bit tighter before deciding to rise.

Seven, Eight and Nine

The pheasant season started to look up. The third day was approaching and I had nine birds to go. It was nice weather so far, but the weather forecast had warned that colder weather was coming in from the west. I thought I would be heading west earlier, but my brother-in-law needed some help the following day and I barely had time to hunt a nearby grove behind some abandoned houses at the edge of the tiny town where they lived. He was the unofficial 'mayor' of the town as he did the winter's snowplowing, so I guess I had 'official' permission to hunt the town's outskirts and no one seemed to mind or complained. A double out of the grove across from a brick church that was mostly abandoned except for one Sunday mass and then one road hunting rooster almost on the outskirts of a slightly larger town named Fulton farther west kept me in my limit margin. Nine roosters, all field cleaned, were placed away in the freezer. The fourth day was predicted to get colder but still comfortable. No stocking caps or gloves had yet to be needed and after you got moving, jackets would come off. I left the Emery/Fulton area and Don Smith's Nirvana, all east of Mitchell, the bigger city in central East Dakota and headed west. The fourth day, I was past Mitchell which crawled with Opener hunters, every motel full. I was getting close to 'Big Muddy'… just east of the Missouri River.

Ten, Eleven and Twelve

At noon, after visiting with a farmer friend and his sick wife near Plankinton, (Both had read my *Mother Earth Spirituality*) I was still east of 'Big Muddy.' I went driving down to the first turn from his house on a gravel road. One rooster was sitting right in the middle of the road as I came up over a slight rise. I slowed the pickup to a stop and backed up to be hidden by the rise as my gun was not even loaded. As I have said earlier, South Dakota is still one of the few states that allow an uncased gun in your front seat. As I remember then, the law was: shells in the magazine are okay, but none in the chamber.

I was stopped by a highway patrol once in that situation. I was with a friend from the Mdewakanton Tribe who are Siouxs also. We were parked on the side of a super highway during hunting season and admiring a sign depicting Indians when the highway patrol stopped us. We were driving a big Ram V-10, that was fairly new. Joe was a 'Casino Indian' who did pretty well outside of Minneapolis – the Little Six Casino. He let me keep that spacious truck for several years but it did consume a bit of fuel. When we answered the state trooper's question if we had any guns in our pickup he told us both to get out of the car but didn't say anything about them having shells in the magazines, and after checking the inside of the V-10, he let us be on our way. Joe was a bit darker than I and a little shorter. I think the trooper at first thought we might be illegal Mexicans, but our English certainly did not have any accent, and we were a bit bigger than the average Mexican who are Indians also, although I find most, practically 100 percent, who deny their Indian heritage. Why, is their business, not mine. This is a sports book, however, and not about politics. To each his own.

I simply ask them in Spanish, "Los Indios (In dee yose)?" In a questioning tone, every one of them so far has replied. "No! No!" I have been told by American citizen Mexicans that I have a natural gift with my pronunciation of Spanish.

"Espana?" Reply: "Si!" (Yes).

"Chicano?" Reply: "Si!" (Yes).

"Latino?" Reply: "Si!" (Yes).

"Catolico? (Catholic) Usual Reply: "Si!" (Yes).

"Indios? (Indian) Reply: "No!" I purse my face and posture my shoulders as if I am not believing. "Indios?" I ask again.

"No, No!" They emphatically deny.

I then point to myself and say,

"El Rojo Indio, Norte Americano."

A blonde airline stewardess of all people taught me to say,

"Estoy. Or goo yoh so.

Dey Sare. Indio Norte Americano."

Basically, all that means is I am a Red Indian from North America and proud of it. "Oglala Lakota." I add in Sioux. My Spanish is not that proficient and I end up by smattering, "In 'Estados Unidos' we 'Rojo Indios' (Red Indians) are 'Or goo yoh so' (Proud)." I leave the conversation at that.

I have to add: It does 'rile' me a bit, when folks will deny their Indian heritage when it is quite obvious that they definitely have Indigenous lineage. I have been to Spain and Portugal and the average Mexican bears absolutely no resemblance to those folks. To me, such disclaiming is rather insulting, to put it bluntly. As for the Mexican people, I strongly believe that by far, most are of 'Indios' descent. My theory is that most are, as we say, full blooded Indians. Our Sioux full bloods laughingly state that they are F.B.I. and I have seen a few T-shirts and sweat shirts stamped with that logo which they wear. I should wear a shirt that states… 'Half F.B.I..' Why the Mexicans are so ashamed of it, beats me. I don't see any wearing our T-shirts.

Last thing I will ever be is being ashamed of what I am. I am a bit more the other way, quite proud of having Native heritage especially Oglala Sioux who have a profound history. Maybe you have to be at least a part Indian to understand why it peeves us a bit to have a whole Nation south of our border not want to be what they really are.

Where were we? – ahhh, loaded guns, or at least with shells in the magazine and not in the chamber. I mention the highway patrol incident to re-verify the fact that in South Dakota you can indeed have a loaded weapon in your vehicle. Out there in Dakota, in the remote rural areas you will see a gun rack right behind the driver. Well, this is one important allowance which is why a state can keep its predator population down, and I hope it is a long time before some candy wimped legislator enters a law banning a non-cased gun or rifle from hanging behind your head in a pickup gun rack so you can readily get at it to pick off a legal predator – skunk, coyote, fox or possum as you do help out the bird population every time you nail one.

This rooster who was about to be #10, allowed me to load my shotgun, drive a bit closer and even get out of the V-10 truck before rising. I dropped him with a field load six shot off the road as he rose and landed into a cut alfalfa field. Rex came out my driver's side and was on him. It was a bit cold for him to be riding in the box where he usually is when we are in the field during decent weather. The rooster lifted once slightly and went back down to run, but a Golden or a Lab can out run a pheasant; a statement that I don't mind repeating in case you are considering a hunting dog.

I was north of Interstate 90 and within a few miles after crossing south over the interstate, I was back in an area owned by the farmer who had read my books; an area that was exceptionally good the year before. The farmer had two separate half sections to hunt on – that is a total of 640-acres. One half section, the northern one, was almost total CRP type land with some alfalfa mixed in with natural prairie, which meant it had extremely productive pheasant cover. I only hunted one of the half sections before sundown, the one with mostly corn and several miles farther south from the north half section. This half section was split by an east/west road with a farm house on the north side occupied by a hired hand. It turned out that the farm hand had a hunting party in ahead of me wherein the south side was not hunted. This land was broken into two quarter sections and I made the mistake of hunting the north quarter section first. I noticed shotgun shells of various sizes strewn here and there which were either fired that morning or the day before. Some one had a lot of shots, I concluded. I should have gone to the south section instead, but I wasted several hours hunting where I started and the sun was heading for the horizon.

Three-hundred-sixty-acres is quite a bit of acreage to hunt, especially when you are by yourself. I finally planned to walk into tall corn on the south end by late afternoon, which is not too productive for just one hunter and a dog, but walking the fence line before you enter and circling back, using your pickup as a blocker at the end does prove fruitful at times. I went into the corn and circled back out again to come out farther down the road. Pheasants were loaded in the corn but it was too tall for a decent shot. You could see them running up ahead but I couldn't shoot those as I was unsure where my dog was and I wasn't that desperate, not with that many birds lifting and running. Sure enough, just as we emerged near the end of the corn, I got a good view of a high rooster. I shot and it faltered, but kept sailing as I placed another round into it and it dropped about ten rows back into the corn. Rex was out of the corn by then and in a good position to see it flying. He went dashing back in its direction. I must have missed, I began to think or maybe it managed to 'fly through my pattern' which is an oft used alibi for a missed shot.

The sun was starting to go down as I waited and I was getting quite apprehensive and wondering what I would do if darkness came. I looked back down the road at the truck. My tank was fairly full of fuel so I was planning to stay until daylight if I had to wait for my dog. I started calling him just as he broke out of the corn and onto the gravel with #11 bird in his mouth. He had been gone about 15 minutes. That corn was loaded with moving birds and how he could find that one was a sheer miracle.

I was about to call it a day as it was getting too close to sundown to attempt to fill out with road hunting, but there were numerous birds in the area, and hens were flushing from the ditch. Rex was indicating birds available as we came down the road, which had a pair of deep ditches on either side, back toward the pickup. Most dogs will have a certain crouch to their stalking when a bird is up front. By now the pickup was not far off, only about 50-yards. Sure enough, a couple hens flushed out of the ditch, the one on the same side as our pickup. I saw a rooster cross over the graveled road just this side of our truck and dart down into the opposite ditch. These were birds which I obviously chased out of the tall corn into the ditches as they were not there when we had passed down earlier, before first entering the corn. We went down into the pickup side ditch with intentions to come right out on the rooster's trail close to our blocking truck but we never got to him. Up came another pair of hens and then a cackle and #12 rooster was dropped onto the gravel.

That cornfield we came out of was pretty big. Joe, my Sioux friend, was with me on the year before hunt and we kind of wandered around inside of it with him mostly staying on the end. I would wander on in and do a semi circle and wound up herding birds back out to him. Naturally we got our limit.

Possum

I remembered coming across a real weird face looking at me when I was in the corn field herding birds for Joe. It was a big possum, biggest I had ever seen and feeding on a pheasant. Years later, my dog after Rex would pick one up. They actually do, 'play possum.' This big one's white face sort of shined in the cornfield. It didn't run and kept its ground as though it was going to finish its meal no matter what. I was close enough for a shot and knew where my dog was so I put in a three-incher and no more possum. They, like skunks and raccoons, eat their share of pheasant eggs. Maybe I saved a 100 or more eggs with that three-incher. If you are going to hunt pheasants, then be able to take out a predator when you get a chance, except for the protected ones, of course, like hawks and owls, which do their share of killing live pheasants. Be cautious when dogs are around, however, when you are going to take out a predator.

The day had started to chill and you could feel winter in the air when Rex picked up my last rooster for the day. It was a red/gold darkening sundown. A large bird sailed across the horizon. Since it was getting dark, I thought it was an owl but it was too high, too large, and heading west so I guessed it had to be an eagle heading back toward the Missouri, which is the road map for their flyway down from Alaska and the Northwest. Obviously it had been feeding among all the wounded and dead rooster pickings which opening weekend produced for them. Rex and I headed out west behind the eagle to the Oasis Motel, Oacoma, by the Missouri in cold gusting wind. We went across the wide Missouri, drawing closer to where I saw quite a few pheasants – preseason.

Wanblee the Eagle

Eagles (Wanblee in Sioux), as far as I know from observation, just do not take out many live Pheasants. I always see them eating on a dead one or see their tracks out in the fields, especially down in the snow or mud of irrigation ditches, which suggest the bird was dead before the Eagle ever got to it. You won't mistake their tracks in the light snow or earlier on creek mud. Man, they are huge! They don't walk far either. They simply land and eat their meal where they find it and never take it to a secluded spot. It is quite impressive when you rarely spook one up close by and also big time startling. I am never out in the field when our year round, and larger Dakota Golden Eagles are Spring nesting and, of course they lift their kills then to their small fry. The bald eagles you see in the fall in pheasant country are mostly migrating and feeding along the way. They are smart and have discovered that many shot pheasants are there to provide a good meal. A coyote would have to think twice before attempting to take its meal away. Everything else in Dakota is too small to even think about attacking an Eagle, except possibly mountain lions which are confined to the Black Hills. When they lift and rise in front of you as you are walking, it is always a shot bird they are feeding on. I have never come across one feeding on a hen, which further suggests it was a wounded or dead rooster that it spotted from the sky.

"Whoof!" Up goes this winged monster, startling your every muscle and nerve endings. Your heart beats wildly for this moment in time. Automatically you press your safe button off then repress it back to on when you realize it is the rarest of moments that you have come up on an eagle feeding on something in heavy cover. It is such a majestic sight as it lifts so much slower than the pheasant or prairie chicken or those swift little Hungarian partridges. It lumbers upward and as long as you keep on walking, it will circle upward and then back around you. You keep on walking with your gun slung back on your shoulder. Out of the corner of your eye you will see this majestic beauty settle back down on its find. I have been blessed with this wonderful, spellbinding happening twice. It makes you close to God, to Creator that made all of this… for those moments.

…this wind has been terrible and it is cold out here!!!!!!! This was an excerpt from my notes I punched out on my laptop at the Oacoma Motel when I settled in for the night.

Thirteen, Fourteen and Fifteen

That's the way it was Wednesday – the last day of my five-day non-resident South Dakota license – a blustery snow opened the day. I waited for the wintry squall to lift as did quite a few other hunters. I was a lone hunter and at a motel that is a gathering hole for out-of-staters near Chamberlain, middle of the state. Most were complaining about the lower bird count. The non-complaining ones were smug as they were 'resort guests' and those places are well stocked. At that time, my only experience was the errant assumption that resort birds were all like the Wisconsin resort where 'Mile' and 'Half –Mile' ranged and Ed K. futilely punched his short ranged shock collar apparatus and blew his whistle. My son Mark and his buddy Todd soon dubbed those kind as 'helicopter birds' meaning they came up fairly slow in comparison to the wild birds. How great my error proved to be in later years regarding resort birds of today which come up like a rocket, and not one bit slower than the totally wild ones. The resort birds are so mixed in with the wild stock that where I hunt, there is no difference. Come out and find out for yourself, if you doubt my words.

I had 12 birds by now, with three to go before heading back to Minnesota, hopefully with a full load. The first nine birds, as I mentioned, were still back in my sister's freezer and it was cold enough by now that I wasn't worried about the three latest additions, which I field cleaned at the motel cleaning station. I placed them in my cooler in the back of the pickup and threw a small bag of ice in with them, although with the lowering temperature, I probably didn't need the bag of ice. Pheasants are much different than chickens and can 'keep' much longer unfrozen.

At noon, I found a cornfield with a dipping road bearing a wide ditch leading to an abandoned railroad track that had proven pretty generous to Joe and me one season. I was on the downwind, south side walking the gravel road while Rex was working the ditch and on up to the slightly stunted corn. West River is always dryer than East River in Dakota and often the inadequate moisture makes the crops suffer. Most pheasants I know, like to sleep out of the wind, especially on the coldest night of the year since the last spring. Sure enough, they were in the heavy grass between gravel road and corn. The ditch slanted from its base upward to an old fence with a few rusted strands of wire. This corn beyond was fairly thin from the obvious dry summer growing conditions and with the cold, the birds just were not about to venture on out into the corn as long as they could hunker down into that warming cover of high grass, especially on the downwind side of a protective slope.

I parked well enough off the road in case a combine would pass by and walked south. That pretty bird can rocket like hell immediately when they leap out and catch the wind, blowing, 20 to 30 mph, maybe more. At that time, you switched to magnum 5's or 6's for your barrel when it is that windy. Many prefer 4's. The higher the wind, the lower the number of your shot. In the tube is a high mag five and two three-inch mag 5's or 6's as #3 and 4 shell. (This was before I came across my Super Eagle and three-and-a-half inch shooting with 1550 fps.) I do use my Super Eagle when I take the blocker's role or a client has fallen in love with the 24-inch Benelli Eagle, and of course for snow geese. Snow geese and Blues were the main reason I bought it. I like the extra round its extended tube provides for me and the three-and-a-half's are added insurance that the long shots can be reached – at least some of them. On snow geese, at that time, the tube was legal, yes, more than three rounds were allowed. Sounds strange, I know, but true.

Why don't I go out and buy a 10-gauge blunder buss for Snows or Blues? I am usually surrounded by them (ten gauges) when I am with Todd Gifford and help guide at the resort but why should I when I have Spring Snows dropping all around me due in part to my Benelli and the 1550 fps steel 2's? Besides, I appreciate the recoil spring in my Benelli's stock which many of the ten gaugers do not have, and there is far less 'give' to one's body or shoulder when you are lying down or sitting and shooting almost straight up. My Benelli saves me from seeing the chiropractor after a hunt.

Back to pheasants. You never want too heavy a mag load on that first shot as you would have to be an Annie Oakley, which I am not. You get more spread and less effective distance for that closer shot without a heavy magnum load. This was hunting when the max fps of 1400 was prevalent and 1500 and 1550 fps were probably just starting to reach the markets, but as yet, for this particular hunt, were unknown to me. Now I understand that 1650 fps exists. You won't need much lead (Not 'led' but 'leed') for that baby. A 30 to 40-yarder crossing shot, no wind, will be right on the bird's beak will be my guess, instead of in front of the beak for that type of round. Maybe fps will get higher yet but right now – 1650 fps seems like a wonder when it comes to shot shells.

I have since changed my loading menu thanks to those recent shell offerings. I do not load my own and can understand now why some did in those days, although maybe the new powders were just emerging then. Opening day in calm conditions in those days, I had a field load, non-magnum seven and a half or six shot up front inside a modified barrel insert. Improved cylinder, a more open bore is popular on opening day which I always threatened to do but never got around to do it then. I do now. Now I have made that move with these new higher fps shells and no longer shoot lighter shot than 6's. For you new hunters, 'spread' is your shot spreading out. A lower explosive load and you have more of a spreading fan in front of you to get or 'pattern' the closer bird, which a good dog makes possible, but in windy conditions lower loads are not as effective. Five shot has fewer but larger pellets or 'shot' than six shot and seven and a half shot. No seven and a half's would be used on this blustery day, no way.

It has been over a decade past now since I carried a 20-gauge Charles Daly-over and under. You get older, you get slower, and admit it. If you don't admit it then you keep wounding way more birds that get away, no matter how good your dog is. For the younger hunter, keep that 20-gauge, it is far more of a challenge than a 12-gauge, however, and while you luckily still have the reflexes. My shorter Benelli has only a three shell tube, so you have four shots in all. They have a reputation for rarely jamming, not even in snow or freezing rain. I hunt in all weather and it is the first automatic I have so trusted that I no longer carry around a spare pump or over and under shotgun. (This was my attitude and practice before I went into muddy water under the broken ice down in Iowa one day.) I fell and went through the ice and shallow water underneath and THAT effectively jammed my Benelli. I now carry another Benelli, a Super Eagle, as a spare, I call it my goose gun as this one is three-and-a-half inch capable. Beretta's have similar jam free reputations as well. You drop a Benelli into muddy water and it is a trip to the gunsmith, unless you happen to be one. He has to clean out the spring and spring receptacle in the stock, which is the reason for the lower recoil of the gun. That operation is a bit beyond my gun-smithing.

By now, the way I am hearing things, all semi-automatics have finally become reliable, at least the new ones with their new actions. Many prefer an over and under gun (two barrels) or side by side with an Improved Cylinder insert and a Modified choke insert, especially at the resorts, but in Dakota and a flock gets up there you are with two shots – your choice. The optional extension tube for the Super Eagle Benelli used to throw me off, so I thought, which proved to be foolish superstition. Now I am used to that extension, but only on the Super Eagle. Five shells in that thing under your barrel is a bit much to be carrying around all day, however, let alone bringing it up as quickly as your reflexes allow you, to sight in. I travel with four total, one in the chamber and three in the tube mostly, except when I am posting and there are quite a few birds coming my way. My arms are also rested when I post so the extra load in the extended magazine is moot. The super critical time sighting seems to get shorter each year, hence a few missed birds – more than a few. When I am by myself, or not with a client who loves to shoot my short barreled Benelli or road hunting, naturally I prefer the shorter Benelli that shoots only two and three quarters or three-inch. The way the Airline security is with guns, more and more resorts are supplying 12-guagers to clients who do not want to go through the security hassle. Once a client shoots my 24-inch Benelli, they usually fall in love with it. I borrowed a resort Pump Benelli, short barreled, one season and that gun seldom missed.

Beretta

Professor Joel Tate is sending me his 26-inch Beretta to break in pre-season mostly on the skeet range and then starting into the season. It will be sporting a sling and its pretty wooden stock and engraved quail scenes will have a few scratches when he shows up this fall. Yes, I know, standing on a skeet platform with a slinged gun while the experts all around you have specialized skeet bangers is a bit unusual but I never was a big worrier regarding impressions. It doesn't hurt to run a couple hundred rounds through a tight gun before the season opens and a few more afterwards. I am sure I will enjoy that piece as well as I do my Benellis. My motto is that a good gun is to be used out in the field and not decorating the inside of a gun closet all its life and Joel agrees.

This will be an unusual hunting story. The author will admit he misses which is rare in hunting stories and hunting books. I have constantly harped on this premise, I know. This author also throws up a lot of lead – tons of it. Again, most all other authors get their bird solidly on the first shot and once in a while you will read where Will Q. Pressed Pants admits to take a second shot on a bird, of course which falls closely for his old faithful and always retrieving dog, Tray. Tray, of course always 'brings the bird to Hand.' Rex simply brings you the bird, even though he may make you wait ten to fifteen minutes while he runs it down from a not too solid hit. Amazing how a good dog in a heavily scented field can find that one wounded running bird out of all those criss-crossing pheasant tracks, and yet locks on to the one he flushes, staying tenaciously on to that one running bird ahead of him. Absolutely amazing, and I have witnessed it – the chase – time and time again. Whups, I am admitting that I did not knock my bird down fatally every time I shot. One hunter told me it is the kicked up fresh earth the running bird makes and even named the elemental mixture of chemicals that gives the bird away. Hmmm, maybe that solves the mystery.

Never Miss Blitzflick

One more short story about a big mouth in Minnesota who claimed he never missed. His kid was a friend of my son's so we purposely took the son with us on an ultra successful Dakota hunt. He came back all aglow, naturally. I was hounded by the father to take him on future excursions but never did. Frustrated, he bluntly cornered me about my reluctance. I stated defensively, "Well, you claim you never miss!"

"That's true. I don't," he adamantly replied. He added. "And I don't have to practice," meaning he didn't shoot at clay pigeons either.

"So you are a 'Natural,' huh?"

"Yup!" He strutted his chin proudly.

"A real live Annie Oakley!" I exclaimed with feigned awe and admiration. He was one of those types that 'knew' everything and of course 'excelled' with 'never-an-error' attitude which the world seems to be full of. Contrariwise he had a neighborhood reputation for just the opposite – a real Blitzflick.

"Never shot many pheasants, I'll admit but I've had my share of North-wood's grouse," he proclaimed with a haughty air.

On a college canoe trip, my good friend John Nordlum from International Falls killed two of those with rocks to add to our walleye supper. I looked him square in the eye and after stating his name, I added in a hushed tone, "I can't take you out to Dakota land." I made up the following with a raised eyebrow and feigned humility. "Our guys just don't want to be embarrassed by such a great shot."

We never did allow him with us but a lot of hunting friends have enjoyed a chuckle over this story.

We were going south, cornfield to our west. Back to the wind, northwest wind (out of the northwest.). Had been lightly snowing, starting out, but had quit when we parked my pickup. Was getting cold. Any colder and I would have had to switch to my heavy field jacket. I had a T-shirt, cotton, long sleeve shirt,

Marine flight jacket, lined, (I want to be buried in that) and my partly red-orange hunting vest over the jacket. Even had on a stocking cap and not the all familiar Vietnam-Phantom F4 baseball cap I usually and purposely wear. (Which incidentally, that hat in warmer weather has also gotten me on some good hunting land from patriotic farmers and ranchers.) I have an ear-covering band for cooler weather for my F4 cap but this was stocking cap time. Real cold, and like spring Snow Geese time in early March, on goes the Korean, Marine fur hat. You want to keep your arms free and be very maneuverable. Loose, flight jacket is just right and keeps my trunk warm. The rubber lined vest insures that. No long underwear yet, just weed burr resistant hunting pants. It has to be darned cold for long underwear as walking generally gives you some warmth. You are not standing in a cold duck blind when pheasant hunting. You move, man, you move. It is not for the lame, lazy, fat and weak! Your tail end moves. You are a Marine grunt for five non-resident, arduous, fat losing, often, wind blowing days. Yes, your wind actually seems to improve when you get out there day in and day out. I mean your lung wind not Mother Nature's wind which howls and gales at times and more than a few pheasant hunters just don't go out in it. Heavy smokers, you poor things, you don't have a chance! Stick to your ducks. I will tell you kids one more time. Do not ever start smoking! You think you will remain young forever but you won't. Few hunters at my age are out there walking as much as I do. Someday you will wish you still had the lung (and leg) power to 'keep on truckin.' Not smoking now will enable you to do so. Get into Sports as well.

My inner underwear top is the kind you seldom wear long if you are moving, especially with the jacket over it and hunting vest as it has a rubberized back and front for carrying your birds. It is the fancy type, (Columbia) with the six rows of shell tubes across the front. It is not for cold weather, however. The shells would not pull out with your gloves on. It was getting That cold. Any colder and I would have had to switch to my old non-red, non-tube, non-rubberized vest, as it sure as heck was not a time to be tugging on shells to reload and pheasants are leaping out of a slough. The plastic shell holders lose their flexibility – temperature wise.

Six rows of shells on the front of the vest? Yup. You get way, way back in on some of those western Dakota areas and you are a long way from your vehicle. The public lands can get huge out there. Many a 'smart' light carrying hunter runs out of shells back in there just about the time the birds start getting up nice and close or he is coming out from a different way he went in. When it is windy, you miss. Yes, MISS. No one wants to admit that word. MISS. Be a nice day wouldn't it, if you are out in real wild country, not where you walk a little ways, but instead sit and rest in a comfortable van, while the driver takes you to another cozy field loaded with birds.

Dakota hunting, real non-resort Dakota hunting, and also at some resorts, you Walk! On the semi-resort, rented land set up, you walk. This means a fatigue factor is now in the game and oh, how it plays into your chances. More on that later. Funny how humans can get. Spend all that money to go way out in Dakota and you think you look cool by carrying five to eight shells in real remote country where you have to go a long ways in and a long ways out. Who in the hell are you impressing? The antelope? Maybe the prairie dogs. Jim Corbett only carried two shells, rarely three when he was tracking a man-eater because he said you seldom get a second shot on one. But you are hunting pheasants not man-eaters! Once, we pumped about eight shells into a possum and two skunks on a way back in there place. On the way down we missed two roosters in the wind, which took six shells. Fourteen rounds gone by and we hit pay dirt in a slough. My partner was out of shells when we made our way back, with two birds to go for our limit and a flock was up ahead of us between our pickup and us. The pickup was in a perfect blocking position. A connecting heavy patch of weeds was right in front of the pickup and my partner tells me he is out of shells. I threw him four rounds and he no more than loaded up and the flock lifted early. Had we kept our steady pace I think we would have broke them much closer to us in front of the pickup which, remember, serves as a blocker. We were lucky to get one. So much for carrying adequate shells.

I also would like to add that I now carry three-inchers in steel 2's or 4's, 1500 or 1550 fps. It is nice to have a degree of choice depending upon the circumstances. These are my choices but I well realize most hunters have their own particular choices as to how many and what type of shells they will employ. I did run a string in Iowa of 22 found birds a few years back using this selection. I did have to rely on my third and fourth shots on more than one bird, but I wound up being convinced that those steel 2's in reserve or steel 4's, can be deadly and provide you with a bit more confidence when you are still firing away whilst' attempting to bring that fading bird down. The three-and-a-half, 1550 fps for back-up, while posting with the Super Eagle, gives you a degree more of self assurance. I have yet to try the 1650 fps shell and will be waiting on next season a bit anxiously to experiment with that round.

All of this high powered talk does not deter me away from the slower burning rounds however. There is always room in your ammunition box for 1200 fps or slightly higher lead sixes for that no-wind day, usually opening day or close to it; when the birds are still sitting comfortably for close flushes. The 1200 fps is going to give you a better spread for a closer shot than that rocket shot coming out at 1550. Farther into the season, the more the birds are shot at and Autumn wind builds up then that is the time I would be using faster shot, almost always. The wind is going to get them (the birds) out there a bit faster and they will usually be flushing a bit sooner and farther out for you and hence making your 1200 fps rounds a bit less reliable, unless of course you are instant reflexed and a Dead Eye Dick, which advancing age will soon dispel for you.

The following is an example where a pair of lower powered shells came through. A season following this Emery, Fulton, Plankinton and Oacoma trip, I was watching two roosters fighting from the road at the edge of a cornfield. The road went on past the opposite end of the not too large cornfield and a short convenient shelter belt bordered the corn and the crossing road at the intersection. I turned left and parked halfway down the road by the shelter belt. My guess was good; the shelter belt ran right at the edge of the corn where the roosters were playing gladiator. I had permission to hunt this land thanks to my generosity of some Black Hills trout earlier that summer, but had never hunted this smaller grove or the smaller cornfield before. I had always concentrated on the larger, tall tree grove farther south, which was generally quite productive. As I carefully crept closer with my dog always behind me, I noticed through the trees that the two roosters had an audience. It was barely no-wind and the fighting must have been so intense to the on-lookers that I was completely unnoticed. Fortunately, a slight rise was in front of the pheasant amphitheater to conceal my approach at the edge of the grove and corn where the two gladiators were combating before their audience – all roosters.

Here was a good chance for a double, as long as things worked out right. Rex III was so good at road hunting which this situation (or rather, opportunity) was similar to, that with an exaggerated almost angry downward thrust of my arm to the ground, (and please notice… no spoken command) he understood he was to 'Stay-put' and not come forward unless I patted my thigh with a come on gesture – no sound, no words spoken. I already had a 1500 fps steel three-incher, first into my tube (magazine) and then a two-and-three-fourths Premium lead six, and two 1200 fps, lead 6's. It was one of the first times I had access to the faster steel three-incher. One of the last two shells was in the chamber, of course. After a 'stay put' I crept around to the back of the rise and brought him forward. He was such an experienced dog he acted like this was all 'old hat' business to him.

Too many dogs get too unrestrained at this state and bolt, as there was just enough breeze coming from upwind that he surely knew birds were just beyond that rise. As we got close, I patted the signal to 'stay put' and got positioned for a charge over the rise. I had the one three-incher in the magazine, the last one of course, for the chance at the unthinkable – a possible triple: the two fighting cocks and what ever else wanted to come up and not melt back into the corn. Pheasants are fairly reliable when they erupt. One goes airborne – most usually– all will go up into the air, despite their cover circumstances. This is the usual procedure for them but always there are exceptions. Just getting a 'double' would be fine with me I thought.

I started to rise and patted my thigh for Rex to come on and we both, like a pair of charging Marines went over the top. At the end of the two–1200 fps rounds, the faster six and the three-incher, three roosters were down but not yet in the bag, or what does that guy say? Ohh yes, "to hand." One was running and Rex ran it down. I threw a shell in my open Benelli, a three-incher and could have put it into the running rooster but was confident that Rex would have him. I picked up my two roosters and sat down on the ground with my heart pumping while Rex brought back the third. Once I wrung its neck, I felt pretty darned good about getting the 'Triple.' In wild pheasant country, many avid hunters seldom have this experience when out hunting on their own. Well, let's get back to the fence line as I was walking with the wind to my right backside on that cold, blustery day.

Two hens got up and went sailing. I took a long practice aim at one of the hens and held it, pressed off my safety, held my aim and said, "Bang. You are dead." I put my safe back on and stood admiring the hen sail on. I stepped back, and at that moment a rooster came up close and with the wind and my weight on the back of my heels on the slope, it was just that fast an action, my position and the wind which the rooster caught, that I did not even get a shot off. Yup, "Bang your dead," even cost me a shot getting off, let alone a chance at a nice close rooster. Live and learn. Have you ever thrown off a couple rounds with an over and under too late at a bird and up comes the second one? All sorts of these non-producing variants happen, don't they?

The year before, I was hunting with Joe on this side (west side) of the big river. A rooster came up from a patch of weed Rex was working. It was with the wind and a gust hit me full force and as I was turning. I just could not get a steady sight picture and he was gone with a few futile shots trailing behind him. Such quick, almost impossible action when a heavy gusting wind blows and you are on uneven terrain. Hmmm, I wonder why gusts just do not blow when Charlie Pressed Hunting Pants with-no-soiling spots or barbed wire-tears arrives at the very situation. You never hear about the gust blowing. Maybe these types do not hunt when the winds blow. On a five-day license, you hunt! Your sighting gets rocked and your position is not like standing on flat ground on a clear, calm day. Sometimes a dirt clod will give, just as you put your forward weight on it and you are at that moment into a critical sighting about to pull the trigger. I guess those never-miss authors somehow avoid these situations. Read their books, is all I can say. Maybe you will somehow acquire this mystical blessing. Shooting at clay pigeon throwing facilities, I notice that the shooting pits or the trails are not covered with crumbling clod or uneven footing. I have read their books but yet the never-miss mysticism never seemed to be bestowed upon me.

Also with certain overcast, and especially the sun in your eyes, hens look like roosters and roosters look like hens and you are damned cautious not to take the chance of shooting a hen. Shooting into the sun at a rising, not completely identified bird just before sun down is the same. This is a real no-no in pheasantdom… shooting hens. This sacred rule is akin to other sacred rules – both no-no's. Number one no-no rule: walking into a brothel or a gambling casino without money and #2 no–no is not refueling an airplane. I guess I could add another and that would be: never attempt to out run a squad car and, just for the heck of it, throw in one more sage bit of advice: never attempt a landing without your gear down and for carrier landings, never try it without your tail hook employed; one damned big no-no for a fighter pilot-Naval Aviator type. It makes no difference whether you are alone or not; this hen precaution. If you hunt a lot, it seems to be just built into your thinking.

A van of hunters drove by going north and must have thought I was pretty dumb to be out hunting on that fence line, with the wind blowing and snow flurries were just beginning. A pair of hens burst out followed by a rooster, right after they passed, crossing over in front of me with the wind from the northwest and I got off two hurried shots as he was above the road, following the hens and was starting to sail. Up and gone. I got off the two too quick rounds, and may have got a piece of him on the second shot. He was across the gravel road, showing a falter, passing the east fence line and about to cross out over a fresh cut hay field. My third shot was a three-incher at 1400 fps and he kept sailing. I had to get him on my last round, a steel two. He was approaching the shell's range but the wind behind me would give me added range. I bore sited on this one, as he was going straight out, no crossing or rising. The steel pellets caught up with him and broke his wing, but he managed a steep glide in front of three hay stacks and my dog was already sailing himself across the field, but unfortunately was after a hen who was a bit left and ahead of the rooster and far enough out to be gliding down. Dogs will do that and not their fault, fixing on one of the flying birds, especially when it is descending. What the heck, it is action time and they are as entitled to the excitement as you are.

So, as the rooster crash landed behind Rex I started yelling. I ran across the gravel road to the fence line and could see the rooster huddled down and when I looked for Rex, the rooster moved away from the dog's tracks and fortunately brought him slightly back to my right, heading south by south west. He was coming back, slightly toward me, at an angle to avoid getting closer to the dog who had gone past where he had landed. Pheasants must have more fear of dogs, (coyotes, foxes) etc, I guess. So that kept him in range. The snow started to come down heavier and I didn't want to get caught out in that open country in bad weather. The morning weather report warned of snowing conditions west of the river but back east where I was the day before, no snow conditions were predicted.

I fumbled for some new shells and tugged on my right side for two three-inchers. (More range). I keep my Magnums and heavy three-inchers on the right side; my lighter shells on the left. Those tubes look funny but are certainly practical for keeping your shells separated properly. The bird was creeping low but moving with an obvious broken wing, so I fired at a golden brown blob in the alfalfa, and saw the red/green, white striped head again moving and let off a round which stopped him. Darn right I will shoot a wounded bird on the ground that is getting away, as long as there are no dogs close by.

I have a reason for keeping the heavier, longer range shell on my right side. When a bird gets out there and you are emptying your gun bringing it down or if you are on a pair of doubles and your gun limit gets expended rather quickly you are going to need fresh shells and usually for the birds that are already down. When birds flush in front of you, mathematical odds dictate that nothing else is coming up. (In most situations.) Get involved with a triple and most generally you are going to realize the need for inserting a long range shell into your gun rather quickly in case one is running. My right hand is more dexterous than my left, as is most folks.' I want to reach down and grab a shell with my right hand and get it into my chamber as fast and as efficiently as possible. Pheasant hunting is often split second happenings and preparation is often key to a successful bagging of the bird.

By this time Rex was heading back and I hand signaled, (body signaled actually) and by the tone of my voice and waving my arm to the right, he knew a bird was on the ground so reacted with his usual enthusiasm. Once he came downwind of the bird's trail, he zeroed in and was soon upon the bird who ran about ten more yards before the dog closed in. In just the short time from when I had first shot at the rooster to when Rex was bringing him to me, a film of snow had covered the hayfield. We headed back to our pickup with our heads down into the wind and falling snow. I headed for I-90 and back to better conditions which would be waiting at the north section of land back near Plankinton where I had permission to hunt. I stopped at Al's Oasis and gassed up, wanting to keep that tank full in possible blizzard conditions. I met an Indian there that I knew and gave him two of my pheasants. Such is South Dakota, a big state yet small in population, seems you are always running into someone that you know.

As I drove east down I-90, I mused on Rex who was resting in the comfortable back inside platform within the pickup cab I made for him so he can watch the world go by as I drive. His running down that last pheasant played in my mind. Why hunters insist on those smaller dogs, or worse, cocker spaniels, etc, which do not have the closing speed, beats me. Do they have the speed to bring down a flat out running rooster? Also, a big cock pheasant can spur the hell out of them and make them reluctant to close in. A bigger dog simply knows how to close in on the shoulders of a bird with one quick efficient gripping bite and hold him down until he quits struggling and he can't get spurred in that position. They don't think twice about spurs if their closing in demonstration is any indication. They don't pause as if they want to think it over. They get initially spurred as adolescents and learn quickly to use the big mouth they were born with. But then I see the efficiency of a much smaller Boykin Spaniel Danny Elkin down in Iowa hunts with. That little guy has a great nose and aggressive durability. He gets up his share of the birds and Danny is a very accurate shooter and doing it with a 20-gauge side by side.

I hear hunters talk about a "soft-mouthed" dog as I have mentioned earlier. I want a dog that can "hook and hold" like the Eagle Claw fish hook motto, I guess. Rex generally will keep the steady clamp until the bird suffocates or passes out before bringing him to me. Although after being gone for about 15 minutes in a monster corn field, he will finally show up with a rooster in his mouth and the bird is swiveling his head from side to side, seeming to enjoy the free ride. Often the rooster just temporarily passes out and stops struggling and goes limp at times, although, mostly they check out totally. I always wring the bird's neck even though it appears dead as when I do not do this, occasionally the bird will climb out of the back of my hunting vest and be on its merry way and the chase begins all over again. Funny feeling when they come alive in the back of your vest. Lose a bird or two like that and you will not be adverse to wringing necks.

I needed two more birds that last day Wednesday, so drove back a good hour to my 'Nirvana' place owned by the farmer and his wife. Few people are allowed on his other half section of pure pristine pheasant heaven. I also have another farmer friend who has similar land in that particular area but planned to 'save' that for my next five-day expedition. I planned to criss-cross into 'Nirvana West' heading up wind, which had abated somewhat. The weather was considerably milder in but a little over an hour's drive. The land had a gentle slope from the north lowering to the south with several mini-sloughs of high wind blocking cattails so it afforded me some natural protection from the northwest wind.

Before starting, my jacket came off, and stocking cap. I had slipped on my underwear top while refueling due to the threatening weather. But now, conditions had abruptly changed and it was more expedient to shed the jacket. My right glove came off too. I wear those little common brown cotton ones when it gets cold and usually have the right one off once it gets a little warmer. I just do not like that right hand covered. Gloves are meant to get lost it seems so I usually buy several pairs at a time. When you wind up with the same two sides you can simply turn one inside out and keep on hunting on a cold day. Those are the little ugly gloves that you can find in every hardware store in America but never in the Cabelos or Eddie Bauer type hunting stores. Will Q. Press Pants, the noted hunting author would not be caught dead in them. It is fun to have them on when you drop your limit off at the cleaning station most Dakota motels provide and five or six guys from the same type of 'chic' group are standing there and often without a full limit. I usually let Rex out of the inside of the pickup at the same time. His tail looks like a rat's from my primitive haircutting and his undersides as well. As he sniffs around they will notice the absence of any kennel on my vehicle. You do have to burr proof your dog, especially Golden Retrievers. He looks like a semi-golden Lab when I get done with him and his suburban fat doesn't drop off in five days. He may not be the Clark Gable of hunting dogs but he sure as hell stays at it and close. Ahh yes, Close! That is why we get our share and at high odds against us compared to the group hunters, not that I am against group hunting. I hunt with two wonderful groups often.

Road hunting I seldom wear a glove, as you are not in the cold that long. I have a nice warm shooting vest pocket which some experienced hunter at Columbia must have thought of. My engineer son once brought along a guy who wore gloves but his problem was that it would take him forever to put his gloves on and then stand there readjusting them when we were road hunting. We alight from the van and there stands 'Gloves' for a full minute or two adjusting his hand warmers. That is the wrong time to be overly applying gloves – like reading your girl friend's letter in the cockpit when red warning lights are flashing or day dreaming while shooting an approach in a fighter jet on instruments on a rainy night. Naturally, he got an Indian nick name – 'Gloves.' Especially after an ass chewing because of some lost birds and he wasn't ready when a pair of roosters came right at him.

A hen came up immediately in the 360-acres. I call this one, Nirvana West. I hope my next book sells big. I'd buy this chunk of land. Within a few yards a rooster got up far to our rear right and crossed left behind us into an area we would be crossing later. By 'us,' I mean, my dog and me. I lined it up with an old red barn and made a mental note. Saw quite a few hens but it looked like we would make our bird count or at least have a fair chance at it. The hens did worry me somewhat as two years before that was about all I happened to see while hunting this same land. Hens, hens and more hens but nary a rooster at this place, that year. Maybe that was why I had initially decided to skip this place and head farther west the evening before. Oddly, that year on this parcel, was also rabbits, rabbits and more rabbits! A disease must have come upon them because I don't recall seeing a single cotton tail that day.

The wind was cold, but at least no snow which seemed to abate as soon as I re-crossed the Missouri. We were more exposed from flat grassland as we approached the northern boundary. I had just put on a glove to warm up my hand and a rooster skyrocketed up and my hand slipped on the safe – too much wind and he was gone. Now don't tell me you have never fumbled with your safe, dear Reader; C'mon, swallow that ego and admit it! Don't be like that Minnesota Northwood's grouse hunter. The glove came promptly off and stayed off. My newer Benelli, I notice, now has a larger safe. Good thinking!

The sun started to pop through the overcast a bit. God, such beautiful sunsets you get to view on the Dakota prairie but this had not started out as a sunny day. I once knew a very beautiful woman, one generation from Sweden. Unfortunately she died of cancer and way too young. She was one of those females who was beautiful in Spirit as well. She held quite a high position at the University where I had gone to law school. As one of the University pilots, my part time job, I flew her to several speaking engagements and we became close friends. I held a sweat lodge for her at her request not long before she passed on. She wanted to return to Sweden one last time to visit relatives. She was aware of some of our Indian ceremonies and asked for spiritual strength to make the trip. Everything worked out fine for her after we held a beseeching lodge together. After the ceremony where she asked the Great Spirit or her concept of a Higher Power for a few more weeks of adequate strength to make her trip overseas, she felt strong and left upon her journey. She told me that when I saw a turquoise sunset, to think of her. Upon her return she was most appreciative for Creator's gift to her and passed on within a short time afterwards. The turquoise in the sky brought her back to me, for a few moments.

We had driven in from the north/south running gravel road on the east side of the field. The terrain and equipment path allowed me to come in to the hayfield about 50-yards to park. Almost a third of the half section was dotted with those big round bales that only tractors can pick up. I remember stacking square bails when I was younger. These big round ones are far more efficient. The north east corner of the half section held a deteriorating, old brick school house with a small corner grove of elm and oak. I parked the pickup in clear grass just south of the school house. I figured that after we would do a big circle, coming back to the pickup from the south, we'd hunt beyond the weed surrounded school house last, in case we did not have that fifteenth bird by then.

From its middle onward the land held a gradual rise in a whole half section of untilled grassland dotted with miniature sloughs and taller grass as we moved inward. The gentle slope coming down from the west and northwest allowed enough water to collect and clumps of cattails to grow. The southwest corner to our right held quite a bit of water which I would soon discover. At each corner except for the school house corner next to the gravel road the cattail growth was considerable. A small hillock beside a slough rose behind the spot I had lined up with the old red barn far across another field. I made this imaginary line to mark that first rooster for a future sweep when we would turn south with the wind for awhile. We entered in the middle and were sweeping into the wind heading for the northwest corner. In the center and running northwest to southeast the sloughs had clumps of cattails and surrounding cover. Because of the season's first cold, many would be sitting tight with corn in their crops and satisfied with the tons of weed seeds all around. This was perfect cover for a lone hunter and the holding weather.

As we were getting closer to the northwest corner, a rooster got up and just as promptly went back down in heavy grass indicating, possibly, it had been wounded from earlier hunters or possibly a field mouse had startled it. Rex was off a ways to the right and did not see the bird and could not pick up the track. Many birds had been in there as in twenty yards a group of hens came up and some more with a couple roosters at the far edge crossing the fence line, out of range. Another pair of roosters came out further south on the fence line and out of range. With all that traffic I could not blame Rex. I should have looked closer at the ground as I found out later it was loaded with grass tunnels. Given more time Rex may have found that obviously hiding bird. The same thing happened at the other corner, the southwest corner. I knocked down a bird out of the slough where a flock of birds had risen and it just disappeared in a portion of heavy grass with tunnels. In between I knocked down a bird in heavy cattails and Rex found that one. No hiding tunnels were in those cattails. We got the rooster to rise we had earlier seen (the one who flew behind us upon first starting out) in the deep slough grass which had an orange-ish hue and fairly close to the line with the old barn I used for marking. I was real ready for that one to come up, especially when Rex went 'birdie.' 'Real birdie' is a certain stance and movement a dog carries when he is hot on a bird in front of him. Three hens happened to come up with him and seemed to cover him pretty well. I think Rex was waiting for me to pull the trigger as the big bird let out a loud cackle.

After watching the rooster fly off into the sunset, I felt movement in my vest and the cattail rooster was coming alive. I dropped my Benelli and swung my vest around to grab the bird and thoroughly wring his neck this time. We then swung down the southern edge of the section heading east. I planned to go east almost to the edge by the road and then turn and come back toward the center and back toward our vehicle into the wind again. We would use the pickup as a 'blocker.' Often birds you are driving will sit tight after sighting a parked vehicle ahead of them. Many birds had flown out of the large south west slough and were heading back to the center of the field. Birds will do that when they have good cover. A big corn field and they simply go from corner to corner.

A farmer on a tractor passed by with two hunting dogs trailing behind and went south across the field to the south. I had permission to hunt the land I was on but ducked down in case his dogs wanted to pick a fight with mine. Hunting dogs are generally friendly with others but no sense taking chances especially with local dogs as they can be 'territorial' and simply are guarding their own turf. I doubt if Will Fancy Pants ever has to duck down low with his dog, in his books. Be a bit beneath his dignity. Me? I simply found it a practical solution to keep on hunting in complete privacy and possibly avoiding an incident. Once the farmer was a half mile away we resumed hunting, heading south and slanting east, then toward the southeast corner we turned back northwest in the general direction of our pickup. A rooster came up and was knocked down going across right to left and back toward the slough we had just come from. He bounced once, close to Rex and bounced back into the air like a bolting fighter plane off a carrier deck. I shot him again. It was my 'final fill' bird and I was a bit over anxious to make the #15 count. Rex dug him out of a tunnel in the grass and brought him toward me after suffocating the bird.

Once Rex almost pulled a wounded bird out of a hollow log the bird chose to hide in. He looked and looked in this clump of thorn bushes and an old dead tree that had a few branches fallen and broken at its sides. Rex was truly puzzled. The scent was there but he couldn't figure out where this bird was. At the last moment, just after Rex figured out the puzzle, I saw the tip of the rooster's tail feathers peeking out from a small hollow log and then Rex jammed his nose into the log and got just enough of the rooster to start pulling him out and off came the roosters tail feathers leaving Rex with a mouthful of feathers. His nose wasn't small enough to go any further into the log so I reached in and got hold of the rooster and pulled him out. I picked up a neat arm scar on a similar situation taking a hiding rooster out of a hole on an Iowa drainage ditch.

A rooster came out of a center slough on the way back to the pickup. A flock came up, mostly hens. Another rooster came up into the wind as Rex was downwind. He chose to fly closer to me than toward the dog. It would have been an easy shot. I was pretty tired by then so we headed back to the truck with my gun at sling. Most hunters avoid slings, it seems, but I find them handy, especially when walking already covered ground a long way back or if you are fortunate to have your limit. "A sling throws off your aim," a hunter claimed to me. Maybe it does and maybe it doesn't but Todd Gifford whom I consider one of the best, never minds them nor do my other sons who seem to have the eye for shooting. They certainly make hunting much more comfortable.

Some of those large hay bales were along our path. I rested my back against a bale and slowly field cleaned the roosters with a small Swiss Army knife. Pheasants are that easy to field clean. Nowadays, thanks to the Middle East, you can't even have a pocket knife aboard an airplane or in your carry on baggage. Such restrictions we modern folk get pegged with. I have lost a few good knives to airport security when I simply forgot to take off a small one from a key chain. A pair of super scissors works best and is kept with my shells and gun oil but I was tired and now no longer in any needed rush to get my limit. A bottle of Mike's lemonade was waiting at my truck but that could wait. Got my last two roosters in this huge field, which made my limit of 15 for five days of tough hunting. What a great feeling! Rex had pulled off some more of his miracles by finding the rooster in the thick cattails and digging down into the grass for another. Two of those 15 roosters he had found in heavy corn, which I never thought he would get. He was gone a good 15 minutes on that last one. Strange how in a cornfield he will get a rooster after chasing it down among many other tracks yet grass can be so baffling. Maybe it is the underground of tunnels in the grass that are often there and like that hunter told me about a running bird kicking up dirt. In the tunnels no dirt is kicked up. Tunnels worked for the Vietcong and NVA. Who knows?

Big Cornfields and Lost Dogs

Many folks won't dare let their dogs go into those huge Dakota cornfields bordered by other large cornfields. In our hunting group, on the two opening days, only a few went into the tall corn. I saw a beautiful Labrador once belonged to a nervous hunter a couple years before who was new to our opening day group – east of Mitchell, South Dakota. (Incidentally – I believe I mentioned that you can not buy a room in those first three opening days of pheasant season in and around Mitchell. (Call them up and see if you can get one for next year. 605 is the area code.) Well, the Lab flat disappeared on our first pass through a big cornfield. Strange thing at the end of the first walk through, with blockers of course, the dog was gone and never seen again and another Lab joined up with us to take his place while his owners from an adjacent cornfield were calling for him. 'Come here Buster. Here Buster,' they called while he was sniffing our dogs. Buster was one of those more rare white Labs. The lost one was a black one.

Just about every year, usually during opening weekend, or less seldom later, you experience a farmer in his pickup approaching with his arm out waving for you to stop. A dog will be beside him. As he draws close, he asks through his open window. "This here your dog?" We reply to the negative and give him as much information as we can as to where we saw other hunting parties with dogs. Come to think of it, seems always the dog is a black Lab. I don't want to rile any feathers however. That may be an indication of how popular that breed is. At least 'Buster' wasn't a black Lab.

Finally, "Come back here, you son of a bitch – Buster," perked his ears. Buster seemed quite pleased with our company however as his tail wagged constantly. We pointed him in their direction. One of our group, yelled, "Buster is over here. Call him again." In response to "Buster, Buster" punctuated with occasional, "You Son of a bitch, Buster!" Buster headed in their direction.

Rex was one of our 'cornfield' dogs as now is my latest one, Puppy. Angus, of Eagle Grove, Iowa, is the best all around dog I have personally experienced. He is a bull of a cross between black Lab and Weimaraner. I am one of the few he will hunt under when his master has to move the pickup and we need him (Angus) in the field. I have seen some great Labs and do not mean to downplay them. Another very effective Lab was one of our Emery 'cornfield' dogs named Molly who has now passed on. Molly lived all her life next to corn and soybean fields. All year long she saw her share of pheasants.

Rex, and now Pup (Rex IV), gets out in front of you in a cornfield but also circles back and comes in behind you. Pheasants do the same maneuver. They circle back and do not always come out the opposite end that you are walking toward especially when they spot blockers up ahead. He brings up a few pheasants on occasion that way also. The pheasant usually breaks and flies when it comes abreast, giving you a nice shot. He is wanting to get away from that dog behind him and seeing humans that close usually puts him in flight. Rex was usually close in corn and often uncanny in finding if he just got a glimpse of when a bird got hit. Many of those big Dakota cornfields have an oasis out in the middle where the corn is stunted by too much water during the growing season and here Pheasants love to congregate. Often you hit one of those and all hell breaks loose. Birds erupt. Dogs can get busy and you need a couple of good 'Finders' when those birds drop back in the deeper corn.

Running Deer

Running deer in a corn row is an unnerving experience. You hear a warning shout from a blocker up ahead or fellow hunters to your side, "Deer Coming!" You can here the hooves drawing closer and the crashing of corn stalks and all of a sudden a large pair of horns goes blasting by within a few rows. It is indeed a startling experience.

I think a Golden has a tendency to want to be around humans more especially if he lives in the same house with you. He just does not want to get too far away from his owner and most will always look back to see where you are at while they are ranging. All four of my Golden retrievers exhibited that characteristic. If you plan to keep your dog kenneled then I suggest you spare a Golden Retriever that kind of life. You may wind up with a great hunting 'robot' but I personally prefer more in a dog. Angus is kenneled but it is a roomy well insulated dwelling and he is free to come and go from his kennel within a spacious yard that adjoins the rear of the house. His owner takes him everywhere either within the truck or free in the box during the season and non-season. Puppy often stays with him overnight as they are close hunting pals. They are an effective duo when it comes to hunting the rewarding drainage ditches which abound with cover and birds. One is on one side and the other on the opposite side. You see more of the dog opposite you than you do your own as the drainage ditches in much wetter weathered Iowa can be fairly steep and your dog disappears from view below you. Your partner calls out point to you as you do for him when your dog comes up on a bird. You peer over the edge and get ready.

Angus: The Legend

I hesitate to bring the following information into this writing mainly because it is almost impossible to believe. Several seasons ago, Angus of Eagle Grove, Iowa, came up with 14 found roosters in his mouth, and more than that amount in hens, who were of course let go. Most of his birds flushed but if the bird didn't flush, Angus simply went in and pinned the bird and brought him to his owner. Angus is a legend in my book. These later seasons he prefers to go on point and gets the bird to flush but that season when he brought out those roosters on his own was a memorable year. He must have had the 'soft mouth' that we spoke of earlier because every hen he brought up flew away unhampered once we released them. Odd thing about Angus. When I first started out hunting with the Eagle Grove group, there were some hunters from Minnesota, distant relatives of John's that made fun of Angus as he was a 'rookie' then. They will have to eat their words now if they ever saw him perform in the field.

Angus and Pup ride in the pickup box when the weather is comfortable. If it is a bit cold, they ride inside on the back seat. Road hunting it is more efficient to have them in the box. Once a guy thought he would have his two dogs ride in the same manner. The first stop light he came to in a small town the dogs jumped out when they saw a squirrel and promptly gave chase. We never worry about Angus or Pup as they are focused only on pheasants.

Distant Relatives and Classmates

I don't know what it is about some distant relatives, not all of course, but some do think they can get away with a bit more than they would with a non-relative. Old classmates fit into this niche as well, it seems. I should relate a bad hunt with an old classmate who had one of the worst dogs I have ever experienced. Toward the end of that miserable journey, I asked him which direction he was going when we were going to do a field. When he pointed, I told him I would go the opposite direction. The worst part was that he insisted he had a good dog even though at times we would have to get in the truck and go find the dog. Anyway, John Jacobson and I were invited to hunt with some of his distant Iowa relatives. Angus was in his prime and Puppy was young yet but well experienced, good enough to be hunting for a South Dakota resort so I didn't mind answering John's invitation by showing up for an Iowa opener. A large public land area was totally ours since this particular hunting group always managed to rise early enough to secure a goodly portion of it by parking their truck and vans in the early hours. The place was loaded with birds.

We stayed at some cabins beside a lake and had a friendly party the night before. I always bed down early before a hunt, however. The hunting grounds were just a few miles away and I discovered that this was an annual event which reached back for several decades. Before we started out to hunt that next morning, one person who happened to be a medical doctor was obviously in charge. John and I were told to take one end of the line just before the shooting would begin. We started out and I was quite thrilled with all the birds that were starting to rise and could have cared less that most were coming up at the opposite end of the line. Eventually Angus started to work and Puppy was doing his share and it wasn't long that we were doing a goodly share of the shooting, so it seemed. Their dogs ranged a bit too much was my conclusion and were no doubt running over and on past sitting birds. By bird count, we were definitely getting more than our share but such is hunting in a group, a bird comes up and if it is a rooster, you take your shots. They all go into a common pool.

Well, it wasn't long before the Doctor came over to our end and politely told us that our dogs were ranging out too far and that we had to pull them 'in,' whatever the hell that meant. I had to ask him for some verification of his statement because our dogs were getting birds up right in front of us and theirs were way farther out than ours and hence hampering their productivity. Wasn't our fault! At that moment Angus and Puppy 'Duo-ed' up a double which we promptly brought down right in front of the exasperated and 'in-error' Doctor. His Indian name became 'Doctor Boss.'

The rest of the group were fairly friendly however and even offered to carry some of our birds.

Next, we both caught hell because we went around wide to block for a small corn field that pheasants were running out of. We got a couple coming out high and several going away and managed to hold a few in for the drivers who would have otherwise never had a chance at them had we not been up ahead. If you don't block while on a grain field drive, especially in stunted corn where every one can see where in the hell you are then you are going to miss out on a bunch of birds, has been my experience. Public land corn is generally of the stunted variety and rarely is the tall, productive field corn which you normally see in modern agriculture. The doctor did not believe in blocking, however. Back in Emery, South Dakota, those boys hunt a lot of corn. They wouldn't think of leaving out the blockers.

Next John took Angus and went to find a downed bird in some tall corn and came out with it. Some how, some way, the Doctor had to make a negative comment about that result. It was getting toward noon and a lunch break had been scheduled. John and I made a rough count and chuckled privately to ourselves that we had gotten well over our share of the birds by then. Good dogs do make a difference.

Relatives or no relatives, John concluded that we had enough hunting by noon. We took only a few of the birds and wished all a polite goodbye and left back to Eagle Grove. The bossy Doctor was a bit too much for our dogs and style of hunting. Hunting is to be enjoyed is our motto. When someone takes away that wonderful enjoyment, it is time to move on; simple as that no matter how good the hunting was.

8

Three Triples

Danger

    I mentioned earlier that pheasant hunting can be dangerous. We were hunting a cornfield where the corn turned scrubby at about the last ten or more rows. There was plenty of visibility as we would drive toward our blockers on the end. A doctor from the east who had hunted with our South Dakota Opener group for several years was one of the blockers. The day before, I had taken him with me along with crack shot Darrell Burckhardt to Don Smith's pheasant 'Nirvana' land during the road hunting break. The Surgeon wasn't the greatest shot and we wanted him to get his share of birds at the productive 'Nirvana' of Don Smith's heavily covered CRP land. I remember Darrell and I dropping him off at the back of a miniature slough that always promised birds. We drove back to the opposite end of the slough and walked in with Rex driving roosters to the doctor. He got his share of chances but just didn't seem to be able to get some clean knock downs.

    That next day I was walking next to Todd's younger brother, Rick, who was just beginning his twenties. Todd Gifford, remember, is introduced in the 'Take a Boy Hunting' chapter and now is one of the most successful hunting guides I have seen and especially for the Spring Snows migration wherein he employs hundreds of Snow and Blue decoys to attract the large flocks in. Rex and Todd's dog Simon, a pointing white Spaniel flushed up a rooster as we came out of the heavier corn. That rooster lifted low and flew straight at the doctor who was one of the blockers just back a ways at the edge of the corn. It seemed time stood still as I saw him come up with his over and under and I actually saw the blast before I heard it and then felt it. I caught the pellets in my right shoulder and it stung and jolted my shoulder back. I heard a yelp beside me and Todd's brother covered his ear with his hand. At first I thought the bottom of his ear lobe was taken off as his hand was red with blood. Fortunately for me, the pellets only bruised me with dents yet never drew blood. I was padded with a T-shirt, a hunting shirt, my flight jacket and best of all a heavier than usual shooting pad on my hunting vest which a sewing lady made for me. I remember looking at Todd's brother and exclaimed, "It doesn't look all that bad. Think of the story you can tell in a bar!" I know! It was a rather odd statement but I think I was trying to say anything positive to keep him from going into shock. Later on, every one had a good laugh over it.

I remember him lighting up with a big smile and agreeing, especially when his older brother came up and looked at it. We both agreed that we could have fared much worse. We then had to deal with the Doc who went into a state of shock. Poor guy, just quit hunting; right then and there. He went back to his room in Mitchell and just stayed there for several days until his airline ticket was due to fly out back east. Dr. Darrell Burckhardt knew him real well and from what I know he still does not hunt.

I have been hit once by a bullet and once was 'rained' on by a shotgun pellet close enough to get embedded under my skin. First thing you notice when you get hit is how it stings like hell. This story needs mentioning to implant upon the mind of the reader to never drop that barrel low at a bird coming at you when you are posting out in front of a group. The Dakota group I hunt with seems to always post experienced hunters as blockers which is a good idea, my opinion. The Iowa group are just as careful also. Todd's brother is of that era that often wears earrings and when he does you can't tell he was hit. He never bothered retaliating in any form against the doctor. We all just felt sorry for the poor guy. It would be one helluva state of utter shock to give up hunting totally.

A Heavy Grove

I was hunting with the South Dakota group. We had the 'Opener' behind us, a good party and on the second day I had suggested we try this one long grove that bordered a good size cornfield. I knew the farmer who unfortunately came down with a debilitating disease and his hard working wife could even drive the combine. They were friends of my sister and brother-in-law. I knew them well enough to offer them fresh trout from my spring and summer forays into the Black Hills where I was raised. Like most folks, they loved eating the trout and told me to hunt the grove and surrounding grain come fall. It was a fairly wide grove and offered good cover for the pheasants.

Our group had a successful hunt through the corn with our dogs and then pushed the grove after two of us who were blockers walked wide at a goodly pace toward the opposite end while the group gave us time to get there before pushing through the grove. A Doctor named Casey was my fellow blocker and as we crossed a new barbed wire fence at the far end, Casey became firmly snagged in his rear on the top wire barb of the fence. He had on the new canvas type that was not very prone to tear loose and there he was bound when the shooting started. Pheasants came streaming through that grove and I had to reload several times. When you are blocking in our country, you shoot what roosters come your way and don't worry about counting. They are all going to get thrown together and divided rather generously by the local shooters, mostly to the out of state guys anyway. The local hunters simply wave their hands and tell you they have plenty of time and days to get more when out-of-staters have to go back where they came from. When it comes to being a blocker, you are not shooting for yourself. You don't stop because you shot three birds. If ten guys are in the hunt and 30 birds, the limit is reached, one guy may have shot four and one guy may have shot two. One guy may have shot five and one guy may have shot one but all go home with their limit. That is just the way it is, sort of like when you see the highway patrol parked along the Interstate, ignoring every one doing 80 on a South Dakota posted 75 mph speed limit, waiting for the speedster who comes by at 85 or 90 mph.

My shooting and movement drove enough roosters back into the grove for the advancing party to get their share while our dogs were working furiously to pick up downed birds. It was quite a memorable shoot and all that time Doc Casey was stuck on that fence line with his two shot over and under, missing most of it. His Indian name dubbed him as 'Fence Sitter.'

The Three Triples

The next day, most of our group who were local went back to work and I was out on my own. I did not have far to go from my brother-in-law's house to wander back to the grove where I wanted to see about several downed birds we couldn't find and which had dropped over into a neighbor's land that was posted. We did not search very hard for those two birds and since it had snowed a bit during the night, I was not adverse to looking for them and bagging them after a night out in the cold snow.

I entered from the roadside of the grove and promptly raised a rooster and a couple of hens. Tree limbs and branches prevented me from downing the rooster but I managed to get off a round. A couple of distant shots rang out as well. When I reached the end of the grove, there were two hunters out beyond the grove and within posted land. They were without a dog and were earnestly searching a small slough about the size of a half a foot ball field or maybe the size of the infield of a baseball diamond; not large as compared to the average slough.

They looked at me and I watched them for awhile as they kept on searching. I asked them if they needed a dog and they waved me on over. They were younger than I and one said he was a brother to the landowner. I mentioned my brother-in-law, whom they knew. I told them about our hunt the day before and one reached into his vest and handed me a semi-frozen rooster. He pointed to where he had found it, assuming it was one of the birds we had shot and never found. My dog had not picked up the scent of the slough rooster yet and when one of us looked in the right direction, there went a rooster and a couple hens scurrying in the opposite direction toward another slough, southeast of the grove which ran west to east where I had come out. They said a whole flock had landed in that slough where the birds ran into and asked me if I wanted to come along with them. We had plenty of room to approach that small slough from downwind, first going wide east and then south. Rex was his usual 'hang close' as we approached, despite what was heavy bird smell up ahead and into the wind. As we approached, we had ten rounds among us. They had semi-automatic Remingtons bearing three rounds each. They told me later that they had never taken out their duck hunting plugs. I had four rounds in my 24-inch Benelli. As we entered the slough abreast from downwind, heading northwest into the slight wind, Rex became extremely 'Birdie.'

For some long moments, we almost held our breaths as we walked slowly into the thicker cover that still afforded us comfortable shooting as the weeds were not over belt high and not yet thick enough to hold us back or impede us. The cover was also fairly thin for a slough. Cattle droppings indicated the cows had foraged within it, thus thinning it out somewhat. It just was not thick enough to conceal a hiding group of pheasants, was my reasoning, although I have seen them hide in what I considered some fairly bare spaces. The suspense began to build with each step. Half way into the slough with Rex carefully working in front of us, still no eruption of 'the flock.' Not even a nervous hen rose. A few more steps and one of the pair said with a bit of exasperation, "They got to be in here. We saw them go in."

A few more steps and Rex would be almost at the edge of the slough which bordered abruptly on short grass not long enough to conceal any bird thinking about sneaking out unseen. "That rooster has to be in here," I remarked as I cautiously held my thumb right above my safe. I wanted to reassure myself that at least one bird had to be in that rather small slough.

I no sooner remarked and the whole world erupted. It was just plain simple to explain – a flat explosion of birds as though every one decided to take to the sky at the same moment, hens and all. I can't talk for the rest of them as I never took notes of their experience and I regret that I did not. I caught the first one high, as it wanted to come back over us, another to my right and back was high as well, and he dropped with my turn toward the rear of the slough, my second round dropping him at the edge where we came in. Guns seemed to be firing from everywhere as I spun back to face the front of the action, searching for #3 which was not much of a problem but getting him isolated from someone else's target was, within all the commotion of noise and sheer excitement. In front, a rooster came out low and rising at the edge and was heading for the grove; I pumped a round into him and he kept trucking; another round, a steel three-inch four and he was down.

The shooting ceased. Suddenly, it was heavy action and now all was silent. Our ears rang. Rex was scurrying like a wild dog retrieving birds. All of a sudden one bird with a broken wing bolted out of cover and headed for the grove. I yelled at my dog and Rex dropped a bird out of his mouth and speeded after that one. No one knew who shot it, such was the action. We counted nine birds, nine roosters on ten shots. That was the only triple/triple I have ever been involved in. Like I say, you cannot get much more real excitement than you can with those cagy, burly, rocket bound "Chinese' roosters of rainbow colors, the feathered citizens of the Dakotas or the sovereign state of Iowa. We three would never be convinced that some other species of bird could give you that much sheer excitement and adrenaline flow. I left that pair with good wishes and a hearty thank you for inviting me in to hunt with them. I never saw them again. All I knew was that they were out-of-staters like me, at that particular time in my life. When this book is finished I will stop by the brother's farm and drop off a copy.

I guess I had to add this episode for another reason, besides mainly utilizing it for its interesting content. I seem to complain a bit much about people who claim to never miss and I do include quite a few of my many misses but in this case – even I had my share of luck.

Top left: South Dakota Tourism photo
Top right: Flushing hen from cattails
Bottom left: Jackrabbit neighbor
Bottom right: South Dakota Game, Fish
      & Parks photo

Top left: Young Lab, Cash
Top right: Pup's first
    long chase retrieve
    (11 months old)
Middle: Holed rooster
Bottom: Finis

Top left: On point
Bottom left: Cattail rooster retrieval

Top: Rex III
Middle left: Angus and John Jacobson
Middle right: Rex IV (Puppy) Iowa Drainage
Bottom: Wolfman, Estelline, South Dakota

Top: Steve, Bob Detterman and Big
    Bird (Dennis Burckhardt)
Middle left: Hunt leader Big Bird
    and Dr. Darrell in Kayser's Bar
Middle right: Dr. Darrell Burckhardt
Bottom: Bonnie and Big Bird,
    Emery, South Dakota

Top: Getting Ready, Eagle
    Grove, Iowa
Middle left: Son, Mark,
    John Jacobson, Danny
    Elkin and dogs
Middle right: Danny's
    Boykin dog is on point
Bottom: Angus, Pup,
    Rooster (Tim Reams)
    and John J. (Few
    know Rooster as Tim.)

Top left: My son, Mark
Top right: Puppy and son, Kyle, who speaks fluent Arabic and types it. Kyle also just won an LBJ State Department Scholarship for a Master's Degree
Middle: Smilin' dog
Bottom: Son, John, and daughter, Mary Pat

Top left: Rooster's Den
Bottom: Puppy and Angus
    enroute to a pheasant field

9

Different Hunting

1967- American flag sent to VMFA Squadron 115 via Headquarters Marine
Corps from Oglala Tribal chairman Enos Poor Bear with request, ("To be
flown over the enemy."). Folded flag was placed under my ejection seat prior
to combat mission and unfurled for photo upon completion and returned to
South Dakota for annual Sun Dance opening ceremony with special honoring
for all returning Vietnam Veterans to the Sioux Tribe.

Being the Hunted—Chu Lai, Vietnam

I mentioned in one of my books the time that I flew five missions back to
back to help rescue two chopper loads of Marines about to be overrun by an
NVA battalion up in the highlands. Those Marines were the 'Hunted.' Our pair
of Phantoms became key rescue factors, beginning one afternoon while serving
on 'hot pad' emergency response duty.

The McDonnell Phantom F4B was the initial production model from the
St. Louis plant. Over 5,000 were to be built, mostly later F4C, D and J models.
These later models had internal 20mm and flight controls in both cockpits. The
Air Force was slow to realize how efficient a bomber it could be besides being

the premium fighter of its day mainly because of the tremendous power its twin J-79 afterburner equipped engines provided. The Marine Corps realized its capability early in the war and happily traded off their prop driven AD (Spad) attack bombers for cancelled Air Force Phantom orders for the McDonnell Company. Air Force AD pilots, (Flying Commandos) were shot down right and left due to its low pull off speed, especially when dropping only one piece of ordnance at a time. When the Spad added power for pull up from a close air support bombing run, it would slow down to around 145 knots. You are pretty vulnerable to ground fire at such a slow speed. The Phantom came in much faster and after hitting their 'burner,' left faster, even on pull up with a full load and consequently saved hundreds of Phantom crews. If a gigantic pheasant could suddenly hit 600 knots, I doubt if even Will Pressed Pants could hit it, not even with a rifle or an AK-47. The B model had only one set of pilot controls, the radar operator sat in back and had no internal Gatling 20mm. An external Vulcan 20mm which had a reputation for jamming was occasionally carried on the bottom MER (Ordnance hook on point.). Rockets were also attached externally but were ineffective compared to our main ordnance. Most of our missions we carried twelve 500 pounders or seven napalm. From experience, we seemed to receive less ground fire when one bird carried nape. In a division flight of four, at least one machine would have nape. In a section flight (two aircraft) we often, but not always, would have one nape carrier.

There were two CH-46 helicopter loads of downed Marines. We fought long into the night, returning at full speed back to them after refueling and reloading out of Chu Lai. Rarely does a pilot ever fly five combat fighter attack missions back to back and never leaving the cockpit. I learned what the Marine helicopter pilots went through, flying long hours, that day and on into the night. I didn't have to hunt my quarry on those missions. They were right there and it was mostly our bombs and napalm that was keeping the NVA from capturing that last helicopter load. We came in so low just to the left of them when bombing seaward that my radar operator said he could see the belt buckles of the troops jumping up and down cheering from the bomb craters they huddled in. After my third mission it was twilight and we were fighting in mountain terrain.

My squadron commander was standing in the loading and refueling revetment when I taxied in. This was usually not a good sign. I knew where I had placed my bombs and usually came in low at times for pin point accuracy which my Skipper (Squadron Commander) had commended me for more than a few times over. Snake Eye bomb configuration allows you to do that without getting your tail blown off from the resultant blast. An umbrella like set of fins springs out from the bomb as soon as it releases from your bomb rack, retarding the big 500 pounder momentarily and therefore allows you to come in real low, drop and get away without getting your tail blown off. A 500 pounder throws out a terrific blast. Before the snake eye configuration, a large bomb just could not be released safely from the aircraft at a very low level. The lower you are, the more accurate you are, and when dropping close to your own troops, pin point accuracy was critical.

I knew immediately why the Skipper was standing there when the plane captain signaled to keep one engine turning to provide power for refueling and reloading. The bomb crews below scurried feverishly with their carts and ordnance. It looked like I was going right back out, such were the dire circumstances the Marines were facing; almost fatally trapped back high on that mountain range. We had already lost an A-4 jet, a Spad AD prop attack aircraft and a Huie gunship. Miraculously, all of these pilots were rescued and were down in those bomb craters with the Marine grunts (Infantry). All three aircraft had managed to crash land at a miniature airstrip cut into the mountain side. Skipper motioned for me to stay in the cockpit, yelling in a loud voice asking how I was feeling fatigue wise. I was damn well fatigued after three demanding missions but I was young and you just do not disobey or get reluctant with a Marine Corps squadron commander. I lied to him however, when I yelled back that I was okay.

"G.D., Chief. I hate to do this to you." He yelled with a relieved tone. Even one Phantom engine running at idle gets a bit loud. The flight surgeon forked up a chocolate malt which I knew was loaded with Imodium to keep you from needing to go to toilet – the #2 one. The pilot could urinate at the back of the Phantom when we had to go right back out. Pilots, even military pilots who have never experienced extreme combat, find this hard to believe. You simply unstrapped and the aircraft was so big and broad that you walked aft and held on to the vertical tail fin that reminded you of a bull Orca while you urinated into the exhaust below you. Helicopter pilots had a convenient 'Pee tube' for that purpose but I think the pressurization requirements of a high altitude Phantom prevented such a necessity. You zipped the front of your flight suit back up and re-strapped yourself to the ejection seat while fuel was being poured into your tanks and the bombs secured below.

"Chief, I will lose a pilot if I send a green one in." He meant that an inexperienced pilot to those mountain passes could easily kill a crew on pullout, especially in the black of night. More than one crew had met that fate. We had to come off low because we had to make sure we would not hit our own troops and yet get to the enemy close by. Often you would dip down a canyon after a drop to be unreachable by the 37 mounted guns. Night would make it all that more difficult.

I yelled back at the colonel below jokingly. "Skipper, if I get back… I want a G.D. Rum and Coke from that Swabbie standing next to you." I added, "If I don't… then have one on me!"

In combat, you often can get away with what you wouldn't dare dream of otherwise. A Swabbie is a slang term for Navy personnel – even Navy Doctors, which our flight surgeons are. Both men gave me a hearty thumbs up while

I attached my oxygen mask back on and prepared to relight my #2 kerosene quencher – the J-79 power plant that could give 17,500 pounds of thrust and allow a take off straight up skyward if you needed it. Power? That baby had plenty of raw power and there were two of those General Electric J-79s attached to it. I wish I could have met some of those trapped troops. This all happened one night in July, high up on a mountain ridge. I knew the return route like the back of my hand, even in the night. As I left the plateau before the mountains, you could see the glow of combat. Flares were being dropped by a C-47.

Like I said, life is not like the movies. It was almost impossibility, but my Skipper was again standing in the revetments with the flight surgeon when I returned back from the fourth mission. I felt like a zombie must feel if there ever was such a thing. We still had not suppressed that stubborn NVA battalion commander enough to get extract choppers in. One more Huie, a gunship, was added to the planes downed. The navy flight surgeon was holding a canteen cup. My Skipper was shaking his head disparagingly. His posture made me wonder for my section leader, Major Duffy, who was flying the same amount of missions I was. 'Had Duff been shot down?' I worried to myself. In combat you do fly to your destination initially together but once the shooting starts you take separation and bomb individually. You also return individually. None of this Hollywood formation joining back up; not on critical situation hot pad duty missions, at least. A plane carrying seven napes (napalm) is going to be empty sooner than a plane carrying twelve 500-pounders and needs to leave the bombing pattern immediately when empty to get rearmed and refueled. An aircraft that burns more fuel may have to leave early and get back again when, or if, the situation below gets hairy.

'Major Tom Duffy had been shot down?' I worried as I taxied to a stop.

The Skipper came over and stood below me. He punched my ladder release and came half way up. He looked perplexed and began with, yelling loudly, "G.D. Chief, Some Marines are going to die tonight if you can't make it back there, one… last-ass-time." He put his words in combat Marine Corps perspective. I took off my helmet to hear better and with it my oxygen mask. I let out a groan. I was one tired, fatigued Son of a Bitch, to put it all in combat Marine Corps terms. The Flight surgeon below added. "That is …if you can make it." If this was a book that kids would never read, I would be more honest and be more truthfully, descriptively, expletive than that… which no doubt will make the politically correct wimps wince as it is. Especially those that would foolishly wish that we Marines would not swear, especially in combat. We all spoke like General Patton when shells were flying and more so when our troops were on the line being killed and captured by a brutal enemy. It is just more precise communication for us and certainly more emphatic. "G.D. Skipper." I replied. "I don't have any choice." I waved to the north. "Folks out there – getting killed…"

"Or captured," he added. "It doesn't look good for one of the choppers." He meant the one that wound up being captured. (They were shot in the highlands, obviously, as they never showed up on POW roles.)

I stretched my feet into my rudders and partially rose from the cockpit. I yelled back boldly. "I can do it, Skipper, but I'd be lying if I said I would turn down a G.D. good shot of something to drink."

The flight surgeon acted like he was about to pull a rabbit out of a hat when he lifted up the canteen cup with a wry smile. The Skipper backed down the ladder and to my amazement, brought out a pharmaceutical bottle of what surely was base dispensary medical alcohol. I had had some before when I had crashed a Phantom on takeoff, due to blown nose tires and no fault of my own. I was spun around backwards after I hit the wires at the end of the runway and my hydraulics caught on fire. I wasn't hurt but such an occurrence does get your attention. The medical alcohol was offered to me in the sick bay clinic right after the crash. I had cut it with orange juice because it is fairly 'wicked stuff.' The flight surgeon talked to me for awhile and deemed I was okay. I was back up flying that afternoon.

" S... of a... B," I voiced out slowly in sheer wonderment. I watched in amazement as the two below mixed up what looked like a goodly strong concoction.

Combat indeed does strange things. Maybe our Skipper knew all about our beloved, yet feared combat General, General Chesty Puller, who did likewise for his troops as a battalion commander on Guadalcanal and then later as a regimental commander in Korea on the Frozen Chosen trail. He would crawl out to a beleaguered and lonely dangerous outpost and give his frontline men a good stiff drink from a bottle of bourbon or whiskey he carried for just such a hairy and dangerous occasion.

"G.D. Colonel, what the hell you doin' out here?" was their most often used and startled reply. Read the book on Chesty Puller; it is all in there what I am relating. If anybody doesn't like what he did then, 'Tell it to the Marines!'

You never, never drink and fly. Those are the rules. But that night I did. They handed up my drink and I savored every G.D. bit of it. It hit my empty stomach like a fireball with a warming glow. It was like spinach to Popeye or 'Shazam' to Superman. When the plane captain gave the start up signal for the second engine, I looked down with a broad cocky smile. I held a thumb's up and put my bonnet (flight helmet) back on, strapping down my mask. I went back out feeling miraculously invigorated and we got the troops out after that final mission.

"You don't mind cutting it with orange juice, do you, Chief," rang in my ears as I headed north under power from those big dependable J-79s, oblivious to the black night and the waiting mountains which we feared more than the enemy's anti-aircraft fire. Flying under those flares you have the added challenge of avoiding hitting your own troops thrown in. You have but split seconds to decide whether to drop or not to drop and you have to get in there and drop and that means right ass on the enemy. It is a damned demanding situation. You absolutely just do not have time for fear or that stupid word, reluctance.

Marine pilots concur – 'You just have to do it, man. You have to ass do it!' Finally we got them out, after dropping our ordnance under the flares which is a fairly hairy, spooky maneuver. I'd take night carrier calls any day …or any night even in rain…over bombing under flares and worse in mountainous terrain.

With deep regret the other chopper load was captured and just disappeared. No POW list – nothing. Success can be bitter sweet. Their names are on the 'Wall' in DC but the rescued lived. Major Duffy was awarded the Distinguished Flying Cross for the same missions I had flown. I was also recommended by my loyal Skipper for the same medal because he knew we were under the exact same conditions, and indeed both fulfilled our challenge placed before us. Major Tom Duffy was killed soon after and I never received my medal because I was getting out and going on to law school. Again, life is never like the movies, life is inexorable. I have told my children, however, that I want that medal pinned to the pillow inside of my casket someday. In my mind I earned it…but life is never like the movies…is it?

Most hunters, especially the NRA (National Rifle Association) ones are deeply patriotic as are most farmers and ranchers as well. As I said earlier, my Marine combat jacket which I still wear considerably has got me on many a choice hunting spot, although lately I seldom have to knock on anyone's door. The Highway patrol has stopped me more than once when I was wearing my jacket and I probably deserved more than one ticket from them but all I ever got was warnings to slow down or to get a tail light fixed or whatever. My last ticket was from a sheriff's deputy. He knew me, as counties are a bit smaller than a whole state. "<u>Ed, Slow down</u>!" was written on my warning ticket. In my older age I want to assure the reader that I am doing pretty good at slowing down, in more ways than just driving. In case you are wondering how one jacket can last so long, down through the years? They don't! You continue to replace them from surplus stores or some flying museums which often feature them in their gift shops. It costs you a significant bundle to have your patches taken off the old and replaced on the new; often more than the jacket costs but what is money? Didn't I mention that life is inexorable …and as long as you buy decent shells and a good dog with your bounty?

Why would I include an actual combat experience in a hunting book?

Because, some of us know what it is like to be the hunted. We, in essence, have paid our dues – so to speak. I respect that wily bird that we hunt simply because I have been tracked by SAM missiles and even have seen several real close ups of those 'flying telephone poles' that obviously missed. Those six aircraft down were mainly the work of some small arms fire but mostly the Chinese 37mm.

I also dearly appreciate that some Divine Force from my own belief system allowed me to return. I have been endowed with a still healthy and capable body that the Great Spirit power has yet allowed me to be invested with and for which I am deeply grateful. I do not want to bring in much religion, especially when the vast majority of my readers have a differing religion than mine, but I feel I do indeed want to express my personal thanksgiving up front and not in the final pages, if anywhere. Extremist groups unfortunately, permeate all religions, thinking that only they know who God, Creator exactly is despite what is obviously a whole lot of Mystery. It took a few years from Nam to fully start hunting again as generally, it is a bit unusual for most combat veterans, especially the ground combatants to return immediately back to hunting. Some, actually many, maybe most...never do.

I never shoot deer anymore and when I was younger I had to get a big doe every fall for my folks who were quite used to eating deer meat (We never call it venison.) I never shot a buck on my sister's land and consequently our herds were very healthy. My sister was pretty strict on that rule, especially to protect the older, big bucks to allow them to do the reproducing according to Nature's laws and we ate every deer we took. If you want to reduce Chronic Wasting Disease then have your state place a moratorium for a couple seasons on shooting the big racked, older bucks. This might be too much common sense however for a state's DNR or Game, Fish & Parks Department.

Back to the Vietnam Vets; we are all individuals, and especially for the Marine infantry, the 'Grunts,' the Airborne, the Rangers and the Army 'Grunts' who experienced heavy combat, I respect those who choose not to hunt. For me, I am glad that I eventually came back to the ringneck. Maybe it was my dogs. Maybe because of them, and of course Dakota, those bird dogs brought me back.

Seven Days of South Dakota Pheasant Hunting November 2006 and 2007

Dr. Joel C. Tate

Gary Black (Blacks Pheasant Farms) and Dr. Joel

Brief Reflections of a Frustrated Quail Hunter

Like many former Virginia quail hunters I have been frustrated and disappointed by our drastically declining numbers of bobwhites, and I really miss following classy Llewellyn Setters or high-tailed English Pointers trailing birds and honoring each other's statue-like point on coveys or singles. When I moved from Tennessee to Central Virginia in 1970, quail were plentiful and if you had good bird dogs and good legs, you could have some wonderful days in the field with dog and man. Occasionally on our quail hunts my friend, Larry, whom I mentioned in the Foreword, would shoot a rabbit, dress it, and prepare it for home-consumption by washing it off in a fresh-running stream. I would pick up a few white quartz Archaic Indian arrowheads along the way. Our primary objectives were to enjoy the outdoors, have good conversation, rib each other as much as we could, find a few covey of quail, and share closeness with man, dog, and nature.

I finally returned to South Dakota after many conversations with Ed who would come out to the college and lecture to my students regarding Native American history, culture and spirituality. We would top off his lectures with a sweat lodge ceremony at my farm where we had plenty of privacy and fire wood that would heat up the stones for the ceremony. Nearby were willow saplings and my students would all pitch in and Lo!, we would have a new structure on my farm and all made rather quickly, cheaply, efficiently without the bother of going down to the courthouse and requesting a building permit. Actually the covered sapling structure is less than five feet tall and about fifteen to twenty feet wide, barely enough for a dozen people or so to huddle inside in a circle. The steam made from pouring water on heated rocks is quite invigorating and was used by various tribes for healing and cleansing. My students all enjoyed the experience.

Talking the Talk: Encounter with Coyote Man

Earlier, in the Foreword I described my first day of successful Dakota hunting with Puppy and Ed. That evening we ate a very hearty supper, compliments of Mama Black, and ran into an interesting group of "farmer-hunters" from Iowa who had come to Eastern South Dakota for some rest and relaxation. We were thoroughly entertained by the lives and times of one "Coyote Man" who described in great detail how he had shot and killed many a coyote predator in the last several years. For a "Back Easterner," I was shocked to hear about his 90 plus miles/hour trip spinning on a large frozen river in pursuit of a wily coyote. According to his own sworn hunting-story testimony, he got his prey while spinning round and round over the ice-encrusted water in a large double-cabbed pickup. And, I thought hunters from my Tennessee homeland were wild and crazy guys! After hearing this and other coyote tales, Ed and I went out to check on the skunks that we had seen the night before. We took a large plastic jug of honey, compliments of Ms. Black's ample kitchen table, opened the lid, and poured generous amounts of its contents around "three skunk gathering" point. Perhaps a new folk tale entitled, "B'rer Skunk and the Honey Baby" would result from our two-night "Predator Patrol Experiment?"

Hunt Day Two: Walking the Walk

During the morning a lot of pheasants were flushing far ahead of us in some CRP cover areas surrounding the corner of a cornfield, and Ed and I were not getting any decent shots. Gary Black decided to take two of his dogs with us early in the afternoon. One was a German Wirehair Pointer, and the other looked like a cross between a hound dog and a German Shorthair. Three dogs and three men moved around one of Gary's favorite hunting spots circling the banks of a good-sized pond. Gary and I went together with his dogs, and Ed took Puppy around the opposite bank. Heavy CRP cover was all around, and Gary and I were walking, or should I say trudging, through some stuff that reminded me of giant Johnson grass outcroppings that I had seen in Tennessee. We had another name for it that was a bit more colorful – "Hell Buck" grass. Going through this "Goliath Hell Buck" made me feel like a tired fullback wading through the outstretched arms of the best defensive line in professional football. Gary, a former star wrestler, seemed to stroll along saying, "Yup," and "You bet" to most of my comments about the thickest grass that I had ever encountered! He told me that pheasants could tunnel under this cover when it snows, but so could the clever coyote or hungry fox. He said that this was Canary Grass and "the thickest stuff around." (Note: For more information on prairie grasses see my interview with Gary in the appendix, and the list of allowable CRP grass varieties that Gary gave to me when we were eating dinner). Later I had missed three or four pretty wild shots at early flushers, and Ed was not doing much better. With Gary's patience and assistance, we had managed to bag one bird apiece under rather trying hunt conditions. After a much needed rest for dog and man, Ed and I decided to return to the same spot where early flushers had greeted us that morning.

Late Afternoon: Four Roosters at Cornfield Corner

As Puppy, Ed, and I returned to where we had started our day's hunt, a huge red sun was beginning its descent on the crimson horizon behind an aging barn and silo. Several early-rising roosters had flushed there early in the morning near a tree-lined thicket cutting through a recently-harvested cornfield. Pheasant food and excellent cover were all around. A deep red bloodlike hue reflected from a small lake framed by the thicket and the corner of the cornfield. Reflections from the lake generated mental reflections of my own on the man/nature connection and beauty of the moment. I had learned the Sioux expressions for the sun (Wiyo), and the west (Wiyopeyata–the sun it goes down) from Ed's books and ceremonies, as well as the contents of Black Elk's vision on the power of the west to make life and death. Something about the moving expression "the sun it goes down" seemed to be more appropriate than the more finalized English expression, sunset. I was moved to replay mental images of late afternoon times like these that I had spent as a young boy in Middle Tennessee when I had hunted rabbits with my first shotgun, a light 16-gauge, variable-choked, bolt action Mossberg that kicked like a Tennessee mule! I wondered, what's wrong with man hunting and killing animals with shotguns and rifles as long as he shows a basic respect for all things? How does one adequately show respect for lives that you are about to take? My mama, Nannie Tate, had taught me many years ago to always eat (or give away) whatever I killed, and then it would be okay. Her teachings about this and many other important matters of existence probably explain my lifetime interests in Indian teachings. Thankfully, I am still able to hunt with these basic views of life and death still with me wherever I go.

Ed walked on the border of the lake, and I walked to his left near a tree line bordered by a thicket of weeds and corn stalks. Puppy flushed a bird just as we entered the "cornfield corner" habitat. True to form, Ed downed him instantly. Puppy retrieved just as another bird flushed behind Ed. He took a long shot and appeared to cripple it as it soared across a small ridge in the cornfield behind me. Puppy searched long and hard to no avail. Just as I was beginning to wonder where "my" pheasants were, Puppy put up a large rooster who appeared to fly directly toward the sun. I dropped this one solidly with my teachers, Puppy and Ed looking directly over my shoulder. Think I got an "A" on that shot. We swung around to the right and headed back around the other side of the lake. It was getting very quiet now, and we only had about 15 more minutes of legal hunting time remaining. There were two more large roosters waiting for us, and as usual, Ed made a clean kill on one of them while I was working Puppy just ahead of me. I guess Ed gets the last shot today? But, once again my confidence told me that this old dog (me) might be tired, but he can still get off the porch. Puppy had not given up either, and as we neared the "Pheasant Mobile" waiting for us near the roadside, Puppy put up the last bird of the day to my right at two o'clock. The dog must have remembered that I could shoot fairly well in that direction. Perhaps he recalled my first shot lesson in the early morning of day one. Guess he figured if I could take one at three o'clock, two was close enough. There was no way that I could miss that bird! Well, more humanly speaking, I could have, but I did not. This episode at Four-Rooster Cornfield Corner had taken no more than the last thirty minutes of a long day of pheasant hunting. As on the morning of the first day, another indelible photograph – "Pheasants at Sundown"– will always be part of my Disc of Life, Ed's very apt terminology for a record of one's life experiences.

The Night of Day Two

A huge pheasant feast from Mama Black and a reconnection with "Coyote Man" and his hunting buddies were followed by a brief visit to our skunk "honey hole" site. Result: the Predator Patrol was "skunked" again by our elusive black and white friends.

Ringneck Pheasant Finale: The Morning of Day Three

Ed had felt pretty rugged for the last two days with lower back pains and some breathing difficulties, so we decided to take it a little easy and go out with Gary Black and his father in their hunt bus. It was an aging school bus outfitted with gun racks, and a wide rustic "lounge area" for man and dog in the middle. The four of us boarded the bus with Puppy and one of Gary's dogs, and went to a real hot spot near Lake Poinsett that Ed and I had run into earlier in the week. We were hunting a very thick and high-weeded pond bank, Ed and Puppy on one side, and Gary and I on the other. Lots of birds were getting up early and once again, first-bird Ed dropped a nice ring neck while I struggled to see in a thick-weed cover two feet over my head. If that is not a good enough excuse for being birdless, my eyes were watering behind fogged-over eyeglasses, and I was hunting in strange territory without my second cup of coffee. After Puppy retrieved Ed's bird, I tried to wake up and focus on "my" bird-to-come.

As I headed down the pond bank from my lofty weeded surroundings, Ed fired two rapid shots – BLAM! BLAM!! I looked in his direction just before all hell broke loose. A wounded pheasant was rapidly ascending into the sky at an estimated angle of 75 degrees. BLAM! Ed shot again. By this time, very high in the air, the pheasant must have become angry or scared enough to attempt to escape earth's gravitational pull and become a pheasant satellite. Perhaps "high-flyer" pheasant was being driven by a highly energized, primal, instinctoid response to the realities of man-created global warming? Anyway, this pheasant was getting the hell out of Dodge, or South Dakota. Ed had evidently loaded or reloaded a "three-and-a-half-incher" magnum anti-aircraft projectile in the Benelli Super Eagle, because with a final cannon blast, BU-UR-UR-RUM!!, the pheasant spacecraft crash-landed at the edge of the pond. Puppy had been watching the skies in obvious anticipation for sometime and was finally able to bring a dead-tired pheasant to his owner. Gary and I looked at one another with a sense of awe and astonishment. We agreed that we had never witnessed such long, high, loud, and successful shooting in our combined wing-shooting histories. Whether Ed's "high-flyer" was hit one out of five times, scared to death, tired of flying, falling for a hen, ready to roost, afraid of the empty voids of Black Holes in outer space, or merely acknowledging Ed's reputation as a Phantom Jet Pilot, we may never know. If I knew Ed's sense of humor a bit better, I might get up enough courage to discuss these and other hypothetical death causalities regarding the demise of "high flyer." No autopsy was performed on this particular representative of *Phasianus colchicus*, and we decided to leave the cause of death to the realms of mystery, speculation, and future fireside hunting stories.

We returned to the hunt bus, told Gary's father about "high flyer," and drove a short way to the side of a hill overlooking Lake Poinsett where a very exhausted Ed went to the end of a cornfield row as a blocker for Gary and me. In about ten minutes Ed had taken his final pheasant for the day while I walked empty-handed with Gary and Puppy, knowing that we only had enough time left in our half-day hunt to make one or two more brief passes through small cornfields near the lodge. So far this day, I had fired a couple of futile shots, and I was beginning to wonder if my last South Dakota outing for 2006 would end with no birds in my hunting vest.

Ten minutes after we boarded the bus, dogs, men, "high flyer," and the rest of Ed's daily limit of pheasant in tow, we made one hunting pass around a small-pond, pheasant hot spot where Gary "always" finds birds. Still feeling a bit under the weather, Ed stayed around the bus silently encouraging me to get that last bird or two. No luck at "hot spot." We re-boarded the bus, and Gary said, "Let's go to the small cornfield up the road and make one more try. You ready Joel?" By then, I had just about resigned myself to the possibility of attaining the unenviable fishing and hunting status known as "skunked." A very light snow was falling as we parked the bus. Gary and I got out of the bus near the end of a small ten to twelve row cornfield, and Gary's father drove Ed to the other end to act as blocker. While we waited on Ed to get ready, I took a few deep breaths of the South Dakota fall air, looked at Puppy and Gary's dog, and decided that there must be at least one more pheasant in South Dakota with my name on it.

The cornrows were very short compared to those we had walked during the last couple of days, and I could see Ed very clearly on the left side at the end of the field. Gary walked a corn row on my left, and his dog worked just ahead of us. Because the field was so small, we were virtually side-by-side. We had just started our walk when Gary's dog went on point to my right. Honestly, this was one of the more solid pheasant points that I had seen in South Dakota and I surely was hoping for a rooster rather than a hen waiting a few feet in front of the dog's nose. Gary said, "Move in. He's solid." I took about five steps, and a beautiful large rooster exploded from the corn and swung around to my right. A good clean shot brought him down with a "THUNK!" Gary's dog brought the bird to him, and he stuck it in my vest.

We moved on down the field toward Ed, Puppy up ahead on the left moving toward his owner, Gary and I nearing the end of the field on the right. Puppy was approaching Ed who was moving slightly across to my side of the cornrows, and they entered their end of the corn rows almost directly ahead of me. As we approached each other, Puppy leaped into a corn row just in front of me. Ed's blocking strategy with man and dog had worked to a tee. Perhaps that last pheasant was a wise old bird that would rather face a neophyte Virginia pheasant hunter rather than a seasoned veteran like Eagle Man. The tone of Ed's voice was very similar to what it had been when he and Puppy had given me my first hunting lesson on Day one. Ironically, Ed and Puppy's positions were almost exactly where they were when I had been given my pheasant hunting "pretest" in "teachable moment" on Day one. As a community college teacher and relatively new pheasant hunting student, I suppose that I was now taking my final exam. Just as had occurred on Day one, confidence and relaxation kicked in on my last, "must-make shot" just before I felt the slight kick and recoil of the Benelli 12-gauge, #6 shot. As Yogi Berra would say, it was deja-vu all over again. The pheasant fell dead, and Puppy retrieved with a wagging tail. Ed said, "Good shot!" Bird #2 in the bag. Final exam passed with flying colors.

Reflections

Three days of pheasant hunting in Eastern South Dakota with Ed McGaa and Puppy burned many memories, affirmations, and re-affirmations onto my Life's Disk. Included among these are:

- The very powerful symbiotic, loyal, deep-bonded, and interdependent relationship that can exist between man and dog when they listen to and communicate with each other in a constant dialogue of mutual caring, sharing, honesty, and trust.
- Learning from man and dog the knowledge, skills, techniques, problems, pitfalls, and promises associated with South Dakota pheasant hunting. Show me a "great hunter" who says that he never misses a pheasant shot and always gets his limit, and I'll show you a great liar!
- The many lessons to be learned through observations of nature by walking freely on the surface of Mother Earth. Breathing the clean air of open prairie grasslands, smelling the black soil of plowed fields, listening and watching as a resplendently feathered pheasant rooster literally explodes from the edge of a cornfield, and watching the sun come up and go down wherever you may be, add joy to your life and replenish your spirit.
- The vital importance of taking time out from a busy life's schedule to connect or reconnect with a compatible friend for relaxation, conversation, intellectual stimulation, and sipping on a couple of bottles of Mike's Lemonade after a great day of pheasant hunting in South Dakota.

Year Two with Ed and Puppy in Estelline, South Dakota: November 2007

The summer of 2007 was extremely dry in the Blue Ridge Mountains of Rappahannock County, Virginia where I live. The Jordan River which normally flows and gurgles along Bean Hollow Road had been reduced to a mere rock-piled trickle, and the foliage on the trees was looking rather "peeked" (pronounced peek-ed, my Tennessee grandma's word for sickly/weak). As the winds of October began to blow the leaves off the Tulip Poplars and Red Oaks on Peak and Big Bastard Mountains enclosing the "holler" that I call home, hunters with bow and muzzleloader were beginning to locate and stalk whitetail deer, wild turkey, and black bear. In another month or so hunters with high-powered rifles and shotguns would enter the woods and harvest a lot of game.

Like other frustrated Virginia quail and grouse hunters who have witnessed the drastically declining numbers of these winged in our midst, I was beginning to get a bad case of a physical and mental malady which I would label the "Winghunter's Blues." Since I play the guitar and five-string banjo, I suppose that I could have composed a song of that title and consoled myself while sitting and singing in my living room by a cozy wood fireplace. Another option would be to get off my duff and contact Eagle Man (Ed McGaa) about a return pheasant hunting trip to his neck of the woods in the Midwest.

Nature and the call of the wild pheasant prevailed, and I e-mailed Ed around October 15th. His blunt reply read, "Birds, hell yeah." I phoned Gary Black, manager of Blacks' Pheasant Fields near Estelline, South Dakota, to arrange room and board for a couple of days, and inquired about pheasant numbers this year. Gary said that he had seen more birds than he had seen in 20 years! "They were all around—everywhere," he exclaimed. That's all the encouragement that I needed to finalize plans with Ed for another great pheasant hunt, booked exactly a year-to-a day from last year's hunt during the third week of November.

Before I left to meet Ed and his Golden Retriever "Puppy" in Sioux Falls, South Dakota, I obtained an on-line five-day out-of-state small game hunting license from the South Dakota Game, Fish & Parks. A few days later, the Game, Fish & Parks forwarded a comprehensive pheasant area map guide to the state, and a summary sheet – "2007 South Dakota Ring neck Outlook." In a "good news/bad news" scenario, the Game, Fish & Parks report for 2007 South Dakota pheasants is as follows:

Good News

The high South Dakota pheasant population witnessed during the last four years should continue in 2007. A pheasant brood survey census conducted every year since 1997 shows pheasant increase of 23 percent from 2006–2007 in 110 survey routes in 13 selected areas. In comparison to a ten-year index, the overall 2007 brood survey is 66 percent higher than the ten-year average. According to Game, Fish & Parks Wildlife Division Director, Doug Hansen, good habitat, cooperative weather, ample rainfall, and the growth of grasses promoted excellent cover for egg hatching and young bird survival. In taking a proactive approach to ensuring pheasant-growth trends, Hansen states:

> Farm programs like the Conservation Reserve Program have provided tremendous habitat and have been a benefit to all wildlife…. It is imperative that wildlife enthusiasts actively involve themselves in the process of making sure Congress fully supports future programs such as CRP.

Bad News

CRP and other federal financial incentive programs for agricultural producers to set aside acreage from crop production face a very uncertain future. South Dakota alone stands to lose at least 296,000 acres (an approximate 20 percent loss), prime CRP pheasant-nesting habitat land in 2007, an additional 110,000 acres in 2008, and more CRP land losses are expected in 2009 and 2010.[1]

My short-term conclusion after reading this report and talking to Gary Black about his pheasant sightings—better get on out to South Dakota and hook up with Ed and Puppy and get some pheasants while the getting is good! Unlike many other landowners in South Dakota and neighboring pheasant states, Gary Black had expanded his CRP acreage for pheasants rather than turn more land into corn crops for ethanol-production dollars. I was very anxious to get to Blacks and check out Gary's wildlife improvements and especially all those pheasants.

Arrival: November 11, 2007

When I arrived at the Sioux Falls airport, I joined Ed and a small group of deer hunters who were sipping some wine, discussing their successes in Western South Dakota, and watching the Green Bay Packers beat the Minnesota Vikings. Ed left our impromptu hunting discussion group at the bar to go to his car and get some copies of two of his books, *Crazy Horse and Chief Red Cloud*, and a recently published work, *Creator's Code*.[2]

(Note: I have read all of Ed McGaa's books, but he had sneaked the last one by me. I highly recommend its "no-holds-barred" exploration of Sioux history and its deep, penetrating analysis of the spiritual world of the Sioux). When Ed returned from the airport parking lot with a box of books, he was accompanied by his friend, hunting companion, and my instant buddy from last year, a Golden Retriever named "Puppy." Puppy was without a leash, and trailed nonchalantly behind Ed. While Ed and I continued to swap stories with deer hunters from Atlanta, Georgia, Puppy went behind the bar to "assist" the Sunday afternoon bartender/cook with his food and drink chores. Everyone around bought books, including the bartender who was very pleased to get autographed copies with explanations about the two works that he had purchased. While these literary transactions were occurring, Puppy was having a steak snack compliments of our intellectual bartender host, who by this time had organized a mini Sunday afternoon seminar on Sioux Indian Culture conducted by Sioux author, Eagle Man (Ed McGaa). Sioux Falls happens to be South Dakota's largest airport and Puppy was being treated just like any other 'customer' as he relaxed behind the bar. Somehow, the football game got lost in all of this shuffle, and we said our warm farewells and went our separate ways. No wonder I look forward to going out west to hunt pheasants with Ed and Puppy. You never know what's coming next.

As we walked across the parking lot I was surprised when Ed said, "Here's the car." Apparently the 1989 Cadillac Pheasantmobile from last year had died and been replaced by a Pontiac mini-Pheasantmobile of newer but slightly lesser stature. Puppy's rear seat throne had gotten small though it still looked very comfortable and cozy. I checked out "my" Benelli 24" semi-automatic shotgun that I used last year, scanned the trunk area making sure that "my" shells were in good supply and, as requested, phoned Gary Black to tell his mama that we would be in Estelline for supper in a few hours. After stuffing ourselves like Thanksgiving turkey, we turned in fairly early with Puppy sleeping at the foot of my bed. I am sure that at least two of us counted pheasants to help us go to sleep.

On Golden Pond: November 12, 2007

After a good night's rest we took our time eating a Midwestern country breakfast, and over a second cup of coffee, we asked Gary where to hunt. His quick answer, "Just about anywhere around here. Birds are all over the place." A hunter from Ontario, Canada and a South Dakota kennel owner would be hunting on one small area of Blacks' approximately two square mile fields, and we decided to take a slow walk around a large pond/small lake directly behind Blacks' hunting cabins. Since we were 'old hat' clients by now, we had a blue pickup at our disposal. But, we elected to take our hunting jaunt beginning with broom and canary grass bordering the pond only a few yards from our comfortable cabin. So far as I know, this small body of water surrounded by thick cattails, and several varieties of CRP grasses bordered by corn fields had no name. Within a few hours and without authorization, I would name it Golden Pond because of all of those ringnecks hanging out around there.

Ever since our hunt last year, Ed and Puppy had convinced me to work slow and methodically and trust four-legged (i.e. Puppy) instincts more than those of mere human (i.e. Ed and myself). I assumed that pheasants would be on the outside rows of the corn, and we did flush some there. As a matter of fact, I dropped the first flushing rooster where the corn came up to the banks of Golden Pond. A good clean shot to begin a morning hunt can get one's day moving with confidence. After that, Puppy took over and led us into very thick cattail cover around and in the water.

Because I played baseball and spent many hours in nature as a child, I knew what "Ducks on the Pond" meant. Now, I was about to experience "Pheasants on the Pond" as instructed by Manager Puppy. After pointing and flushing four or five hens, a couple of nice roosters boiled up directly out of the water. Just after their wings slapped the cattails, they were downed by Ed's Super Eagle Benelli. I shot a rooster who fell dead in the water. A little later, unfortunately, I unloaded my gun across Golden Pond at a large rooster ring neck. Dropping wings, many feathers and one dangling leg later, and the rooster still flies. Two days later, I fired at this guy again, I believe, and unless a coyote, owl, or other predator has found him, he may still be waiting for me.

Appropriately, the most memorable action of day one involved my South Dakota hunting hosts – Ed and Puppy. My last year's description of the man/dog relationship was confirmed in one of those magic moments when one hunter stands motionless and watches another hunter work a good dog gently into the wind where the scent of pheasants abounds. Beautiful blue sky, rustling cattails, sun reflecting off Golden Pond, Ed and Puppy slowly stalking in the cattail/canary grass cover, Ed talking to Puppy, Puppy walking the walk, too busy to talk. Puppy points solidly at the water's edge. Ed hollers at me to come on down. I respond, "Go ahead, take him."

Ed moved in slowly and a large rooster flushed and squawked just in front of Puppy's nose. I believe that Ed's gun was loaded with a lead #6, two-and-three-fourths-inch shell in the chamber and a lead #5 in the tube, followed by #3, a steel #2 or #4, "three-incher," and at least one steel #2, "three-and-a-half-incher" as a backup shot for high flyers, fast flyers, and long flyers, as he would say. Both of the last two shells were 1550 or 1550 fps. I asked him why he didn't use lead for the longer shells and his response was simply – "too hard to find." He elaborated, "I shoot my geese with steel 2's at 1550 fps if I can get them. The faster the shell for a long shot, the better are your chances." This is one of the many lessons that Ed has tried to teach me in my two years of hunting with him—keep shooting and use the right shells.

In a rapid-fire sequence Ed empties his Benelli as the large bird soars across the pond. Puppy gets very excited as he watches his companion hit the bird with several shots. If you know Ed, you know that he never gives up! Just as I think, well another wounded bird gets away, Ed's last "three-and-a-half-incher" brings the pheasant down smack dab in the middle of Golden Pond. In the meantime, Puppy had not given up either. He was in the water just as the bird hit. The pheasant was literally swimming like a duck on the pond, and Puppy had to exert lots of energy for the retrieval. He returned the water-logged bird as Ed proudly watched while standing up to his knees in the cold water. Last year, I had witnessed Ed make "the highest flyer" pheasant shot that I had ever seen or heard of. This year, I would have to record this one as the "longest flyer" over water shot that I have personally seen. The only thing missing on our morning on Golden Pond was my digital or video camera. But, as is hopefully obvious from this written account, I have added this experience to my Disc of Life on the track marked notable hunting episodes with man and dog. Total pheasants in bag, six.

Bad Bird Day: November 13, 2007

Our second day of hunting was frustrating at best. We had started our morning with a long walk in very thick pheasant cover near Lake Poinsett. We had heard that this was a real hot spot for ring necks, and it looked really good to us in terms of habitat. Under very grey skies the three of us walked, walked, and walked. The wind was blowing, dark clouds were rolling, and early flusher hens were everywhere. Ed managed to knock a rooster down in a thicket cover near a fence line and with Puppy in the lead, the three of us searched heavy cover over and over again to no avail.

As we were returning to Black's for lunch, the farm mechanic waved at us from a large garage, near our cabin. As a matter of fact, he was trying to get us to come over and see a very large ring neck rooster plucking around a green grassy area underneath some rusty, abandoned farm machinery. The noon day sun was bright, the wind had slowed down, and this bird stood there before us as big as life. The old saying came to mind—"A bird in the hand is worth two in the bush." Well, this bird was not in our hand, but with a good dog, two good Benelli 12-gauge autos loaded to the hilt, one excellent shooter (Ed), and one average plus shooter (me), our chances of "bird in hand" were very good. The large rooster seemed to be tied underneath the old farm machinery. As we approached "Big Bird" with Puppy in the lead, Ed and I got ready. The rooster ran a few yards and took flight right in front of us, this time larger than life. Two empty guns later, and Bin Laden bird had escaped. Ed looked at me; I looked at him; Puppy looked a bit disgusted at both of us. I felt that the farm mechanic and a co-worker were laughing at us. They told us to go on the other side of a thicket where Bin Laden bird had flushed because they had seen another rooster fly in that direction. I could sense the determination in Ed to get at least one bird for our morning's efforts.

As we rounded the thicket and approached the top of a ridge overlooking Golden Pond, Puppy flushed a rooster just ahead of Ed. Ed swung his Benelli, fired a couple of rounds, and the squawking bird joined Bin Laden bird as a hunter escapee. Disgusted, two hunters and dog returned to Blacks with empty hunting bags, and a borderline sense of temporary powerlessness over escaping pheasants. After a short lunch and conversation with Gary over missed shots and elusive birds, we drove around late in the afternoon, sighted a large rooster by the side of the road, and followed him into some cattails along a small pond. Ed worked Puppy cautiously as I followed to one side. Ed seemed determined to get that rooster to end what has thus far been Bad Bird Day. Since I was Ed's guest from the east, he was trying to make sure that I got my share of birds. But, somehow I knew this one was his. Just about 30 minutes before the sun went down, Puppy leaps into the cover, Ed makes a swift clean shot, an instant retrieval followed, and as if proof were needed, Ed reconfirmed that his instincts, eyes, gun, ammo, and golden retriever were still in excellent working order for the next day's hunt. Ten minutes after Ed made his shot, I followed Puppy into a cattail thicket and knocked down my one and only rooster for the day. Total pheasants in bag, two.

"(S)hootnanny": A Musical Interlude After Supper

Evidence from European caves, Mayan pyramids, buffalo and deerhide skin drawings from the Great Plains, African wood carvings, Southwestern sandstone petroglyphs, and current outdoor channel TV programs indicates that man the hunter not only enjoys the quest and conquest related to the hunt, the kills, and the eating of game; but, that he also enjoys after-the-hunt celebration with fellow hunters and their families. We had not had a good day of hunting, but we had a wonderful night of eating, drinking several bottles of Gary Black's best wine, and singing many songs. Members of the Black family (Gary, Gary's son, Ma and Pa Black) gathered around the table. At my request, Gary's son found a guitar which had obviously not been played in a long time, and our lead singer, Ed, reared back in his chair and, as they would say down in my native Tennessee, "really let her rip." I got the worn-out-from-lack-of use guitar strings tuned up, and played song after song until my fingers hurt! Our instant and very improvisational music repertoire evolved into a rather large assortment of tunes from the 1940s onward. A few of our "hits" as my wine-clouded memory recalls were: "Ghost Riders in the Sky" (Ed–most all of the words); "Folsom Prison Blues" (Ed–some of the words); a 1944 version of "Sioux City Sioux" (me–all words learned from my Tennessee mom); several sing-along hymns with Ma Black taking an occasional lead; Janis Joplin's "Bobbie McGee" (me for Gary Black); old Hank Williams' classics; a Bluegrass medley; and a most surprisingly old Irish folk song from Gary's son that none of us, including his dad and grandparents, knew or had ever heard. He could really sing, and he really knew all of the words!! Subjectively speaking, like Garrison's Keillor's Kids of Lake Woebegone, we were all above average. After our Bad Bird Day, this was a great family night with friends. I will never forget Gary's statement "This is the best week of hunting that I have ever had." Gary, a big man of few words, spoke volumes for those of us sitting around and singing at Ma Blacks' table after supper. Somehow, missing a few pheasants on "Bad Bird Day" became almost insignificant.

Windwalkers: November 12, 2007 (a.m.)

Today's weather forecast for the Estelline, South Dakota area had been warm and windy with predicted gusts of 40 plus mph. Although I had seen this forecast just after our family music concert at Blacks,' and had heard about these western winds all of my life, I had never experienced them before, much less tried to shoot a fast-flying pheasant aided and abetted by wind power. Given these hunting conditions, Gary decided to go with us and provided some extra experienced dog power answering to the names of "Wolfman" and "Al." Dark, billowing grey clouds looked foreboding as we loaded up in two pickups with guns and dogs. Gary was right at home in these conditions, and Ed seemed to be on a pheasant mission to make up for our two-bird-only day the day before.

Gary took us through a very green field of oats as we approached a mixture of corn rows and thick CRP grass surrounding a pond. Our hunting strategy was as follows: Ed would take Puppy up ahead and block for us as Gary and I worked his two dogs down the corn rows and into the wind. (Later that evening after our hunt, I found out that these winds were 50 plus mph rather than the predicted 40 plus mph!) Many pheasants were getting up ahead of us. I noticed that those moving into the wind hung like kites on a string while those sailing with the wind looked more like the Phantom jets that Ed used to fly in Vietnam. To be honest, it was okay by me that these pheasants were "early risers" because my eyeglasses were clouding up and my eyes were watering with a mixture of sleet and rich black soil from a South Dakota cornfield. Excessive winds, cloudy glasses, watering eyes, and a borrowed Benelli – I had all of the excuses necessary for missing if a pheasant happened to launch in range.

Our first bird that day was a double kill with Ed shooting with the wind while I shot at the same time, swinging my gun counterclockwise against the wind. Although one should leave ego behind while hunting, I was glad to think that I put a few shots into the first pheasant for a little confidence under such challenging hunting conditions. Before we left this very rich hunting ground, Puppy pointed a pheasant at the pond's edge, and Ed downed it cleanly before it entered a tree-lined thicket. Although I really enjoy hunting with Gary and Ed, by this time I was ready for some soup and crackers from Ma Black's kitchen. This is exactly what was waiting for us when we took our noon break. If Ed had said let's give it up for the day, I would not have argued. He had just given me a copy of his new book, *Creator's Code – Planetary Survival and Beyond*. I was ready to stay in the cabin for some R & R – reading and rest.

Mission Accomplished: November 14 (p.m.)

As most of you who are reading this know, the pheasant bag limit in South Dakota is three birds per person per day. Ed and I now had bagged two pheasants, and my intuition told me that a little wind, grey skies, and a non-ideal hunting day would not deter a determined Eagle Man who had still not shaken off what he perceived as a poor pheasant shooting venture yesterday and on this windy morning. After a warm bowl of soup and a boots-off hour respite, we were ready to roll (or at least walk) about 2:00 p.m.

In the early afternoon we hunted an area of thick cover behind Blacks' cabins. We had seen pheasants there on day one and Gary had told us to try our luck there. We jumped lots of hens and I got one long shot at what I thought was the rooster that got away on day one. His leg was dangling, but he still was able to escape my shots and fly across Golden Pond to the other side. Ed dropped a rooster after Puppy flushed him out of a thick cattail-covered marshland. We then entered one of South Dakota's public access areas where we got up a solitary hen and got into Gary's pick up which we had parked adjacent to the public access land (For those of you not familiar with this type of open-to-all small game licensed hunters, you can consult the South Dakota Game, Fish & Parks website at www.sdgfp.info). The wind had died down slightly but the skies remained dull and grey as we contemplated our remaining hour or so of hunting before the sun went down.

As we rode along a back road which accessed a large Black Angus cattle operation containing corn fields, prairie grass pasture lands, and bountiful CRP lands, pheasants were crossing the road in droves. This sight reminded me of my youth in Middle Tennessee when World War II veterans had taken me dove and quail hunting on excellent bird cover which has since all but vanished in this part of my native state. Gary had described the land along this South Dakota back road as a pheasant "honey hole," and all of those road-crossing birds had suggested that he knew what he was talking about. I was looking at what could be called a veritable pheasant airport! Ed let me out of Gary's pickup (or, by this time was it Ed's truck?) upon a ridge overlooking "honey hole," and drove back down to the main road. He told me to come down through the corn and CRP rows and that he would be blocking near the intersection of the back and main roadways. By this time, I would estimate our remaining hunting time to be 20 minutes at best. I was also beginning to think that this day would close with less than a half of our daily pheasant bag limit realized. But once again, my less than optimistic outlook on a cloudy, windy, and now approaching dark day had to be temporarily put aside as Ed waved his arms for me to come on down to the corner where dog, truck, and an experienced pheasant hunter were blocking.

I jumped a few hens as I proceeded toward the main road. As I approached Ed and Puppy standing near the pickup truck, Ed started firing and yelled up at me—"We got all kinds of roosters flocking down here-come on down, they are scattered everywhere in this thick stuff." Within a couple of minutes, both of us were filling the air with shot many of which found their mark at the assembled cockbird covey. Puppy was jumping all around and he was having a tough time trying to decide which of our four downed pheasant roosters to pick up first. Ed and I have hunted together enough not to worry about who shot what and scorekeeping. I have a suspicion that he got more than I did. But just as the sun was going down, the time of Wiyo (the sun) – peyata (it goes down) in the language of the Lakota Sioux, we tossed the birds into the back of Gary's (Ed's) truck. Puppy jumps up in the truck bed with the six roosters. Did I sense a look of canine accomplishment on his face, to match Ed's countenance as we drove off down the road?

"Cornfield Corner" and Return to Golden Pond: November 15, 2007

After "windwalking" under the previous day's grey skies, we awoke to an absolutely beautiful morning of warm weather, clear blue skies, and very little wind. We decided to limit our hunt to a half-day so we could rest the muscle and bones of dog and man. Ed is 71 years old and I am 66, and we admit our ages and our need for rest. In dog years, Puppy is middle-aged, but he too looked as if he could use a limited day's hunt.

We began our hunt at last year's "Cornfield Corner" where we bagged four roosters late one November afternoon just before the sun went down. Marshland and two ponds surround this corner just down the road from Blacks,' but this year the former cornfield had already been plowed. Ominously, we spotted a large rooster on the left side of the public highway as we parked our vehicle. I knew that Ed would want to pursue this just-sighted ring neck before we proceeded any further.

We moved away from the highway and Puppy closely searched the cattails where we had seen "first bird" go in. Ed worked Puppy into the wind, and I knew that he wanted me to take the first shot. As I anticipated, the rooster took flight on the pond bank near where a back road met the main road. I swung to my left at ten o'clock, and "plop" the beautiful rooster fell dead in the middle of the access road. Puppy retrieved it to me, and I proudly put it in my hunting vest. Somehow, I knew that the three of us were beginning a fantastic morning of wing shooting.

Bird two was downed about 15 minutes after Bird #1. Ed worked one side of a pond/marshland, and I went with Puppy down the other. Just as Puppy and I came to our end of the pond bank, he absolutely froze in the thick cattail cover. I mean <u>froze</u>! He was shaking with intensity, and I bent over within a foot or so of the end of his pulsating nostrils. I really thought that I would be able to see an anticipated hen crouching with fright. I kicked the cattails one time, and a giant rooster zoomed directly over my head to the shouts of Ed's "Take him!" Though startled, I swung the 24" Benelli around counterclockwise as the ring-neck headed directly over the center of the pond. I fired a two-and-three-fourths-inch #6 and got feathers. This was followed by two three-inchers, #2 shots which may have hit the pheasant both times. On the last shot, the pheasant dropped in a median cover strip at the pond's center. From years of dove and quail hunting, I thought that this pheasant acted as if he had been hit in the head by the way he soared upward just before he fell. I was fairly sure that Puppy and I would locate this bird as Ed walked to the car to get his camera. We went all the way to the other end of the pond, and Puppy brought me the results of my longest, successful, pheasant shot ever made. Ed had been trying for two years to get me to load my gun properly, and "keep shootin'." This time I listened, and it paid off…great point, decent persistent shooting, great Puppy work on retrieve, and a good photograph of Puppy, Joel, and downed "longshot ringneck."

Return to Golden Pond

With two pheasants in tow, we returned to the site of day one's hunt on Golden Pond just behind Blacks' cabins. With any luck, there would be some big old roosters hanging out in all of that good cattail/canary grass cover and marsh surrounding the pond. Our approach would be to slowly work the pond's edge under Puppy's instincts and guidance. Ed and I decided to stay close to one another and Puppy because he had put up many birds there just four days earlier.

After three hens flushed at the corner of the pond near our parked pickup, Puppy got real birdy just ahead of Ed. A large rooster splashed and squawked just to Ed's right. Ed made a good clean shot, and Puppy brought him his first pheasant for the day. We eased on around Golden Pond, and Ed and I fired at the same time and dropped a large rooster about ten feet into the water. Just as this rooster fell, another one flushed behind Ed and headed into a cornfield on a small rise above Golden Pond. He turned and made what I thought was a dead shot a few rows into the corn. He told me to "get that bird outta the weeds, and Puppy and I will find that one in the cornfield." As the sun shown brightly on Golden Pond, my "walk in the grass" changed into wading in the water following a trail of feathers floating on the still icy pond. After much persistence, I saw the pheasant's gleaming multicolored breast reflecting the noonday sun. I picked up the water-logged bird and temporarily ignored my totally soaked pants, underwear, and soaked, layered leather boots. I went up to check on Ed's progress in his and Puppy's bird search in the cornfield. He told me that they had used a grid search pattern and covered many square feet of cornrows to no avail. Another elusive "dead falling" pheasant had escaped. Ed's theory was that the bird may have made it into an animal's hole where it would probably die and/or be consumed by a wily predator coyote.

On our return to Blacks, we hunted a narrow strip of marsh cover just across from Cornfield Corner. I knew that Ed wanted one more bird in the bag. As we walked side by side behind Puppy, a big old rooster exploded straight ahead of Ed. One shot, one bird. Ed finishes the hunt clean and solid. Actually the anticipated half-day hunt had lasted about one-and-a-half-hours. Five pheasants to show and one at-large escapee. A great hunting morning had ended, and four days later, after I returned to Virginia, my waterlogged hunting boots were still drying in front of the fireplace.

Public Access/Walk-In

After four great days of hunting at Blacks,' Ed, Puppy, and I headed toward Brookings, South Dakota to have dinner with some of Ed's family, and find a hot tub to soak our weary bones and muscles. On our way to Brookings, and later the next day, on our way to Sioux Falls for my return flight, we decided to see if we could find a few more roosters in three of South Dakota's General Hunting Access Walk-In Areas. We met and communicated with a few pheasant hunters, but did not put up a single rooster in a couple of long walks in good cover which seemed to have been hunted very heavily during the past month.

For 15 years the South Dakota Game, Fish & Parks has worked with private landowners to provide hunting access to approximately one million acres of CRP or other wildlife habitat areas. In exchange for a small payment/acre and immunity from non-negligent liability, private South Dakota landowners (who control about 80 percent of the state's land base) open their land to unlimited, free public hunting on a "foot-traffic only" hunting basis. Other activities such as target shooting, camping, horseback riding, fishing, or dog training are prohibited, and the Game, Fish & Parks requests that hunters should not contact cooperating landowners to hunt other portions of their lands. All South Dakota Access Program Lands are clearly marked with white, green and white, and yellow markers which read respectively, "Walk-In Area Foot Traffic Only," –Game, Fish & Parks "Waterfowl Production Area" –United States Department of the Interior, Fish and Wildlife Service, and "State Game Production Area" –Game, Fish & Parks.[3]

Year Two Reflection

Yes, endless cover for game birds is about as close to nature as a person can get.[4]

See the tall grass prairie for itself, and you begin to suspect that grasses are what hold this world together.[5]

It is imperative that wildlife enthusiasts actively involve themselves in the process of making sure Congress fully supports future programs such as CRP.[6]

My return trip to South Dakota for a few days of pheasant hunting with Ed and Puppy eliminated the "Winghunting Blues" illness (a debility common to former quail and grouse in the state of Virginia) that I was experiencing in late October and November of 2007. With good Benelli auto 12-gauges, appropriate mixed loads of two-and-three-fourths-inch, three-inch, and three-and-a-half-inch shells, and a clipped, close stalking and careful working Golden Retriever, Ed McGaa and I bagged about 19 birds at Blacks' Pheasant Fields in the Eastern Prairie Region near Estelline. I recycled many fond memories from the previous year, made some decent shots, and continued my pheasant-hunting lessons from Ed and Puppy. This year, I learned to be more attentive in regard to shell loads and their proper sequencing in the chamber of "my" borrowed Benelli. I learned, or re-learned to always be on the lookout for big old roosters who seem to dare you to come after them as they proudly strut on South Dakota roadways. On more than one occasion each year, a roadway-rooster sighting was our beginning bagged bird for the day's hunt. I also re- learned to persevere until just before sunset. Never be surprised after a long day of unproductive hunting to bust four pheasant roosters in the last 20 minutes of legal hunt time. Ed McGaa, pheasant hunter, would agree with my dad, Ed Tate, who taught me not just to keep on, but to "keep on keeping on" whether chasing a baseball in the outfield or hunting quail and pheasant. Ed is still trying to teach me to be ready to roll with my gun as soon as we exit the Pheasantmobile or Gary Black's blue pickup. Ed reverently calls it, 'Ol' Blue.' I mean Really ready, shells-assorted-in-hunting-vest, gloves-on, boots-tied, gun-ready, ready. I may have to come back next year (and specialize in readiness training) for a Junior year in the pheasant field with my two Pheasant Professor friends.

Direct hunting experience on well-managed CRP, and research on CRP, prairie vegetation, pheasant population trends for 20 plus years, and the man/pheasant connection have shown me that, like global warming, the pheasant hunting future depends on both nature (climate, floods, and droughts), and human nurture (e.g. wildlife habitat preservation/enhancement such as CRP, public/private conservation efforts such as the South Dakota Game, Fish & Parks and private landholder walk-in access agreements; and continued hunter/non-hunter support for wildlife conservation efforts at the local, state, and national levels). A very recent draft report, and strategic plan from the South Dakota DFP (November 27, 2007) includes the following issues, challenges, and opportunities for promoting private lands habitat and access programs for the foreseeable future.[7] These include among others:

1. Support for the National 2007 Farm Bill and future funding for USDA programs such as CRP.
2. A local level involvement process to maintain/increase wildlife populations by the improvement of respective habitat. A synergistic relationship between South Dakota Game, Fish & Parks wildlife, Pheasants Forever, Farm Bill biologists, and local partners should facilitate effective program delivery.
3. Habitat loss–Issue areas here include increased urban sprawl, degradation and conversion of native grasslands, loss of wetlands, pollution, and increasing property values/taxes.
4. Landowner demographics–A reduction in the "tie" to the land. This is related to the aging of the farming community and the extent to which agri-business is replacing agriculture.

5. Ensure South Dakota Game, Fish & Parks's program of hunting access to private lands. Maintain the Walk-In Area program and monitor payment rates to private landowners, hunting pressure levels, and qualitative hunting areas.

6. Biofuel/ethanol challenges–Basically the question is: Will the ethanol production process (i.e. more corn acreage) put undue pressure on CRP lands and native grassland?

7. Funding sources for habitat–"As a result of prospering wildlife populations, especially the ring-necked pheasant, hunting license sales have provided adequate funding to support habitat programs that compliment CRP..."[8] Alternative funding sources should be explored by the Game, Fish & Parks to ensure optimum habitat requirements for game/non-game species.

8. Public outreach and education programs on habitat–Citizens are urged to use the Internet (especially Game, Fish & Parks's private lands habitat program webpage) for information and communication on South Dakota wildlife.

9. Promote habitat with conservation partnering–The South Dakota Game, Fish & Parks should continue to work closely with such entities as the USDA, Pheasants Forever, the Nature Conservancy, and private landowners to complete habitat programs on private land.

10. Potential challenges as a result of global climate change–Changes in rainfall patterns, length of growing seasons, and species distribution will impact habitat and associated wildlife populations, including the expansion/contraction of species range and the loss of certain species sensitive to climate change.[9]

Conclusion

Habitat has been defined as "the natural environment of an organism; place that is natural for the life and growth of an organism."[10] Unlike Indian Grass and Big Bluestem, the ring-necked pheasant is not a species indigenous to the fertile prairie lands of the Great Western Plains. Pheasants came to the New World because human brought them here. With Creator's assistance, Human can help to keep them here, and promote their continued survival on Mother Earth.

Food for Thought: Pheasants and the Conservation Reserve Program (CRP)

While hunting on the property maintained by Blacks' Pheasant Fields, I noticed the extent to which these fields had been planned and planted to balance and maintain the food and cover requirements of South Dakota ringnecks. Blacks' "About the Hunt" brochure reveals a working with nature approach so vital to present and future pheasant populations of South Dakota and other Pheasant Belt States.

We have taken land out of agricultural production and planted millet, milo, sorghum, sudan grass and corn strips for some excellent hunting and food for the birds. Through the winter, with the abundance of food and natural habitat and hundreds of acres of CRP, we can maintain a very healthy number of birds.[1]

I told my hunting partner, Ed McGaa (Eagle Man), that when I returned to Virginia, I would research CRP and explore the extent to which my observations and discussions with Gary Black regarding pheasant food and CRP cover were representative of what's happening elsewhere in pheasant country in and around what has been called, arguably, the "Pheasant Capital" of the world – South Dakota.

CRP - Past, Present, and Future?

Created in 1985 with the passage of the Food Security Act and administered by the USDA's Farm Service Agency (FSA), the Conservation Reserve
Program (CRP) is the nation's largest conservation program designed to protect
the natural resource bases of soil, water, and wildlife on private land. Annual
rental payments and cost-share assistance are offered to agricultural land owners
and farm operators who volunteer former cropland or marginal acreage deemed
eligible by local FSA offices in consultation with state and federal agriculture
and conservation officials. CRP participants enroll in contracts for ten to fifteen
years based upon an Environmental Benefits Index which relatively weighs the
following environmental criteria for the proposed CRP allotment/benefits:

1. Air quality benefits from reduced wind erosion.
2. On-farm benefits of reduced erosion.
3. Wildlife habitat benefits that encourage covers and habitats on contract acreage that will be most beneficial to wildlife.
4. Water quality benefits from reduced erosion, runoff, and leaching.
5. Benefits of enrollment in conservation priority areas where enrollment
   would contribute to the improvement of water quality, wildlife habitat, or air quality.
6. Benefits that will likely endure beyond the contract period (e.g. later
   enrollment in Wetland/Grassland Cost Share Programs, Prairie Pothole Wetlands and Associated Upland Habitats, Non-Cropped Wetland Restoration Initiatives, Food Habitat Plots Establishment, and
   Native Warm Season Grass Establishment Projects).[2]

P.F. (Pheasants Forever) is a non-profit wildlife conservation and habitat
improvement organization which works closely with local, state, and federal
agencies to promote CRP initiatives, including those programs connected to the
enhancement of quail, grouse and pheasant populations across the United States.
A recent newsletter from Pheasants Forever, contains a CRP timeline, highlight-
ing the development and current status of the Conservation Reserve Program.

Timeline:
  1970s – End of Soil Bank Era
  1985 – Passage of the Food Security Act establishing CRP
  1986–1989 – Over 34 million acres are enrolled in CRP
  1990 – Reauthorization of CRP in the Farm Bill
  1991 – 1994–2.5 million acres added to CRP
  1996 – Continuation of CRP in Farm Bill
  1997 – Largest CRP re-enrollment sign up with over 16 million acres
     accepted

2002 – Increase in CRP available acres from 36.4 million to 39.2 million in the Farm Bill

2006 – Current Enrollment is 35 million acres out of 39.2 million

2007 – More than 16 million acres of CRP will expire.[3]

According to nationwide CRP data released by the United Department of Agriculture (USDA) for September through November 2006, there were approximately 740,000 active CRP contracts existing with approximately 425,000 farms, whose combined CRP acreage allotment totaled just over 36 million acres. Producers holding these contracts were scheduled to receive slightly less than $1.8 billion (United States dollars) in 2006, based upon an average expenditure of $48.88/acre. These payments allow participating producers to earn an average of $4,143 per farm enrolled in CRP. Comparable statistics for the state of South Dakota for the same time period were: approximately 28,500 active CRP contracts, on just over 14,000 farms, totaling 1.5 million acres. For the year 2006, South Dakota CRP enrollees were to receive approximately $63 million.[4] Future projections and speculations regarding the 2007 Farm Bill proposals from the USDA, and a tentative commitment from President George Bush suggest that CRP expenditures, and acreage allotments will total respectively $1.8 billion (United States dollars) and about 36 million CRP acres for fiscal year 2007. According to USDA Secretary Mike Johanns, President Bush is "committed to fully utilizing the 39.2 million acre enrollment authority under CRP."[5]

CRP Acre Allotments: The Top 12 States

As of September, 2006 USDA CRP data revealed that the top 12 states in the United States in terms of CRP acreage enrollment were in approximate CRP-rank order-Texas (four plus million acres); Montana (3.4 plus million acres); North Dakota (3.4 million acres); Kansas (3.1 million acres); Colorado (2.4 million acres); Iowa (1.9 million acres); Minnesota (1.8 million acres); Missouri (1.6 million acres); South Dakota (1.5 million acres); Washington (1.4 plus million acres); Nebraska (1.3 million acres); and Oklahoma (one plus million acres).[6]

The rounded-off combined CRP acres for these 12 states is 26.8 million acres, (equivalent to my home state of Tennessee), which constitutes three fourths (74 percent) of the total United States CRP allotment of 36 million CRP acres, a land area equal to the size of Iowa.[7] Many of these states contain the most bountiful pheasant populations in this country. Is there a connection or correlation between CRP and the number of pheasants born and harvested? What are the benefits of millions of CRP acres and a $2 billion investment in this program?

CRP: (Not Just) For the Birds

Two thirds of all United States conservation payments go to producers participating in the CRP and CREP (Conservation Reserve Enhancement Program), a federal-state partnership to further local conservation goals including planting tree and grassland buffers along stream banks. Most of the remaining third is distributed through the Wetland Reserve Program which restores and preserves wetlands that have been converted to cropland; the EQIP (Environmental Quality Incentives Program) which provides financial and technical assistance to install conservation practices on eligible agricultural land; and the CSP (Conservation Security Program) which pays producers to conserve and to protect watersheds. An Executive Summary on Conservation and the Environment (USDA June 2006) and recent fact sheets from Pheasants Forever, and the Theodore Roosevelt Conservation Partnership show how these programs have accomplished many environmental goals related to the following:

- **Soil Erosion and Productivity** – A drop of 1.3 billion tons per year of soil erosion between 1982 and 2003, and estimated soil productivity benefits of $162 million with CRP, EQIP, and changing production factors as the major contributing factors.[8]
- **Wetlands** – Agriculture experienced a net gain of over 260,000 acres from 1997–2003 with CRP and WRP as major contributors to wetland restoration. Two million acres of wetlands and adjacent buffers were restored.[9]
- **Water Quality** – In addition to soil erosion reduction, the annual CRP water quality benefit of reduced sediment load is an estimated $266 million. EQIP and similar programs have also reduced nutrient and pesticide runoff. WRP and CREP filters sediment and nutrients from cropland runoff before they reach streams or lakes. 170,000 stream miles have been protected.[10]
- **Air Quality** – The air quality impact of agriculture includes odor, ozone precursors, ammonia, particulate emissions, and greenhouse gases. The USDA is giving increasing emphasis to these concerns. Since 2003, the USDA targeted greenhouse gases through EQIP and related efforts, and estimates that an additional 12 million metric tons of carbon dioxide will be reduced from the atmosphere by 2012. 48 million metric tons of carbon dioxide have already been reduced by these USDA programs.[11]
- **Wildlife Habitat** – The USDA concludes that its conservation programs "have made major contributions to establishment of wildlife habitat and enhancement," including increases of waterfowl and grassland bird populations on current CRP land that had experienced a serious decline in these populations during the 1970s–1980s. In the

Western states, which include most of the "top 12" CRP states noted above, the animal population increase includes big game elk, white-tailed deer, mule deer, pronghorn antelope, and, especially for those of you reading this work, ringneck pheasants.[12] Spin-off economic benefits to wildlife population increases and habitat improvement include estimates of at least $4.7 billion of hunting expenditures, and $629 million expenditures for wildlife viewing. Large portions of these funds directly benefit local communities.[13]

• **Wildlife Habitat and the Future** – Key challenges for the future of CRP and its supporting network of conservation efforts include controlling excess nutrients in rivers, streams, lakes, and estuaries of the Gulf of Mexico and Chesapeake Bay; insuring water avail-ability for agriculture, environmental, and urban use; protecting existing and endangered flora and fauna species; lowering rising greenhouse gas emissions, and exploring the future environmental implications of tapping renewable energy sources such as biodiesel fuels and ethanol production from agricultural lands.[14]

The USDA recognizes that farm income may be adversely affected in the short-run if conservation measures such as CRP reduce crop production, in-crease crop prices, and decrease the purchase of local agricultural supplies by farmers, but a 2004 study concludes that "the negative effects of the CRP on rural economies tend to be small and transitory." According to the USDA, future conservation policy must balance farmer production and income with the quali-tative environmental benefits previously described.[15]

CRP: "Really for the Birds" (Literally)

Without question, CRP is probably the single most important wildlife habi-tat program in modern times. In 1986 South Dakota had an estimated pheasant population of 2.1 million birds, one of the lowest numbers in 15 years. Since the establishment of CRP, pheasant populations have hit a 45-year high and pheas-ant hunting supports a $153 million per year industry.

A variety of wildlife species benefit from CRP. For example, CRP provides nesting habitats and is the main reason our pheasant hunting has been so good.... Without CRP, or a program that duplicates its wildlife values, we all lose...John Cooper, Secretary, South Dakota Department of Game, Fish, and Parks.[16]

...record harvests are a direct result of CRP acres, Pheasants Forever habi-tat projects, mild winters, and favorable spring nesting conditions. CRP equals more pheasants. It is that simple. Dave Nomsen, Pheasants Forever Vice Presi-dent of Governmental Affairs.[17]

Hunting in South Dakota is as good as it gets because three essential ele-ments are present: habitat, habitat, and habitat.... Those components are:

1. Habitat for breeding.
2. Habitat for avoiding predators.
3. Habitat for winter survival.[18]

Counting Pheasants Scientifically

In August 2006, USDA Secretary Mike Johanns announced the findings of a comprehensive, scientific investigation which statistically documents the quoted assertions above.[19] The 53-page study was conducted and prepared for the USDA Farm Service by Western EcoSystems Technology, Inc. and represents pheasant survey data within the ring-necked pheasant range of these states: Minnesota, North Dakota, South Dakota, Nebraska, Kansas, Missouri, Utah, Idaho, and Oregon. The entire report, entitled, "Estimating Response of Ring-necked Pheasant (*Phasianus colchicus*) to the Conservation Reserve Program" is not light, bedtime reading, but its overall findings and implications are significant for CRP benefits in general, and for those of us interested in the maintenance and enhancement of *Phasianus colchicus* populations.[20]

Using complicated statistical models related to percentages of major habitat types (e.g. nature of vegetative cover, forested, developed, agricultural field, and wetland), the research team computed Breeding Bird Survey (BBS) counts of ring-necked pheasants along 388 survey routes in the sample states from 1987–2005. The primary objective of the report was the assessment of how pheasants have responded to CRP practices on sensitive cropland, including pasture. In statistical terminology, habitat features including CRP categories were the independent, predictor variables in the study, and the dependent variable was pheasant populations as counted along BBS routes. In other words, how are pheasants responding to the habitat development and land use modifications associated with the implementation of CRP practices?[21]

Research Findings and Implications

The major findings of the study which can be replicated in this and other CRP impact regions in the future was an estimated 22 percent increase in ring-necked pheasant count along a survey route associated with every 788 acre increase of CRP herbaceous vegetation. The acreage increase was 4.05 percent for an average buffer zone. In layman's terms, this translates into a 22 percent increase in ringneck pheasant counts for every four percent increase in CRP enrolled acres along the route.[22] In response to this study, Pheasants Forever created a statistical model and a pheasant number predictor equation which includes number of pheasant nests per CRP acre, eggs per nest, nest success, and brood survival. *Pheasants Forever estimates that 25.5 million CRP acres within the pheasant range produce an estimated 13.5 million pheasants per year.* [23] That CRP lands might generate population increases in the habitat breeding ranges of other grassland species of birds such as the sharp-tailed grouse and sedge wren is also suggested in the USDA study.[24] In the future, CRP lands may be prime visiting spots for bird watchers and photographers and not just pheasant hunters. However, Pheasants Forever biologists and officials recognize that habitat criteria may be strongly influenced by harsh winters, wet springs, and summer droughts such as occurred during the summer of 2006.[25]

Pheasants Forever pheasant harvest studies for 2005 and for the 2006 hunting season, including many of the "Top 12" CRP-acreage states, and the nine states sampled in the Ecosystems Technology Study CRP pheasant study, seem to corroborate the CRP/pheasant population connection as well as the vagaries of Plain states weather patterns.[26] Pheasants Forever forecasts reported and predicted the following pheasant conditions in six of these states:

- **Kansas** – The 2005 harvest of around 800,000 roosters. Predicted "landmark season" for 2006. Realities of drought conditions and late wheat harvests negatively impacted nesting success and brook survival. The 2006 pheasant harvest estimate of 600,000–700,000 roosters or a return to 2003–2004 pheasant population conditions. CRP acres released for emergency haying/grazing may modify walk-in hunting acres.
- **Minnesota** – In 2005, the best pheasant harvest in 40 years, 586,000 roosters. Half a million plus pheasants bagged in two of the last three years. Mild winter and increase in broods for 2006. Gains in grassland areas, accounting for six percent of the Minnesota landscape, and farm programs working with Pheasants Forever chapters may be responsible "for returning Minnesota's bird numbers to the 'good old days.'"
- **Missouri** – Northeast and northwest corners have the most CRP acres, and "consequently the most birds." Favorable winter and spring should lead to a pheasant harvest within the range of the state's 30,000 bird average.
- **Nebraska** – In 2005, 437,000 roosters taken, the highest total in five years. Mild winter, normal spring, similar season for fall 2006. Excellent hunting offered on private lands through CRP MAP (Managed Area Program) Cooperation. Public access to nearly 200,000 CRP acres/year. CREP (Conservation Reserve Enhancement Program) and Focus on Pheasants Programs are increasing wildlife habitat.
- **North Dakota** – In 2005, estimated harvest of 809,000 roosters. Year 2005 reported as "the best pheasant season since the Soil Bank Era over 40 years ago" (State Biologist, Stan Kohn). Extremely mild winter and three plus million CRP acres of pheasant habitat are plus

factors for 2006. Dry conditions in the summer may be negative for brood size. Numbers of pheasants should be increasing elsewhere.
- **South Dakota** – Year 2006 prediction that "The Pheasant Capital" will not disappoint pheasant hunters. A relative mild winter and good spring nesting conditions in 2006 were favorable. Stage set for a "Monster" 2006 season, but a summer drought hit central/north-central South Dakota. Perhaps 2006 will produce a similar pheasant harvest to 2005 which set a 40-year high-harvest number of 1.9 plus million roosters, double the size of any other state. No secret to these numbers 1.4 plus million acres of CRP land. Pheasants Forever recommends reauthorization of CRP in the 2007 Farm Bill. Total pheasant harvest for 2006? If 2006 is not the "Monster year" for pheasant populations, perhaps we should "blame" the weather, not CRP. [27]

Note: Pheasant hunters and anyone else supporting wildlife conservation or hunting interests should check the excellent Pheasants Forever website (http://www.pheasantsforever.org/hunting/lifecycle) for continuing pheasant forecasts for each state and pertinent CRP developments. In addition to this, Pheasants Forever provides detailed illustrative diagrams of pheasant biology, including the four major phases of a pheasant's annual life cycle (nesting, brood rearing, foraging, and winter survival) roughly aligned with the spring, summer, fall, and winter seasons.[28] Pheasants Forever should be recognized for its outstanding contributions toward the maintenance and enhancement of pheasant populations in South Dakota and neighboring states.

CRP for Other Birds: Grouse, Quail, and Waterfowl

Two other scientific investigations show that USDA/CRP efforts have increased the populations of sage grouse in eastern Washington State, and quail in Nebraska, Kansas, and Missouri. In October, 2006 the Washington Department of Fish and Wildlife issued a detailed report entitled, "Use of CRP Fields by Greater Sage-grouse and Other Shrubsteppe Associated Wildlife in Washington." Data on sage-grouse populations were analyzed for the years 1992–2006.

In summary form the central findings and suggestions were:

- The sage grouse population grew approximately 12 percent after covers matured on CRP acreage, even though the region concerned had witnessed a 25 percent sage grouse population decrease between 1970–1988, prior to CRP availability.
- Without CRP, populations of the same species continued to decline in the years of the investigation.

- Sage-grouse increase may be explained by the abundance of big sage-brush, growth of perennial grasses and the increasing success of sage-grouse nesting in CRP and/or grouse recognition of CRP as a potential nesting habitat.
- It is likely that the population in the study would be "severely impacted if the CRP program ended."[29]

A similar study of northern bobwhite quail conducted in 2005–2006 by Mississippi State University in Nebraska, Kansas, and Missouri concluded that populations of this species increased approximately three percent in CRP-enrolled lands.[30]

The relationship between duck populations and CRP is currently being documented in studies of wetlands in the Prairie Pothole Regions of Minnesota, Montana, North Dakota, South Dakota, and Iowa. CRP enrollments in the Duck Nesting Habitat Initiative have restored approximately 100,000 acres of wetland ecosystems in these states with the primary aims of protecting water quality and increasing quality nesting habitat. According to John Johasson, FSA/USDA spokesperson, duck populations are to increase by an estimated 60,000 birds/year. Johasson estimates that CRP has restored two million wetland buffer areas in the United States, and that CRP has added 2.2 million new ducks/year to our waterfowl flyways. Program sign-ups will terminate at the end of 2007. (See Conservation Reserve Program, "Wetlands Will Further Increase Duck Numbers" News Release-USDA at http://www.fsa.usda.gov.)[31]

CRP Farmer/Pheasant Success Stories

During my three-day pheasant hunt with Ed McGaa on Blacks' Pheasant Fields I had many pleasant conversations with Gary Black, the overall manager of the food plots, ground cover, and pheasant hunting operations at Blacks.' The following questions were posed in my earthy Middle Tennessee dialect, slightly diluted by my 37 years of residence in Central Virginia. His answers were spoken in that guttural Midwestern, "You bet," "Noooo," and "YEP!" that I cannot effectively duplicate orally, or in writing. Nevertheless, here's what he had to say about land, pheasants, and CRP (JCT=me; GB=Gary Black):

> JCT: Gary, what is the total size of your pheasant hunt area here?
> GB: 2000 acres.
> JCT: What is the approximate acreage of your milo, corn, sorghum, or other planted food crops?
> GB: 300–500 acres. It varies.
> JCT: You have mentioned CRP quite often. How many acres do you have enrolled in CRP?
> GB: About 600 acres

JCT: What type of grass or cover crops does the CRP support, and what kinds of sowed grasses do we see around here? How can I recognize them? (See Appendix A for a list of "Allowable Grass Varieties for South Dakota CRP," compliments of Gary Black and distributed by the USDA-NRCS October 7, 1998). Pipestone National Monument and the National Park Service distribute a very informative brochure entitled, "Tallgrass Prairie" which describes and illustrates many of these and other grasses native to the Midwestern Prairie regions. (See Appendix B attachment or contact the Pipestone National Monument office for more details).

GB: Mainly Switchgrass, Indiangrass, Sideoats, Big Bluestem, and Canary grass. Switchgrass has those tiny seeds at the top that get into a dog's eye. Indian grass has thin stems, is kinda gray-looking, and has fuzzy tops with small seeds. Sideoats looks like small regular oats, and the tiny oats grow on the side of the head. Big Bluestem is that real tall, thick stuff that grows chest-high or more. Canary grass is that real thick stuff that is really hard to walk through.

JCT: Is Canary grass that stuff that we had to trudge through around those small ponds?

GB: YEP!! It'll really wear you out when it's wet with rain or snow!

JCT: Knowing that Gary was quite a wrestler and football player in his day, I commented that walking or jogging through Canary grass would get you ready for a bout with Hulk Hogan or for a linebacker position with the Minnesota Vikings.

GB: You bet!!

JCT: Who pays for the CRP grass seed?

GB: This is done on a cost-share basis with the farmer or land owner.

JCT: How much of a CRP payment do you get per year?

GB: About $70/acre total.

JCT: When was CRP started on your land?

GB: About 20 years ago, when CRP first came in.

JCT: When does your enrollment end?

GB: 2006.

JCT: Will you re-enroll?

GB: Absolutely!

JCT: What have been the biggest contributions of CRP to the number of pheasants that you see on the land that you hunt?

GB: We would not have nearly as many pheasants without CRP.

JCT: When you re-enroll, will you try to increase your CRP allotment, or keep it the same?

GB: I hope that I can increase the WRP a little bit – maybe by 30-acres or so.

JCT: What is WRP?

GB: That means Wetland Reserve Program.

JCT: What is that?

GB: This helps to restore and protect wet areas around cropland. It has some cost share involved.

JCT: About how many pheasants are harvested here each year?

GB: About 1,000. We release at least 600 birds per year which we raise here.

JCT: How do you think 2006 will compare with the past?

GB: We should be about the same. I would say that the number of wild pheasants here has about doubled since the 1980s. We will continue to use CRP and do the best we can.

JCT: Does CRP have any negative features?

GB: Nope!

JCT: Thanks Gary. Enjoyed our talk.

GB: Yep! You bet![32]

In commemoration of CRP's 20th Anniversary year in 2006, the USDA published habitat and game success stories for CRP enrolled lands across the United States. The stories of two South Dakotans, Steve Halverson of Lyman County, and Keith Krull from Hushes County show the positive side of CRP from the farmer perspective.

"CRP Helps Farmer Manage Bird Habitat and Population"

Active farmer Steve Halverson manages several thousand acres in the White River bottom in Lyman County, South Dakota. The area may likely produce more birds per acre than anywhere else in the State. Steve constantly strives to find the balance for land use among crop rotations, hay, and CRP devoted to grass practices or woody habitat, with the latter helping to maximize bird production and survival.

Steve is first and foremost an active farm producer. He strategically enrolls CRP acres on his wheat and feed grain farm in blocks to maximize bird production and survivability. Several offers to enroll cropland in CRP during the last general CRP sign-up were not accepted. As a result, Steve continues to crop corn, winter wheat, and sorghum in rotation on those acres, leaving adequate wildlife food plots for winter food at his own expense.

Steve continually monitors the conditions of birds and habitat and develops his acreage to improve both. He has seen a large decline in bird numbers in the river bottom and continues to try to solve that puzzle. It may be that his crop areas are so attractive that the birds no longer need to utilize the river bottom as extensively as they once did. Another concern for him is whether or not the birds on his property have enough quality winter cover to survive the harshest of winters in the future.

Hunting provides supplemental income for the Steve's operation. Despite drought conditions, he harvested 1,800 wild birds last season.

Steve's hope is that CRP will continue to play a useful role in his operation in the future.[33]

"CRP Integral In Creating Prairie Restoration Showcase"

The Krull Ranch in Hughes County, South Dakota, is a showcase for the restoration of grasslands and prairie wetlands on private land. Recent restoration work has earned Keith Krull a national wetlands conservation award from Ducks Unlimited.

Several years ago, a farmer from Montana bought land in South Dakota and broke it out to plant to wheat. According to Keith Krull, the land in Hughes County was ground "that never should have been farmed." Brothers Keith and Kip Krull bought 1,100 acres of what they called "bruised and beaten" acres to add to their ranch. Then they immediately set out to repair the damaged land.

"We couldn't have done this on our own. The government programs were there to help us put this together," said Keith Krull.

Many of those 1,100 acres were offered and accepted for enrollment in CRP.

With CRP cost-share assistance, plus additional assistance from Ducks Unlimited; United States Fish and Wildlife Service; and the South Dakota Department of Game, Fish, and Parks the Krulls restored or created nine wetlands on the property. They seeded several acres to grass and have initiated several other conservation practices in order to restore and repair the grassland.

"What we have out here on all those wetlands now is a duck factory," says Keith as he drives from one patch of water to the next. "And CRP has really brought the pheasants back." In addition, there are sharp-tailed grouse, wildflowers, and deer in abundance.[34]

A neighboring farmer from North Dakota extols the multiple benefits of CRP in his letter written to United States Secretary of Agriculture Mike Johanns. In support of the 2007 Farm Bill Jim Kurle says, in part:

My name is Jim Kurle. I am a South-Central North Dakota farmer, as was my father before me, as was his father before him. I am sorry that I missed the farm bill forum at Minot on July 26, because I heard there were some negative comments about the CRP program. I can't imagine who would be against the program; it couldn't have been a CRP farmer. I would like to express my thoughts on this CRP program, since I am aware of the upcoming 2007 farm bill and I know your hands are full.

You know, some people say, CRP hurts the local Cenex station. Our local Cenex in Wilton, North Dakota is not only profiting but expanding. CRP surely hasn't affected them negatively. Some say CRP hurts rural towns. Rural towns have been drying up since the 1940s. Since then, farmers can commute with better automobiles on improved highways for cheaper and better quality products. Farmers are simply more mobile. CRP has nothing to do with it.

Some say CRP has hurt our local bank. Our local bank stands solid. With CRP as a stable income for farmers, we can repay our loans more easily. The CRP program has made a tremendous difference in my life, personally. I farm land that is not like the Red River Valley Land. My land is hilly and rocky with much of it highly erodible. A heavy rain would move my soil and cause large ruts in the field. CRP has stopped this erosion. A windstorm would move my soil to another location and CRP has stopped this.

In the late 1990s I developed health problems. At that time, I placed an ad in the paper for rental of my land. I received few inquires, but nothing solid developed. After studying the CRP program, I voluntarily bid most of my farm into the CRP program. I saw myself going deeper and deeper into debt-seeing a possible foreclosure or forced sale of my land-to a new hope with CRP. Our CRP acres are flourishing. I have upheld my share of the contract. I have cut and sprayed any existing weeds on all of acres, preventing any spread of weeds to the property of others. The grass is a great place for wildlife. We have seen a huge growth in the number of deer and birds for the sportsmen. I have had hunters from all over the nation, such as Florida, Georgia, Arkansas, Washington, Minnesota, and Wisconsin. These hunters have thanked us for providing a place to hunt. The CRP program has brought in $300 million to North Dakota's economy from recreational activities. During drought, the CRP program has provided ranchers with needed hay, preventing a possible tragic sale of their herds. CRP is a safeguard for them, our CRP is a value to them; it gives us a chance to help someone else. I know what some "people" say about the CRP program, but as a CRP farmer, I know what I see. I see my banker smiling, because I am repaying what was a heavy debt load in 1998 to a manageable debt load today. I see the Cenex manager smiling because we are debt free to him. I see my farmland produce tall, lush grasses. I see my soil staying in one place. I see the wind and rains unable to cause soil and farmland erosion. I see wildlife back in its rightful place, where deer can walk into a field of grass so tall that they will visually disappear. I see a wildlife refugee, and I see a hunter's paradise. I see a positive relationship developing between CRP farmers and America's hunters. I see drought stricken ranch managers coming to my door, asking for help. I see what they see, acre after acre of tall grass that will save their livelihood. I see their smiles as they drive away with load after load of hay bales. I see CRP as being a great program–for me it sure has been. I see CRP as being a win, win deal, and don't let anyone tell you otherwise.

*I would like to see my government keep CRP intact, so that in 2007 I will
have the option to automatically reenroll my land in to the CRP program...*[35]

Pheasant Futures: Now and Forever??

Three days of South Dakota pheasant hunting with Ed McGaa and Puppy
in November 2006 and 2007, and follow-up CRP research both re-affirmed and
enhanced my existing knowledge base regarding the complexity of nature, and
the extent to which the creatures of nature are entwined and intertwined in mutual feedback loops with nature and with each other. Since 1966 when I took 20
high school students to the Yucatan Peninsula of Mexico, I have explored the
origins and evolution of corn (also known as teosinte, wild maize, or Zea mays),
and I use its story often in my college classes to illustrate how corn "makes"
man, and man, in turn helps to "make" corn in its almost infinite variety. Corn's
beginnings go back to a time period somewhere between 9,000–7,000 years
ago when, according to famed archaeologist Richard MacNeish, man began to
bring a wild plant under his "control" (another word for domestication, since we
all know that man's "control" over such matters is very limited indeed!) in the
Puebla-Oaxaca region of Mexico.[36] Indeed, Maya creation mythology reveals
that creator-beings could not get man's creation "right" in three prior attempts
until, on the fourth try, they fashioned man/woman from corn. Man/woman,
in turn, used creator-driven "brain power" to grow and improve the yields of
domesticated corn through proper cultivation, seed selection, and the ritualistic
observances of spiritual ceremony. In short, the Maya and other traditions claim
that man could not exist without corn; nor could corn exist without man; and on
and on, and on in a repetitive cycle of reciprocating interdependence.

When I examine the present status of pheasant populations, habitat, and
man-intervention, I see limited parallels between the corn/man relationship and
the man/pheasant relationship as currently manifested in the fields of South Dakota and neighboring states. Those of us who have dressed pheasants harvested
in South Dakota and other pheasant cornbelt states can attest to the extent to
which most pheasant craws are literally stuffed with the agricultural gold of
prairie state corn. Outdoor Life contributing writer, Mark Kayser notes that
"pheasants are granivores, or seed-eaters," and that corn meets a good portion of
the pheasant food requirements in the pheasant belt. Does the pheasant live by
corn alone? The intricacies of pheasant habitat suggest otherwise. A pheasant's
corn-rich diet is supplemented by man-grown soybeans, wheat, milo, and sun-
flowers, with a medley of weed seeds and grasses thrown in by nature, and CRP-
enhanced nature.[37]

Studies of pheasant population estimates and harvest records in many pheasant states reveal an up and down pattern that currently is largely the resultant of
the basic elements of weather and habitat. (For these figures see Pheasants For-

ever and the Department Game Fish, and Wildlife for the various pheasant states. For the state of South Dakota, 1919–2005, consult the South Dakota Game, Fish & Parks Websites).[38] Other than acknowledge and follow the admonitions and advice of those who strongly believe in the man-made and man-generating components of global-warming facts, (not opinions anymore) as they relate to the consequences for various species – including the ring-necked pheasant – man cannot control the weather. But, Homo sapiens may be able to intervene and modify some of the long-term, man-impacted causes/consequences of drought, excessive rain, extreme temperature fluctuations, and the increasing extinction of vast numbers of species. (For detailed, insightful commentary on all of this, see Nature's Way,[39] especially chapters eight through eleven by McGaa, and An Inconvenient Truth by Al Gore.)[40] In a more immediate, near-term time period we must acknowledge, support, and cooperate to promote those ideas and actions that work to maintain and increase the pheasant population base now and in the future.

Observations and Acknowledgements

- The Conservation Reserve Program created in the 1985 Farm Bill [supplemented by such ancillary wildlife support programs as the Wetland Reserve Program and the Environmental Quality Incentives Program] has done more to promote wildlife habitat, in general, and increase the pheasant population, in particular, than any government program in the recent history of the United States.
- CRP nesting habitat initiatives including the sowing of native warm-season grasses such as big bluestem, Indiangrass, and switchgrass are perhaps the major reasons for very good hunting seasons and pheasant population increases in the Pheasant Belt, with 40–60-year harvest highs reported in such states as North Dakota, Minnesota, Kansas, Nebraska, and South Dakota (South Dakota's 2005 bird harvest count was 1,949,000, the highest number recorded since 1963).[41]
- Scientific analysis, commissioned by the USDA, data from pheasant hunting support groups such as Pheasants Forever, and various studies from state departments of game, fish, and wildlife collectively report that "CRP equals more pheasants."[42]
- CRP is a win, win, win, win situation for many farmers, conservationists, pheasant hunters, wildlife watchers, and Mother Earth.

Needed Cooperation

CRP is a living laboratory of federalism at its best. CRP federal initiatives achieve their maximum intents and purposes for the ecosystem and pheasant populations when combined with state and local political and economic support programs such as South Dakota's Walk-In Hunting Access Program (WIA), Nebraska's CRP-MAP (Management Access), Kansas' Walk-In Hunting Area Program (WIHA), and North Dakota's Private Land Initiative (PLI) Conservation PLOTS (Private Land Open to Sportsmen) Programs. Basically, all of these programs (combined with the efforts of State Game and Fish Commission projects, Pheasants Forever, Ducks Unlimited, and other private hunting support agencies) piggy-back CRP dollars and advice with economic support and expert consultation on land-use, conservation, and wildlife promotion initiatives and incentives. The South Dakota Game, Fish, and Parks WIA has opened vast hunting opportunities (primarily on the 90 percent of privately owned South Dakota farmland) to hunters on where and when to hunt on a "walk-in, foot-traffic only" basis after landowners, and Game, Fish & Parks representatives sign a contract providing financial renumeration and long-term land use rewards/advice from Game, Fish & Parks. South Dakota hunting license fees assist in landowner payment contracts. The Kansas WIHA works in a similar fashion, and an estimated 60 percent non/resident, and 55 percent resident population of hunters use WIHA acres. In Nebraska, the CRP-MAP has resulted in a "terrific response from hunters," has "opened a lot of acres to a lot of folks," pleased landowners, and taken hunting pressure off public lands. North Dakota's PLI and PLOTS are North Dakota's GFD's central mechanisms to enhance wildlife habitats (including pheasants) through cost-share assistance programs with landowners. With hunting access to private lands as the primary goals, PLI and PLOTS subsidize grass plantings, wildlife water developments, and CRP/CREP lands through a Community Match Program sponsored by groups such as local chambers of commerce, city councils, and community wildlife organizations. All of these are designed with the idea that communities benefit when more hunters come into North Dakota.[43]

Predictions on the future of the CRP/Pheasant connection are all but impossible. Ben Shouse, a writer for Pheasant Country, describes CRP as "a tiny boat in the sea of the larger agricultural policy debate."[44] Some of the issues driving this debate include:

The possible expiration of millions of CRP contract acres between 2007–2022; the uncertainties of Farm Bill 2007 appropriations; land use and economic competition issues involving conservation, livestock production, farm commodity subsidy programs, food production for a growing human population; and, the possible future demands for more corn, and soybean oil for ethanol and biodiesel fuel generation.[45]

The Future – Native Prairie Grasses: Biofuel For Pheasants and Automobiles?

A ten-year study recently reported by David Tillman, Professor of Ecology at the University of Minnesota concludes that diverse mixtures of native grasses (i.e., great pheasant habitat) produce more biofuel energy than either corn-based ethanol or soybean-derived biodiesel fuel. Not only do native grasses supply 238 percent more usable energy per acre than any single plant species, fuels made from prairie grass biomass are "carbon negative" as contrasted with "carbon positive" corn ethanol and soybean biodiesel. Carbon negative plants actually reduce the amount of carbon dioxide in the atmosphere, and could contribute to the reduction of greenhouse gases, and thereby assist in the battle against global warming. In the future Tillman's research suggests that biofuels from native grasses grown on the world's 1.25 billion acres of old or marginal farmland could also replace approximately 13 percent of global petroleum transportation consumption, and as much as 19 percent of global electricity consumption. Side benefits of increasing the amount of native grass would include other benefits of the CRP, including soil and water restoration, and wildlife habitat preservation. Although Tillman acknowledges that current CRP practices do not allow CRP-enrolled farmers to sell native grasses for fuel generation, he suggests that the 2007 Farm Bill could be modified to accept such practices.[46]

Future Food For Thought

An exploration of the CRP/Pheasant connection raises broad and important questions regarding land use strategies on millions of acres, the economic interests of landowners and business corporations, recreational opportunities and economic costs/benefits for the general public, future energy requirements for spaceship earth, governmental policy priorities, and such qualitative environmental concerns as clean water, clean air, soil nutrition, and global warming.

• Is there enough land available to meet the physical, economic and social needs of a growing human population?

- Will resource utilization conservation strategies be conducted in a spirit of cooperation rather than competition and designed to benefit the many as opposed to the few?

- Will future cost benefit analyses include long-term qualitative environmental concerns as well as short-term economic interests?

- Will we be able to balance the future needs and lifestyles of the landowner, the farmer, the pheasant hunter, the wildlife enthusiast, and the general citizenry in an atmosphere of tolerance, trust, harmony, and mutual interdependence?

A Future Farming and Pheasant Hunting Scenario
Location: Somewhere in the Pheasant Belt, USA
Time: November 2016

John, Sam, and their three-year old Golden Retriever, Doc had just finished a three-day pheasant hunt on 4000 plus scattered acres of Prairie State's Pheasant Habitat Program (PHP) lands. John had downed nine ringnecks, and Sam had seven plus a wounded bird that Doc could not locate. Three local farmers had signed PHP agreements in 2010 and so far it seemed to be a win, win, win situation for the farmers, pheasant hunters, and Prairie State citizens. Local, state, and federal matching funds combined with generous contributions from Pheasants Forever (Pheasants Forever) and Ducks Unlimited (DU) had been forwarded to the Prairie State Game and Fish Commission which in turn disseminated these funds to landowners holding choice properties for pheasants, ducks, and grouse. Wildlife food plots were abundant, native grasses were growing vigorously in surrounding wetlands, and more pheasants had been harvested so far this year in Prairie State than in any other year since the "boom" pheasant year of 2005. The three farmers had been enrolled in CRP for eight years, but more relaxed USDA guidelines were now allowing them to judiciously harvest a larger share of the native grasses for hay, especially in drought periods. A couple of their farmer neighbors had dropped out of CRP because they thought the guidelines on cutting grass for hay were too rigid. Twenty years of extensive study on prairie grass varieties had paid off, and now proper mixtures of grass types were being chosen based upon such specific characteristics as soil type, soil moisture content, rainfall pattern, predator populations, and the preferred habitat for selected wildlife species.

John, Sam, and Doc were tried and true pheasant hunters, and they had passed up shots at huge mule deer in the past decade. It seemed to them that deer liked CRP almost as much as pheasants. Six years ago they had met a very outgoing farmer at the Prairie Town Crossroads Convenience store, and they usually tried to work in a hunt on his property after they finished their trek on the PHP lands. Honestly, PHP had plenty of birds, but Sam and Doc really liked the privacy and personal attention of the George Hunt farm family and their in-laws. After purchasing a three-day supply of snacks, beer, shotgun shells, and some extra clothing at the store, they drove north approximately ten miles and entered the gate to George Hunt's property. For a negotiable and reasonable per man daily fee, they would hunt pheasants during the day and eat and sleep at the Hunt Bed and Breakfast spread which had evolved from an abandoned dairy barn constructed by Mr. Hunt's grandfather. A warm fireplace was the focal point for the rustic kitchen and dining area. The Hunts try to limit the number of hunters at the B&B at any one time, but their total number of hunters has greatly increased since they got permission from the Prairie State GFC to release 1,000–1,200 pheasants per year to supplement the native population. In 2001, research conducted by the Department of Animal Husbandry at Prairie State University had determined the compatibility of wild pheasants and stocked birds, and the brood size and hatchling survival rates had been rated as very good for over a decade. Mr. Hunt owned 800-acres, and he leased the hunting rights to another 1,000 acres from his son, Rather (400-acres) and neighbor, Mr. Byrd (600-acres). For the past three years Mr. Hunt had depended upon Mr. Byrd for his pheasant supply since he would rather concentrate his time and energy on his hog operation which he has run for the last twenty years. Over breakfast Mr. Hunt described in detail the boundaries of their hunting area which were well-marked with orange signs and the initials H&B (Hunt and Byrd).

As John, Sam, and Doc rode into their designated one square-mile hunting area, they saw a mixed area of cornfields, wetlands, small ponds, and wooded thickets geometrically interspersed with ample CRP native grassplots sowed ten years earlier. The essential differences in this property and the PHP land that they had hunted the week before was in the variety of vegetation growing on the more obvious nesting and food plots. Milo, varieties of grain sorghum, millet, and row-upon-row of recently harvested corn served as major food sources for pheasant, and at least ten to twelve varieties of native grasses had been sown along the banks of several small creek beds and ponds. More native warm season grasses such as Big and Little Bluestem, Tomahawk Indiangrass, and Summer Switchgrass had been added to the usual grass mixture to accommodate Prairie State's overall increasing temperature ranges during the last ten years. Recent data from Prairie State University verified rising temperatures, but additional analyses seemed to indicate that soil and atmospheric temperature were slightly less on and around the land area where native warm grass species were dominant.

Mr. Hunt's son, Rather, and Mr. Byrd's daughter, Fonda Green graduated from Prairie State University in 2010 with respective degrees in Biofuel Engineering and a double major in Animal Husbandry and Granivore Ecology. They were married in the same year and, lucky for them, Rather's rich, unmarried uncle had left him 750-acres of land which contained the old homestead where he and Rather's father had grown up. After debating what to do with this inherited acreage, the young couple decided to enroll in CRP and plant 80 percent of this land (600-acres) in a variety of native grasses that had been approved by the USDA and State Department of Natural Resources and Wildlife. The remaining 20 percent of the land (150-acres) would be used to grow corn and other grain foods to grind and convert into a balanced customized pheasant food mix created by Fonda Green. Fonda gave her father a "good deal" on this custom mix to feed the pheasants that he in turn sold to her father-in-law, Mr. Hunt.

In 2012 Rather and Fonda had borrowed $5,000 to match local and state funds supplemented by support from Pheasants Forever and Ducks Unlimited. They used these funds to install a pilot, mini-biofuel processing system in an abandoned corn crib located on the Hunt homestead. An ecology professor and Rather's major academic biofuel engineering advisor were conducting a five-year research project on the feasibility and costs/benefits of an experimental biofuel production project involving 25 farmers within a 30-mile radius of the Hunt and Byrd homesteads. Under a temporary CRP modification agreement permitting harvesting of native-grasses for fuel generation, 70 percent of the native grass acreage (420-acres) would be used for the biofuel project, and the remaining 30 percent of the native grass acreage (180-acres) would be left for pheasant cover and land restoration. Also, Rather and Fonda were currently working with the State University and Fonda's former advisor to explore the extent to which the planting and harvest time for biomass native grass fuel crops could be coordinated with pheasant brooding, nesting, hatching, and young pheasant chicks' survival rates. The major research question posed by the research team of biofuel engineers and granivore experts would be, in simple terms – can native grass biomass fuel and pheasants be "generated" on the same land in a way that is compatible, profitable, efficient, and non-polluting?

In the meantime, John, Sam, and Doc got their pheasant limits, stopped at the Prairie Town Crossroads Convenience Store, grabbed snacks for man and dog, and filled up the tank of their FFV (Flexible Fuel Vehicle) truck with 25 gallons of a 2015 mixology of 90 percent ethanol/biomass-enhanced gasoline. (Note: In addition to the traditional cornstarched-based ethanol additive, the ethanol plus component was a cellulosic ethanol made from hybrid poplar woodchips from Virginia, and the biomass fuel was a derivative of a variety of big sagebrush harvested in the median strips of interstate highways and from selected stands of Indiangrass found on Sioux reservations in South Dakota.) As they headed east on I-70 they were already discussing next year's pheasant hunt in Prairie State. Perhaps they would be able to hunt on Rather and Fonda's 450-acre native grass/biomass experimental plot if those professor/science types could ever get all this pheasant/fuel stuff straightened out.

Avid pheasant hunter/writer Ed McGaa recounts many of nature's lessons in his book, Nature's Way: Native Wisdom For Living In Balance With The Earth among them the lesson of balance in all things. The man/pheasant relationship in North America illustrates this balance as well as other important natural lessons including animal habitat, conservation practices and the power and wisdom to be derived from walking upon and observing the bounties and benevolence of Mother Earth. I will give Ed the last shot on my pheasant hunting excursion. Chapter One of Nature's Way, "Wisdom Through Observation" contains several lessons that Ed learned from being a good student in nature's classroom. He writes:

> I also learned from seeking the wily ringneck pheasant in fall cornfields. The Dakotas are dotted with such fields-corn, hay, soybeans, along with shelterbelts of trees and other seemingly endless cover. The many sloughs, creeks, and gullies are edged by brush, hedges, weeds, thicker weed beds, thicker weed stands, and cattail clusters. One of the delights of Dakota living is experiencing a pheasant eruption anywhere from a couple of roosters to a hundred from a crowded slough full of cattails. That sight gives a person a pretty good idea of the power and complexity of Nature.[47]

Hetch etu aloh. It is so indeed.

South Dakota Hunting Business Directory

BATH
Tacoma Park Place
12954 396th Avenue
Bath, SD 57427
http://www.dakotariverranch.com
jonesfarms@nrctv.com

BIG STONE CITY
Schmidt's Landing Resort
48140 Schmidts Road
Big Stone City, SD 57216
http://www.schmidtslanding.com
schmidts@tnics.com

The Grocery Basket
P.O. Box 96
Big Stone City, SD 57216
http://silentfallsresort.com
silentfalls@bigstonelake.net

BURKE
Buryanek Bay Bunkhouse
27495 Buryanek Road
Burke, SD 57523
http://www.buryanek.com
buryanekjdj@yahoo.com

CHAMBERLAIN
Thunderstik Lodge Inc.
24931 Thunderstik Road
Chamberlain, SD 57325
http://www.thunderstik.com
info@thunderstik.com

CRESBARD
Fest Inn
P.O. Box 95
Cresbard, SD 57435

CUSTER
Custer Mansion Bed & Breakfast
35 Centennial Drive
Custer, SD 57730
http://www.custermansionbb.com
cusmanbb@gwtc.net

Dakota Badland Outfitters
P.O. Box 852
Custer, SD 57730
http://www.ridesouthdakota.com
ehusted@earthlink.net

DEADWOOD
Deadwood KOA Campground
P.O. Box 451
Deadwood, SD 57732
http://www.deadwoodkoa.com
deadwoodsd@mykoa.com

Turneffe Flats
P.O. Box 36
Deadwood, SD 57732
http://www.tflats.com

EDEN
Joe's All Season Guide Service
P.O. Box 137
Eden, SD 57232
http://www.joeguidesyou.com

EDGEMONT
Fort Igloo LLC.
11122 Fort Igloo Road
Edgemont, SD 57735
funranch@gwtc.net

ESTELLINE
Black's Pheasant Field/
Outskirts Lodge
19630 459th Avenue
Estelline, SD 57234
(605) 873-2719
(605) 881-0393 (cell)
www.blackspheasantfields.com
info@blackspheasantfields.com

EUREKA
Hoffman Angus Ranch
34328 106th Street
Eureka, SD 57437
hmanangus@valleytel.net

FORT PIERRE
Chantier Creek Resort
20214 S.D. Hwy. 1806
Fort Pierre, SD 57532
chantiercreek@aol.com

Triple U Buffalo Ranch
26314 Tatanka Road
Fort Pierre, SD 57532
http://www.tripleuranch.com
uuubuff@gwtc.net

GEDDES
The Barn Bed & Breakfast
37191 284th Street
Geddes, SD 57342
http://www.bbonline.com/sd/thebarn
thebarn@midstatesd.net

GETTYSBURG
Bob's Resort
29336 U.S. Hwy. 212
Gettysburg, SD 57442
http://www.bobsresort.com
bobsresort@bobsresort.com

Paul Nelson Farm
P.O. Box 183
Gettysburg, SD 57442
http://www.paulnelsonfarm.com
cenelson@sbtc.net

South Whitlock Resort
29500 U.S. Hwy. 212
Gettysburg, SD 57442
http://www.southwhitlock.com
southwhitlock@southwhitlock.com

Whitlock Bay Supper Club/
Chuck Krause Guides
29504 U.S. Hwy. 212
Gettysburg, SD 57442
http://www.whitlockbay.com

GREGORY
Biggins Hunting Service Inc.
33451 U.S. Hwy. 18
Gregory, SD 57533

Mulehead Ranch Adventures
34122 S.D. Hwy. 44
Gregory, SD 57533
http://www.muleheadranch.com
duling@gwtc.net

GRENVILLE
Pickerel Lake Lodge
2356 Miotke Road
Grenville, SD 57239
http://www.pickerellakelodge.com

HARROLD
Tumbleweed Lodge
20210 322nd Avenue
Harrold, SD 57536
http://www.tumbleweedlodge.com
michael@tumbleweedlodge.com

HAZEL
Racota Valley Outfitters
18252 442nd Avenue
Hazel, SD 57242
http://www.racotavalley.com

HERRICK
**Bob's South Dakota
Hunting Service**
34880 U.S. Hwy. 18
Herrick, SD 57538
http://www.bobshuntingservice.
com

HILL CITY
Palmer Gulch Lodge
P.O. Box 295
Hill City, SD 57745
http://www.palmergulch.com
info@palmergulch.com

HITCHCOCK
**Swarming Pheasant
Hunting Preserve**
39184 196th Street
Hitchcock, SD 57348
http://www.swarmingpheasants.
com
appelorchard@sbtc.net

KADOKA
Bilmar Expressions
820 S.D. Hwy. 248
Kadoka, SD 57543
bilmar@gwtc.net

KIMBALL
Ashley, Todd
Kimball, SD
(605) 778-6716
(605) 680-9467 (cell)

Pheasant Crest
23625 365th Avenue
Kimball, SD 57355

Pheasant Hunt
24665 356th Avenue
Kimball, SD 57355
(605) 778-6716

Wings of Thunder
35786 244th Street
Kimball, SD 57355
http://www.wingsofthunder.com

MECKLING
E Circle Hunting Farms
45345 311th Street
Meckling, SD 57044
http://www.ecirclee.com
ecirclee@aol.com

MITCHELL
Famil-E-Fun Campground
25473 403rd Avenue
Mitchell, SD 57301

Rooster Roost Ranch
117 S. Lawler
Mitchell, SD 57301
http://www.roosterroostranch.com
perryneugs@mit.midco.net

Thunderbird Lodge
P.O. Box 984
Mitchell, SD 57301
http://www.thunderbird-lodge.com
thunderbird@santel.net

MT. VERNON
Rosewood Barn
24882 397th Avenue
Mt. Vernon, SD 57363
http://www.rosewoodbarn.com
rosewoodbarn@santel.net

ORAL
Dakota Hills Inc.
14129 Ringneck Road
Oral, SD 57766
http://www.dakotahills.com
dakhills@gwtc.net

PIERRE
Broken Arrow Farms
1405 E. Wells
Pierre, SD 57501
http://www.huntbrokenarrow.com
info@huntbrokenarrow.com

**Cattleman's Club
   Steakhouse & Lodge**
29608 S.D. Hwy. 34
Pierre, SD 57501

**Cheyenne Ridge
   Outfitters & Lodge**
101 Ridge Road
Pierre, SD 57501
http://www.cheyenneridge.com
anglers@dakota2k.net

**Lighthouse Pointe/
   Oahe Trails Golf**
19602 Lake Place
Pierre, SD 57501
http://www.lighthousepointe.com
bp@mncomm.com

Oahe Marina & Resort
20250 Hyde Road
Pierre, SD 57501
oahemarina@mncomm.com

Okobojo Resort
204 Garrigan Drive
Pierre, SD 57501

Outpost Lodge Inc.
28229 Cow Creek Road
Pierre, SD 57501
http://www.theoutpostlodge.com
leswulf@aol.com

Pike Haven Resort
27645 Pike Haven Place
Pierre, SD 57501
pikehaven@venturecomm.net

Spring Creek Resort
610 N. Jackson
Pierre, SD 57501
http://www.springcreekresortsd.
  com
springcreekresort@msn.com

POLLOCK
West Pollock Resort
P.O. Box 17
Pollock, SD 57648
http://www.westpollockresort.com
westpollock@valleytel.net

SENECA
R & R Pheasant Hunting LLC.
33635 171st Street
Seneca, SD 57473
http://www.r_
  rpheasanthunting.com
r_rpheasants@venturecomm.net

SPENCER
Pheasant Creek
Bill Lehrman
35542 431st Avenue
Spencer, SD 57374
(605) 246-2475

STURGIS
Rush No More Campground
21137 Brimstone Place
Sturgis, SD 57785
http://www.sturgiscamping.com

VIBORG
Paradise Valley Adventures
44666 289th Street
Viborg, SD 57070
http://www.
  paradisevalleyadventures.com
paradisevalleyrides@hotmail.com

WINNER
R.H. Turnquist
31522 285th Street
Winner, SD 57580
http://www.winnersd.
  org/chamberbus/
  turnquist_hunting.htm
rhnturnq@gwtc.net

Notes

Pheasant Photos –
> ftp://ftp.state.sd.us/tourism/CHAD/1-30-08McGaa
> Chad Coppess, Senior Photographer
> South Dakota Tourism & State Development
> 711 East Wells Ave.
> Pierre, SD 57501
> (605) 773-3301
> chad.coppess@state.sd.us

Preface
1. Chris Dorsey, "Pheasant Days" (Stillwater, MN, *Voyageur Press*, 1992) p. 89.
2. ibid p. 151
3. Steve Grooms, *Modern Pheasant Hunting* (Harrisburg, PA: Stackpole Books, 1982), p. 41.
4. Ibid p. 41.

Introduction
1. Associated Press, Dec. 28, 2007. (*Rapid City Daily Journal*) p. 1.
2. Senator Inouye (D. Hawaii) Study. U.S. Senate Record, 1986.
3. Chris Dorsey, "Pheasant Days" (Stillwater, MN, *Voyageur Press*, 1992) p. 121.

Chapter 10
1. South Dakota Game, Fish, and Parks, "2007 South Dakota Ring Neck Outlook."
2. Ed McGaa, *Crazy Horse and Chief Red Cloud* (Minneapolis, Four Directions Publishing, 2005).

   Ed McGaa, *Creators Code* (Minneapolis, Four Directions Publishing, 2007).

3. South Dakota Game, Fish & Parks. www.sdgfp.info.
4. Ed McGaa, *Nature's Way*, p. 8.
5. *National Geographic*, April 2007, pp. 134–135.
6. Game, Fish & Parks Wildlife Division Director, Doug Hansen.
7. South Dakota Department of Game, Fish & Parks. "Private Lands Habitat & Access Programs: Strategic Plan" November 27, 2007.
8. ibid p. 20.
9. ibid.
10. Random House Webster's College Dictionary, 1995.

Chapter 11
1. Brochure entitled "Blacks' Pheasant Fields"
2. Pheasants Forever, "Conservation Reserve Program (CRP)," http:///www.pheasantsforever.org/conservation/farmbill/?crp.

   United States Department of Agriculture, "Conservation Reserve Program," http://www.fsa.usda.gov/FSA.

   South Dakota Private Lands Programs and Information, "South Dakota Game, Fish & Parks Private Lands Programs," http://www.sdgfp.info/Wildlife/privatelands/Index.htm.
3. Pheasants Forever, "Conservation Reserve Program (CRP)," http:///www.pheasantsforever.org/conservation/farmbill/?crp.
4. United States Department of Agriculture, "CRP Enrollment Data as of September 2006 with Projected Rental Payments for Fiscal Year 2007."

   Erik Schubach and the US50.com, "Fast Facts Study Guide," http://www.theus50.com/area.shtml.

   Steven Westcott and Kristin Scuderi, "Johanns Announces $1.8 Billion In Conservation Reserve Program Rental Payments," United States Department of Agriculture, http://www.fsa.usda.gov/FSA.

   United States Department of Agriculture, Farm Service Agency, "Conservation Reserve Program– Monthly CRP Acreage Report Summary of Active and Expiring CRP Acres By State," http://content.fsa.usda.gov/crpstorpt/10Approved/rmepegg/MEPEGGR1.HTM.

   United States Department of Agriculture, "Budget Summary and Annual Performance Plan," pp. 26–31.

   Agriculture Online, "Johanns announces $1.8 billion in CRP payments," October 2, 2006, http://www.agriculture.com/ag/story.jhtml.

5. Steven Westcott and Kristin Scuderi, "Johanns Announces $1.8 Billion In Conservation Reserve Program Rental Payments," United States Department of Agriculture, http://www.fsa.usda.gov/FSA.

Ed Loyd and Stevin Westcott, "Johanns Announces CRP Re-Enrollments and Extensions for Eligible Producers in 2007," United States Department of Agriculture, Release No. 0030.06, http://www.usda.gov/wps/portal/ (p. 2).

6. United States Department of Agriculture, "CRP Enrollment Data as of September 2006 with Projected Rental Payments for Fiscal Year 2007."

Erik Schubach and the US50.com, "Fast Facts Study Guide," http://www.theus50.com/area.shtml.

7. Erik Schubach and the US50.com, "Fast Facts Study Guide," http://www.theus50.com/area.shtml.

8. United States Department of Agriculture–2007 Farm Bill Theme Papers, "Conservation and the Environment, Executive Summary, June 2006." (p. 3).

Lynn Tjeerdsma, Theodore Roosevelt Conservation Partnership, "Elimination of Conservation Reserve Program Proven Costly to Taxpayers," September 7, 2006, http://www.trcp.org/pr_crpreport.aspx.

9. Ibid.

Pheasants Forever, "Conservation Reserve Program (CRP)," http:///www.pheasantsforever.org/conservation/farmbill/?crp.

10. United States Department of Agriculture–2007 Farm Bill Theme Papers, "Conservation and the Environment, Executive Summary, June 2006."

Lynn Tjeerdsma, Theodore Roosevelt Conservation Partnership, "Elimination of Conservation Reserve Program Proven Costly to Taxpayers," September 7, 2006, http://www.trcp.org/pr_crpreport.aspx.

11. Ibid.

12. United States Department of Agriculture–2007 Farm Bill Theme Papers, "Conservation and the Environment, Executive Summary, June 2006." (p. 3).

13. Lynn Tjeerdsma, Theodore Roosevelt Conservation Partnership, "Elimination of Conservation Reserve Program Proven Costly to Taxpayers," September 7, 2006, http://www.trcp.org/pr_crpreport.aspx.

Dave Nomsen and Bob St. Pierre, Pheasants Forever, "Latest CRP Sign-Up is a Victory for Pheasants," http://www.pheasantsforever.org/press/release.php?releaseID=84.

14. United States Department of Agriculture–2007 Farm Bill Theme Papers, "Conservation and the Environment, Executive Summary, June 2006." (p. 3).

Lynn Tjeerdsma, Theodore Roosevelt Conservation Partnership, "Elimination of Conservation Reserve Program Proven Costly to Taxpayers," September 7, 2006, http://www.trcp.org/pr_crpreport.aspx.

15. United States Department of Agriculture–2007 Farm Bill Theme Papers, "Conservation and the Environment, Executive Summary, June 2006." (p. 4).

16. "CRP and the Future of Hunting in South Dakota," www.sdgfp.info (p. 6).

17. Bob St. Pierre and Dave Nomsen, Pheasants Forever, "Pheasants Forever Says CRP Produces 13.5 Million Pheasants Annually," http://www.pheasantsforever.org/press/release/php?releaseID=276.

18. South Dakota, "Pheasant Management in South Dakota," http://www.sdgfp.info/Wildlife/hunting/Pheasant/ManagementQ&A.htm.

19. Steven Westcott and Kristin Scuderi, "Johanns Announces $1.8 Billion In Conservation Reserve Program Rental Payments," United States Department of Agriculture, http://www.fsa.usda.gov/FSA.

20. Ryan Nielson, Lyman McDonald, and Shay Howlin, "Estimating Response of Ring-necked Pheasant (*Phasianus colchicus*) to the Conservation Reserve Program," June 19, 2006.

21. Ibid pp. 1–7.

22. Ibid, pp. 1–4, 18.

23. Bob St. Pierre and Dave Nomsen, Pheasants Forever, "Pheasants Forever Says CRP Produces 13.5 Million Pheasants Annually," http://www.pheasantsforever.org/press/release/php?releaseID=276.

24. Ryan Nielson, Lyman McDonald, and Shay Howlin, "Estimating Response of Ring-necked Pheasant (*Phasianus colchicus*) to the Conservation Reserve Program," June 19, 2006 (p. 29).

25. Bob St. Pierre and Dave Nomsen, Pheasants Forever, "Pheasants Forever Says CRP Produces 13.5 Million Pheasants Annually," http://www.pheasantsforever.org/press/release/php?releaseID=276.

26. Pheasants Forever, "2006 Pheasant Hunting Forecast," http://www.pheasantsforever.org/hunting/forecast.php.

27. Ibid, pp. 2–5.

28. Pheasants Forever, "Pheasant Biology," http://www.phesantsforever.org/hunting/lifeCycle.php?pg=courtship.

South Dakota Game, Fish, and Parks, "How to Design a Pheasant Management Area."

29. State of Washington, "Use of CRP Fields by Greater Sage-grouse and other Shrubsteppe associated Wildlife in Washington," October 2006 (pp. 29–32).

30. United States Department of Agriculture, Farm Service Agency, "Studies Show USDA Conservation Efforts Increase Northern Bobwhite Quail and Sage Grouse Populations," http://www.fsa.usda.gov/FSA.

Complete research results can be found on the Farm Service Administration's website at http://www.fsa.usda.gov/Internet/FSA-File/quail_study.pdf. For summary conclusions of the grouse and quail studies, see the home page of the Farm Service Agency of the United States Department of Agriculture.

31. United States Department of Agriculture, Farm Service Agency, "Conservation Reserve Program Wetlands Will Further Increase Duck Numbers," http://www.fsa.usda.gov/FSA.

32. Oral Interview with Gary Black, November 14, 2006.

33. United States Department of Agriculture, Farm Service Agency, "CRP Helps Farmer Manage Bird Habitat and Population," http://content.fsa.usda.gov/pas/absolutenm/templates/crp_success_story_template.asp.

34. United States Department of Agriculture, Farm Service Agency, "CRP Integral in Creating Prairie Restoration Showcase," http://content.fsa.usda.gov/pas/absolutenm/templates/crp_success_story_template.asp.

35. Email from Jim Kurle to Mr. Johanns, "Farm Bill 2007 Official Comments," August 21, 2005.

36. Michael D. Coe, *Mexico* (New York: Thames and Hudson, Inc., 1982), p. 39.

37. Mark Kayser, *Field and Stream*, "Sidestepping Pheasants: Find your own hunting territory off the beaten path to enjoy great shooting for ringnecks," http://www.outdoorlife.com/outdoor/hunting/upland/article/0,19912,702471,00.html. (pp. 2–3).

38. South Dakota Game, Fish & Parks Private Lands Programs, "Ring-necked Pheasant Statistics for South Dakota," http://www.sdgfp.info/Wildlife/hunting/Pheasant/Stats.htm.

39. Ed McGaa, *Nature's Way: Native Wisdom For Living In Balance With the Earth* (New York: HarperCollins Publishers, 2004).

40. Al Gore, *An Inconvenient Truth: The Planetary Emergency of Global Warming and What We Can Do About It* (Rodale, 2006).

41. South Dakota Game, Fish & Parks Private Lands Programs, "Ring-necked Pheasant Statistics for South Dakota," http://www.sdgfp.info/Wildlife/hunting/Pheasant/Stats.htm.

Pheasants Forever, "2006 Pheasant Hunting Forecast," http://www.pheasantsforever.org/hunting/forecast.php.

42. Bob St. Pierre and Dave Nomsen, Pheasants Forever, "Pheasants Forever Says CRP Produces 13.5 Million Pheasants Annually," http://www.pheasantsforever.org/press/release/php?releaseID=276 (Remark by Dave Nomsen, Pheasants Forever Vice President).

43. South Dakota Game, Fish & Parks Private Lands Programs, "General Hunting Access (Walk-In Areas) Fact Sheet," http://www.sdgfp.info/Wildlife/privatelands/HuntingAccess.htm.

Marc Murrell, *Great Plains Game and Fish*, "A Footrace with Ring-necks," December 2006, pp. 25–27.

North Dakota Game and Fish Department, "Private Land Initiative (PLI)," 2005, http://www.gf.nd.gov/info/pli-program.html.

44. Ben Shouse, Pheasant Country, "Farm bill changes might hurt hunting," January 17, 2006, http://www.pheasantcountry.com/news/Story.cfm?ID=623.

45. United States Department of Agriculture, Farm Service Agency, "Conservation Reserve Program-Monthly CRP Acreage Report Summary of Active and Expiring CRP Acres By State," http://content.fsa.usda.gov/crpstorpt/10Approved/rmepegg/MEPEGGR1.HTM.

Pheasant Country, "Pheasant populations look good but will need help for the future," June 1, 2006, http://www.phesantcountry.com/news/PrintStory.cfm?ID=660.

Keith Good, Organic Consumers Association, "Military Spending, Deficit, & Ethanol Subsidies Threaten Farm Conservation Program," November 6, 2006, http://www.organicconsumbers.org/2006/article_3321.cfm.

Stu Ellis, Agriculture Online, "Corn, soybeans or CRP in 2007?," September 11, 2006, http://www.agriculture.com.

46. Deane Morrison, University of Minnesota, "Corn Ethanol Yields an Energy Dividend But Gains Are Higher With Soy Biodiesel, A New Study Shows," July 18, 2006, http://www1.umn.edu/umnnews/Feature_Stories/Ethanol_fuel_presents_a_cornundrum.html.

Deane Morrison, University of Minnesota, "Back to the future: Prairie grasses emerge as rich energy source," December 8, 2006, http://www1.umn.edu/umnnews/Feature_Stories/Back_to_the_future_prairie_grasses.html.

David Ruth, EurekAlert!, "Mixed prairie grasses are better biofuel source, U of M study says," December 7, 2006, http://www.eurekalert.org/pub_releases/2006-12/uom-mpg120406.php.

47. Ed McGaa, *Nature's Way: Native Wisdom For Living In Balance With the Earth* (New York: HarperCollins Publishers, 2004), p. 8.

Appendixes

Appendix A

NATIVE WARM SEASON	NATIVE COOL SEASON	
Alkali Sacaton	**Green Needlegrass**	**Tall Wheatgrass**
Common*	Common*	Common*
	Lodorm	Alkar
Big Bluestem		Orbit
Common*	**Thickspike Wheatgrass****	Platte
Bison	Common*	
Bonilla	Critana	**Smooth Bromegrass**
Champ	Elbee	Common*
Pawnee		Bounty
Sunnyview	**Western Wheatgrass**	Carlton
	Common*	Cottonwood
Blue Grama	Flintlock	Fox
Common*	Rodan	Lincoln
Bad River	Rosana	Manchar
Willis		Rebound
	Reed Canarygrass	Sac
Indiangrass	Common*	Signal
Common*	Frontier	
Holt Tomahawk	Loreed	
	Palaton	
Little Bluestem	Rise	
Common*	Vantage	
Badlands	Venture	

	INTRODUCED COOL SEASON	
Blaze		
Camper		
	Creeping Foxtail	**Intermediate Wheatgrass**
Nuttal Alkaligrass	Common*	Common*
Common*	Garrison	Chief
	Ratain	Clarke
Prairie Sandreed		Oahe
Common*	**Crested Wheatgrass**	Reliant
Goshen	Common*	Slate
Pronghorn	Hycrest	
	Fairway	**Pubescent Wheatgrass**
Sand Bluestem	Nordan	Common*
Common*	Ruff	Manska
Garden	Summit	MDN-759
Goldstrike		Greenleaf
		Luna
Sideoats grama		
Common*		
Butte		
Killdeer		
Pierre		
Trailway		
Switchgrass		
Common*		
Dacotah		
Forestburg		
Nebraska-28		
Pathfinder		
Summer		
Sunburst		
Trailblazer		

*The origin of non-varietal native and introduced grass seed will be limited to North Dakota, South Dakota, Minnesota, Nebraska, Montana, and Wyoming. All foreign seed, including Canadian, must be adapted named varieties

**Thickspike wheatgrass may be substituted for western wheatgrass when the latter is not available and only west of the Missouri River.

USDA-NRCS 10/7/98

Appendix B

This brochure, along with plant signs located along the trail, will aid you in the identification of some of the more prominent prairie grasses found at Pipestone National Monument.

Big Bluestem (Andropogon gerardii) The most common of the prairie grasses reaches a height of four to six feet. It is commonly called "Turkey foot" because the seed head branches into three parts resembling a turkey's foot. Seed stalks appear in July and August.

Buffalo grass (Buchloe dactyloides) This grass is usually found in the drier areas of the prairie. Seeds are produced throughout the growing season.

Sideoats Grama (Bouteloua curtipendula) This grass is distinguished by the seeds which occur on one side of the seed stalk - hence the same "sideoats." Seed stalks flower in July and August

Blue Grama (Bouteloua gracilis) This grass is often bluish in color. The seed head is thick and often curved when mature. Seed stalks flower in June, July and August.

Prairie Cordgrass (Spartina pectinata) This is one of the tall grasses of the prairie. The seed heads resemble short strands of rope or twine. Usually found in marsh areas, the seed head appear from July to October.

Little Bluestem (Andropogon scoparius) This grass grows in dense clusters reaching four feet in height. Stems may be brown, tan or wine-red in late summer and into fall.

Indiangrass (Sorghastrum nutans) A warm-season perennial grass with stems reaching six feet. The flower head is branched, soft and slightly fuzzy ranging in color from chestnut to grayish brown.

Switchgrass (Panicum virgatum) Found in large clumps, typically two to four feet high, occasionally reaching heights of six feet. Flower heads may appear to be purple or auburn in summer, then turn to tan in the fall.

Source: Tallgrass Prairie, Pipestone National Monument, Minnesota National Park service, United States Department of the Interior.

Other Books written by Ed McGaa

Mother Earth Spirituality:
Healing Ourselves and Our World

Rainbow Tribe:
Ordinary people Journeying on the
   Red Road

Native Wisdom:
Perceptions of the Natural Way

Eagle Vision:
A Sioux Novel of a Tribe's Return

Nature's Way:
Native Wisdom for Living in Balance
   with the Earth

Crazy Horse and Chief Red Cloud

Creator's Code:
Planetary Survival and Beyond

These titles are available at www.edmcgaa.com, at most Barnes and Nobel and Borders bookstores, and Amazon.com

To order copies please go to www.edmcgaa.com. (Price ($15.00 + 3.00 S/H)

For Mail Orders please send a check or money order in U.S. Funds to:
Four Directions, 1117 Silver Street, Rapid City, SD 57701.

Correspondence: eagleman4@aol.com or order@edmcgaa.com

I am often asked where one should send their donations regarding the Sioux. My recommendation is Crazy Horse Memorial – A fascinating project with the best Indian museum in the nation, in my opinion.

   Crazy Horse Memorial
   Avenue of the Chiefs
   Crazy Horse, SD 57730-9506